Kraków

Krzysztof Dydyński

LONELY PLANET PUBLICATIONS
Melbourne • Oakland • London • Paris

Kraków
1st edition – March 2000

Published by
Lonely Planet Publications Pty Ltd A.C.N. 005 607 983
192 Burwood Rd, Hawthorn, Victoria 3122, Australia

Lonely Planet Offices
Australia PO Box 617, Hawthorn, Victoria 3122
USA 150 Linden St, Oakland, CA 94607
UK 10a Spring Place, London NW5 3BH
France 1 rue du Dahomey, 75011 Paris

Photographs
All of the images in this guide are available for licensing from
Lonely Planet Images.
email: lpi@lonelyplanet.com.au

Front cover photograph
Rynek Główny   with statue of Adam Mickiewicz in foreground, Kraków
(Krzysztof Dydyński, Lonely Planet Images)

ISBN 0 86442 698 4

text & maps © Lonely Planet 2000
photos © photographers as indicated 2000

Printed by The Bookmaker Pty Ltd
Printed in China

Contents – Text

THE AUTHOR   **4**

THIS BOOK   **5**

FOREWORD   **6**

INTRODUCTION   **9**

FACTS ABOUT KRAKÓW   **10**

History 10	Government & Politics 18	Society & Conduct 28
Geography 17	Economy 18	Religion 29
Climate 17	Population & People 18	Language 30
Ecology & Environment 17	Arts 19	

FACTS FOR THE VISITOR   **31**

When to Go 31	Radio & TV 43	Disabled Travellers 47
Orientation 31	Video Systems 44	Senior Travellers 47
Maps 31	Photography & Video 44	Kraków for Children 47
Tourist Offices 31	Time 44	Universities 48
Documents 32	Electricity 45	Cultural Centres 49
Embassies & Consulates 34	Weights & Measures 45	Dangers & Annoyances 49
Customs 35	Laundry 45	Legal Matters 50
Money 35	Toilets 45	Business Hours 50
Post & Communications 38	Left Luggage 45	Public Holidays 51
Internet Resources 41	Health 46	Special Events 51
Books 42	Women Travellers 47	Work 54
Newspapers & Magazines 43	Gay & Lesbian Travellers 47	

GETTING THERE & AWAY   **56**

Air 56	Car & Motorcycle 62	Organised Tours 64
Train 60	Bicycle 63	
Bus 61	Hitching 63	

GETTING AROUND   **65**

To/From the Airport 65	Taxi 66	Walking 67
Public Transport 65	Boat 67	Organised Tours 67
Car & Motorcycle 66	Bicycle 67	

THINGS TO SEE & DO   **69**

Old Town 69	Northern Suburbs 98	Activities 108
Wawel 82	Eastern Suburbs 101	Language Courses 109
Southern Suburbs 89	Outer Suburbs & Outskirts 102	
Western Suburbs 96	What's Free 108	

PLACES TO STAY   **111**

Budget 111	Mid-Range 114	Top End 115

2 Contents – Text

PLACES TO EAT   118

Food 118
Drinks 120
Budget 121
Mid-Range 123
Top End 124
Cafés 125

ENTERTAINMENT   126

Pubs & Bars 126
Discos 127
Gay & Lesbian Venues 127
Jazz & Blues 127
Folk & Ethnic Music 127
Classical Music 128
Cabarets 128
Cinema 128
Theatre, Opera & Ballet 128
Spectator Sports 129

SHOPPING   130

Crafts 130
Amber 130
Contemporary Art 130
Antiques 131
Books & Maps 131
Music 131
Photography & Film 131
Camping & Outdoor 132
Markets 133

EXCURSIONS   134

Oświęcim (Auschwitz) 134
Ojców National Park 137
Zakopane & the Tatras 138
Dunajec Gorge 145
Częstochowa 146

LANGUAGE   151

GLOSSARY   156

INDEX   165

Text 165
Boxed Text 168

COLOUR MAPS   see back pages

MAP LEGEND   back page

METRIC CONVERSION   inside back cover

Contents – Maps

THINGS TO SEE & DO

St Mary's Church 73   Wawel Cathedral 85

SHOPPING

Shopping 132

EXCURSIONS

Oświęcim 135   Tatra National Park 142
Zakopane 139   Częstochowa 147

COLOUR MAPS   back pages

Around Kraków ....Map 1   Old Town & Around ......Map 4   Wawel ....Map 6
Greater Kraków ....Map 2   Stradom, Kazimierz
Inner Kraków ....Map 3   & Podgórze ....Map 5

The Author

Krzysztof Dydyński

Krzysztof was born and raised in Warsaw, Poland. Though he graduated in electronic engineering and became an assistant professor in the subject, he soon realised that there's more to life than microchips. In the mid-1970s he took off to Afghanistan and India and has been back to Asia several times since. In the 1980s a newly discovered passion for Latin America took him to Colombia, where he lived for over four years and travelled throughout the continent. In search of a new incarnation, he has made Australia his home and worked for Lonely Planet as an artist, designer and writer. He is the author of *Poland*, *Colombia* and *Venezuela* and has contributed to other Lonely Planet books.

FROM THE AUTHOR

This book was written with a great deal of help from old and new friends, who generously contributed information, advice, inspiration, hospitality and much else. Warmest thanks to Ewa, Jaga and Janusz Mączka, Ela Lis, Kazimierz Stagrowski, Angela Melendro, Wayne Paulter, Grzegorz Słącz, Olga Jaros, Jacek and Grażyna Wojciechowicz, Maciek and Ewa Gajewscy, and Leszek Żebrowski.

This Book

Some of the text and illustrative material from the third edition of *Poland* has been used in this book.

From the Publisher

This first edition of Krakow was edited in Lonely Planet's Melbourne office by Jocelyn Harewood with help from Darren O'Connell and Anne Mulvaney. Mapping, design and layout was done by Celia Wood with help from Yvonne Bischofberger and Tim Uden. Thanks to Marcel Gaston and Mark Griffiths for guidance, to Matt King for arranging the illustrations and to Quentin Frayne and Agata Sternalski for the Language and Health sections.

Photographs were provided by Lonely Planet Images. The front cover was designed by Guillaume Roux.

Foreword

ABOUT LONELY PLANET GUIDEBOOKS

The story begins with a classic travel adventure: Tony and Maureen Wheeler's 1972 journey across Europe and Asia to Australia. Useful information about the overland trail did not exist at that time, so Tony and Maureen published the first Lonely Planet guidebook to meet a growing need.

From a kitchen table, then from a tiny office in Melbourne (Australia), Lonely Planet has become the largest independent travel publisher in the world, an international company with offices in Melbourne, Oakland (USA), London (UK) and Paris (France).

Today Lonely Planet guidebooks cover the globe. There is an ever-growing list of books and there's information in a variety of forms and media. Some things haven't changed. The main aim is still to help make it possible for adventurous travellers to get out there – to explore and better understand the world.

At Lonely Planet we believe travellers can make a positive contribution to the countries they visit – if they respect their host communities and spend their money wisely. Since 1986 a percentage of the income from each book has been donated to aid projects and human rights campaigns.

Updates Lonely Planet thoroughly updates each guidebook as often as possible. This usually means there are around two years between editions, although for more unusual or more stable destinations the gap can be longer. Check the imprint page (following the colour map at the beginning of the book) for publication dates.

Between editions up-to-date information is available in two free newsletters – the paper *Planet Talk* and email *Comet* (to subscribe, contact any Lonely Planet office) – and on our Web site at www.lonelyplanet.com. The *Upgrades* section of the Web site covers a number of important and volatile destinations and is regularly updated by Lonely Planet authors. *Scoop* covers news and current affairs relevant to travellers. And, lastly, the *Thorn Tree* bulletin board and *Postcards* section of the site carry unverified, but fascinating, reports from travellers.

Correspondence The process of creating new editions begins with the letters, postcards and emails received from travellers. This correspondence often includes suggestions, criticisms and comments about the current editions. Interesting excerpts are immediately passed on via newsletters and the Web site, and everything goes to our authors to be verified when they're researching on the road. We're keen to get more feedback from organisations or individuals who represent communities visited by travellers.

Lonely Planet gathers information for everyone who's curious about the planet – and especially for those who explore it first-hand. Through guidebooks, phrasebooks, activity guides, maps, literature, newsletters, image library, TV series and Web site we act as an information exchange for a worldwide community of travellers.

Research Authors aim to gather sufficient practical information to enable travellers to make informed choices and to make the mechanics of a journey run smoothly. They also research historical and cultural background to help enrich the travel experience and allow travellers to understand and respond appropriately to cultural and environmental issues.

Authors don't stay in every hotel because that would mean spending a couple of months in each medium-sized city and no, they don't eat at every restaurant because that would mean stretching belts beyond capacity. They do visit hotels and restaurants to check standards and prices, but feedback based on readers' direct experiences can be very helpful.

Many of our authors work undercover, others aren't so secretive. None of them accept freebies in exchange for positive write-ups. And none of our guidebooks contain any advertising.

Production Authors submit their raw manuscripts and maps to offices in Australia, USA, UK or France. Editors and cartographers – all experienced travellers themselves – then begin the process of assembling the pieces. When the book finally hits the shops, some things are already out of date, we start getting feedback from readers and the process begins again ...

WARNING & REQUEST

Things change – prices go up, schedules change, good places go bad and bad places go bankrupt – nothing stays the same. So, if you find things better or worse, recently opened or long since closed, please tell us and help make the next edition even more accurate and useful. We genuinely value all the feedback we receive. Julie Young coordinates a well travelled team that reads and acknowledges every letter, postcard and email and ensures that every morsel of information finds its way to the appropriate authors, editors and cartographers for verification.

Everyone who writes to us will find their name in the next edition of the appropriate guidebook. They will also receive the latest issue of *Planet Talk*, our quarterly printed newsletter, or *Comet*, our monthly email newsletter. Subscriptions to both newsletters are free. The very best contributions will be rewarded with a free guidebook.

Excerpts from your correspondence may appear in new editions of Lonely Planet guidebooks, the Lonely Planet Web site, *Planet Talk* or *Comet*, so please let us know if you *don't* want your letter published or your name acknowledged.

Send all correspondence to the Lonely Planet office closest to you:

Australia: PO Box 617, Hawthorn, Victoria 3122
USA: 150 Linden St, Oakland, CA 94607
UK: 10A Spring Place, London NW5 3BH
France: 1 rue du Dahomey, 75011 Paris

Or email us at: talk2us@lonelyplanet.com.au

For news, views and updates see our Web site: www.lonelyplanet.com

HOW TO USE A LONELY PLANET GUIDEBOOK

The best way to use a Lonely Planet guidebook is any way you choose. At Lonely Planet we believe the most memorable travel experiences are often those that are unexpected, and the finest discoveries are those you make yourself. Guidebooks are not intended to be used as if they provide a detailed set of infallible instructions!

Contents All Lonely Planet guidebooks follow roughly the same format. The Facts about the Destination chapters or sections give background information ranging from history to weather. Facts for the Visitor gives practical information on issues like visas and health. Getting There & Away gives a brief starting point for researching travel to and from the destination. Getting Around gives an overview of the transport options when you arrive.

The peculiar demands of each destination determine how subsequent chapters are broken up, but some things remain constant. We always start with background, then proceed to sights, places to stay, places to eat, entertainment, getting there and away, and getting around information – in that order.

Heading Hierarchy Lonely Planet headings are used in a strict hierarchical structure that can be visualised as a set of Russian dolls. Each heading (and its following text) is encompassed by any preceding heading that is higher on the hierarchical ladder.

Entry Points We do not assume guidebooks will be read from beginning to end, but that people will dip into them. The traditional entry points are the list of contents and the index. In addition, however, some books have a complete list of maps and an index map illustrating map coverage.

There may also be a colour map that shows highlights. These highlights are dealt with in greater detail in the Facts for the Visitor chapter, along with planning questions and suggested itineraries. Each chapter covering a geographical region usually begins with a locator map and another list of highlights. Once you find something of interest in a list of highlights, turn to the index.

Maps Maps play a crucial role in Lonely Planet guidebooks and include a huge amount of information. A legend is printed on the back page. We seek to have complete consistency between maps and text, and to have every important place in the text captured on a map. Map key numbers usually start in the top left corner.

Although inclusion in a guidebook usually implies a recommendation we cannot list every good place. Exclusion does not necessarily imply criticism. In fact there are a number of reasons why we might exclude a place – sometimes it is simply inappropriate to encourage an influx of travellers.

Introduction

The royal capital for half a millennium, Kraków has witnessed and absorbed more of Polish history than any other city in the country. Moreover, unlike most other Polish cities, it came through the last war unscathed, hence it has retained much of this past, which is guarded in its walls, works of art and traditions. The postwar period seems to have had little impact; the tallest structures on Kraków's skyline are not skyscrapers but the spires of old churches.

In appreciation of the town's exceptional historic and artistic values, in 1978 UNESCO included the centre of Kraków on its first list of the world's cultural heritage. No other city in Poland has so many historic buildings and monuments (about 6000), and nowhere else will you encounter such a vast collection of works of art (2.5 million).

Yet there's more to see than ancient walls. Kraków is alive and vibrant, with the past and present mingling harmoniously. The continuity of its traditions gives the town its own peculiar atmosphere, and countless legends have added their aura. Kraków is a city with character and soul.

Traditionally the major centre of Polish culture, Kraków's cultural status remains very high. Many leading figures of contemporary arts and culture – Andrzej Wajda, Roman Polański and Krzysztof Penderecki, to name just a few – are associated with the city. The two Nobel prize winners in literature, Czesław Miłosz (1980) and Wisława Szymborska (1996), live here. The city also gave the world its first Polish pope.

Kraków is Poland's best educated city. With its renowned six-century-old Jagiellonian University and 12 other institutions of higher education, it has over 70,000 students, a tenth of the city's population.

Give yourself plenty of time in Kraków – this is not a place to rush through. The longer you stay, the more captivating you'll find it and there's almost always a festival or other special event happening. However, if you feel like escaping from the urban grit there's a fair choice of national parks and significant sights not far from the city, including the chilling Auschwitz death camp and the 700-year-old Wieliczka salt mine, both UNESCO World Heritage List sites.

Facts about Kraków

HISTORY
Prehistory

The area of present-day Kraków hosted nomadic tribes for at least 50,000 years – that's what the archaeologists determined after they had examined primitive flint tools and other remains found on the Wawel hill and its environs. In the nearby Ojców caves, traces of human habitation go back even much further, to about 200,000 BC. However, it wasn't until the Neolithic period (4000 to 2000 BC) that permanent farming communities began to evolve in this part of Europe and trading routes started to crisscross the thick forests which covered the area.

In the last millennium BC and the early centuries AD, such diverse groups as Celts, Balts, Goths, Huns and various Germanic communities invaded, crossed and sometimes settled in the region, before the Slavs arrived from the south-east in the course of the 6th or 7th century AD and gradually pushed the existing inhabitants off. Different Slavonic groups eventually conquered and settled different regions of what is now Poland.

Kraków's Origins

The first traces of Kraków as an organised village date from the 7th century, and by the 9th century it grew into one of the main settlements of the Wiślanie (Vistulans), a Slavonic tribe which had spread around the region known as Małopolska (Little Poland). The earliest written record of Kraków dates from 965, when an Arabian traveller and merchant of Jewish descent, Ibrahim ibn Yaqub from Cordova, visited the town and referred to it in his account as a trade centre called Krakwa.

By that time, Poland was slowly emerging in Wielkopolska (Great Poland), after diverse Slavonic tribes inhabiting the region had been united into a single political unit under the domination of the group known as Polanie (the people of the fields). The first recorded ruler, Duke Mieszko I of the Piast dynasty, was converted to Christianity in 966. This date is recognised as the formal birth of the Polish state. The first capital and archbishopric were established in Gniezno and, in 1000, three bishoprics were founded in three key locations across Poland. One of these was Kraków, which

The separate walled cities of Kraków and Kazimierz, in the late 15th century.

gives an indication of the town's importance in those early days.

The son of Mieszko I, Bolesław Chrobry (Boleslaus the Brave, 992-1025), enlarged the empire to the size and shape similar to that of Poland today. Shortly before his death he was crowned the first Polish king by the pope bull, thus introducing Poland into the family of European monarchies.

Medieval Times

Sandwiched between two expansive powers, Germany (the Holy Roman Empire in those days) and Russia (which was then hundreds of small principalities dominated by Kievan Rus), from its dawn Poland was engaged in numerous armed conflicts with one or the other, or with both at the same time. Due to these pressures, particularly the constant German invasions of the northwest, the administrative centre of the country was moved from Great Poland to the less vulnerable Little Poland. By the middle of the 11th century, Kraków was established as the royal seat. The Wawel castle and several churches were built in the 11th century and the town, initially centred around the Wawel hill, grew in size and power.

In their devastating 13th century invasion, the Mongol tribe of Tatars conquered Kiev and most of the Russian principalities, then pushed farther westward into Poland. In 1241-42 they had ravaged much of Little Poland, including Kraków, which was largely burned down. In 1257 the new town's centre was laid out on a grid pattern, with a vast market square in the centre. Brick and stone largely replaced wood, and Gothic became the dominant architectural style.

Poland gradually became a mighty, prosperous state under the rule of King Kazimierz III Wielki (Casimir III the Great, 1333-70), and the capital of Kraków flourished. Two new towns were founded in Kraków's neighbourhood: Kazimierz in 1335, to the south, and Kleparz in 1366, to the north.

The king was a generous patron of art and scholarship. In 1364 he founded the Kraków Academy (later renamed the Jagiellonian University), the second university in Central Europe after the one in Prague. Nicolaus Copernicus (Mikołaj Kopernik), who would later develop his heliocentric theory, studied here in the 1490s.

As the city grew, so did its cosmopolitan community, which comprised a host of minorities, the most significant of which were the Jews, who began to appear in Kraków as early as the 12th century. Their numbers grew quickly from the 1330s when, amid the increasing religious persecution of Jews in the rest of Europe, King Kazimierz Wielki offered them shelter in Poland. Their community in Kraków soon became strong enough to be the focus of conflict, and in 1494 King Jan Olbracht (John Albert, 1492-1501) expelled them from the city. They moved to nearby Kazimierz, where they were assigned a small area.

When King Kazimierz Wielki died heirless, the throne passed to the daughter of the king of Hungary, Princess Jadwiga, who in 1386 married Duke Władysław Jagiełło of Lithuania. He accepted the Catholic faith and became the first ruler of the Jagiellonian dynasty. As a result of his

King Kazimierz III Wielki (the Great), a caring ruler and generous patron of the arts.

political marriage, Poland's territory expanded five-fold overnight, and the Polish-Lithuanian alliance would last through the following four centuries.

Under Jagiełło (1386-1434), Polish territory continued to increase. The king led a series of successful wars, including the Battle of Grunwald in 1410, when the Polish-Lithuanian army defeated the Teutonic Knights, marking the start of their decline. In the Thirteen Years' War of 1454-66, the Teutonic Order was eventually disbanded and Poland regained access to the Baltic Sea. The Polish empire now extended from the Baltic Sea to the Black Sea, making it the largest European state.

The Golden Age

The early 16th century brought the Renaissance to Poland. The incumbent king, Zygmunt I Stary (Sigismund the Old, 1506-48), was a great promoter of the arts. The Latin language was gradually supplanted by Polish and a national literature was born. Printing presses came into use and books began to appear. In 1543, Nicolaus Copernicus published his immortal work, titled *On the Revolutions of the Celestial Spheres*, which altered the course of astronomy by proposing that the earth moves around the sun.

The next and last king of the Jagiellonian dynasty, Zygmunt II August (Sigismund Augustus, 1548-72), continued his father's patronage of arts and culture. Thanks to their inspiring and protective policies, the arts and sciences flourished and the two reigns came to be referred to as Poland's golden age. Kraków's economic and cultural expansion reached its peak in that period. The medieval Wawel castle gave way to a mighty Renaissance palace, and the town's population passed the 30,000 mark.

The bulk of Poland's population was made up of Poles and Lithuanians, but included significant minorities of Germans, Ruthenians (Ukrainians), Tatars, Armenians and Livonians (Latvians). Jews constituted an important and steadily growing part of the community, and by the end of the 16th century Poland had a larger Jewish population than the rest of Europe com-

bined. By 1800, Poland was home to three-quarters of the world's Jews.

Religious freedom was constitutionally established by the Sejm (or Diet – the Polish parliament) in 1573 and the equality of creeds officially guaranteed. Such diverse faiths as Roman Catholic, Eastern Orthodox, Protestant, Judaic and Islamic were able to coexist relatively peacefully.

Decline

During the reign of Zygmunt August, the threat of Russian expansionism increased. In the hope of strengthening the monarchy, the Sejm convened in 1569 and unified Poland and Lithuania into a single state. There was no heir apparent to the throne, so it established a system of royal succession based on election by a popular assembly of the gentry, a class of local nobility which had attained significant political power. In the absence of a serious Polish contender, a foreign candidate would be considered.

The experiment proved disastrous and eventually led to Poland's three partitions two centuries later. During this period (known as the Royal Republic), Poland was ruled by 11 kings, only four of whom were native Poles. The first elected king, Henri de Valois, retreated to his native France after barely four months on the Polish throne. His successor, prince of Transylvania Stefan Batory (Stephen Bathory, 1576-86), proved to be a much wiser choice. He conducted a series of successful battles against Tsar Ivan the Terrible.

After Batory's premature death, the crown was offered to the Swede Zygmunt III Waza (Sigismund Vasa, 1587-1632), the first of three kings of Poland of the Vasa dynasty. As a ruler of two countries, he wanted to be closer to his motherland. An opportune moment came in 1595 when a fire consumed Wawel castle, and he moved the court from Kraków to Warsaw.

The transfer of the capital, completed by 1609, brought an end to Kraków's good fortunes. Though the city remained the place of coronations and burials, the king and the court resided in Warsaw and political and cultural life was centred there.

Meanwhile, wars continued unabated. The most disastrous of these was the Swedish invasion of 1655-60, known as the Deluge, in which Poland lost over a quarter of its national territory. Cities were burned and plundered, and the economy destroyed. From the population of 10 million, four million people succumbed to war, famine and bubonic plague. Kraków was captured and looted.

The last bright moment in the long decline of the Royal Republic was the reign of Jan III Sobieski (1674-96), a brilliant commander who led several victorious battles against the Ottomans. The most significant of these was the Battle of Vienna in 1683, in which he defeated the Turks and forced their retreat from Europe. Ironically, the victory only strengthened Austria, a country which would later take its turn at invading Poland.

The 18th century saw the agony of the Polish state. Kraków's glory was long over and its population dropped to a mere 10,000 people. Wawel castle was in such poor shape that the Sejm allowed Stanisław August Poniatowski to be crowned in Warsaw, not in Kraków as was the rule up to that time. As things turned out, he was the last Polish king (1764-95).

The Partitions

When anti-Russian rebellion broke out in Poland, Russia entered into treaties with Prussia and Austria, and in 1773 the three countries annexed three substantial chunks of Poland, amounting to 29% of Polish territory. The partition had the effect of an icy cold shower and led to immediate reforms in the administrative, military and educational spheres. In 1791, a new, fully liberal constitution was passed. It was known as the Constitution of the 3rd of May, and was the world's second written delineation of government responsibility (the first was that of the USA).

In response, Catherine the Great sent Russian troops into Poland and crushed resistance. The reforms were abolished by force. The second partition came in 1793, with Russia and Prussia strengthening their grip by grabbing over half the remaining Polish territory.

Patriotic forces under the leadership of Tadeusz Kościuszko, a hero of the American War of Independence, launched an armed rebellion in 1794. The campaign gained popular support and the rebels won some early victories, but the Russian troops were stronger and better armed and they finally defeated the Polish forces. This time the three occupying powers decided to eradicate the troublesome nation altogether, and in the third partition, effected in 1795, divided the rest of Poland's territory among themselves. Poland disappeared from the map for the next 123 years.

Kraków fell under Austrian rule, which proved to be the least oppressive of the three occupants. The city enjoyed reasonable, and steadily increasing, cultural and political freedom. By the closing decades of the 19th century it had become the major centre of Polish culture and the spiritual capital of the formally nonexistent country, a focus for intellectual life and theatre. The avant-garde artistic and literary movement known as Młoda Polska (Young Poland) developed here in the 1890s. It was also here that Józef Piłsudski, the prophet of Poland's independence, began to form armed squads in 1908, which later evolved into the Polish Legions.

WWI

WWI broke out in August 1914. On one side were the Central Powers, Austria and Germany (including Prussia); on the other Russia and its western allies. With Poland's three occupying powers at war, most of the fighting was staged on the territories inhabited by the Poles, resulting in staggering losses of life and livelihood. About one million Poles died. Since no formal Polish state existed, there was no army to fight for the national cause, apart from Piłsudski's poorly armed Polish Legions.

Paradoxically, the war eventually brought about Polish independence. However, it came mostly by a combination of external circumstances rather than through the direct participation of the Poles. After the October Revolution of 1917, Russia, then plunged into civil war, no longer had

Lenin in Kraków

Following the defeat of the revolution of 1905, the tsarist authorities carried out mass arrests of the leaders and participants of the failed revolt. To avoid the danger, Vladimir Lenin decided to flee the country and went to Paris in 1907, from where he directed the communist movement for the next five years.

In April 1912, *Pravda,* the communist paper, was launched in St Petersburg. It was locally organised by Stalin, but he was arrested after publishing the first edition. Lenin tried to co-ordinate further editions from abroad but it wasn't easy because of Paris' political climate and its distance from Russia. He sought to be closer to the motherland and chose Kraków as the base for his further activities.

Kraków was a much better option than Paris for various reasons. While the French police collaborated at that time with Russian security services, the attitude of the Poles towards the Russian police (and towards the entire Russian government) was extremely hostile, so Lenin could carry out his activities with more ease and less risk. Kraków's other great advantage was its proximity to Russia – meetings with Russian activists could be held easily and frequently and the mail was delivered quickly. In fact, parcels and letters (including discourses and articles for *Pravda*) were carried by local peasants from Kraków across the border to Russia then sent domestically, avoiding suspicion.

Lenin came to Kraków with his wife and her mother in June 1912 and lived in the city for two years and one month. He first resided in Kraków's central Hotel Victoria (no longer existing), and later lived in rented houses around the city, changing his address several times. During the summers of 1913 and 1914, he spent several months at Podhale at the foot of the Tatra Mountains because of his wife's health problems. In August 1914 he was arrested in Poronin and jailed in Nowy Targ, but was released after just 11 days in prison, following a petition by some renowned Polish artists. To avoid the risk of possible further arrests he soon moved to Switzerland.

After WWII, a Lenin Museum was opened in Kraków, but it was closed in 1989 when the communist rule crumbled. In the same year, a massive Lenin statue that stood in Nowa Huta was removed and later sold to a Swedish businessman for 100,000 Skr (it's now in Värnamo's museum in Sweden).

the power to oversee Polish affairs. The final collapse of Austria in October 1918 and the withdrawal of the German army from Warsaw in November brought the opportune moment. Marshal Piłsudski took command of Warsaw on 11 November 1918, declared Polish sovereignty, and usurped power as the head of state.

Between the Wars
The newborn country covered about 400,000 sq km and was populated by 26 million people, one-third of them of non-Polish ethnic background, mainly Jews, Ukrainians, Belarusians, Lithuanians and Germans. Warsaw took over most political

and administrative functions, but Kraków retained much of its status as a cultural and artistic centre. Marshal Piłsudski retired from political life in 1922, but seized power in a military coup in 1926, and held on until his death in 1935. Under his rule, Poland gained a measure of prosperity. By the outbreak of WWII, Warsaw had grown into a city of 1.3 million, including 350,000 Jews. Kraków at that time had 260,000 inhabitants, 70,000 of whom were Jews.

WWII
WWII began on 1 September 1939 with a massive German invasion of Poland. Despite valiant resistance there was simply no

hope of withstanding the numerically over-whelming, well armed German forces; Warsaw surrendered on 28 September, and the last resistance groups were quelled by early October. Hitler intended to create a Polish puppet state on the newly acquired territory, but since no collaborators could be found, western Poland was directly annexed to the Reich while the central regions became the so-called General Government, ruled from Kraków.

Hans Frank, the notorious Nazi governor, took the royal Wawel castle for his residence and began a reign of terror, with mass arrests, imprisonments and deportations. In an attempt to eradicate the Polish nation and Germanise the territory, the Polish education system was dismantled. The most valuable works of art, including Veit Stoss' famous altarpiece, were taken to the Reich. In November 1939, 183 Kraków university professors were arrested and deported to forced-labour camps in Germany. Jews were at first segregated and confined to the ghetto established in Podgórze suburb until they were taken to the death camps. Kraków, like all other Polish cities, witnessed the silent departures of Jews who were never to be seen again.

The death camps were probably the most horrifying and inhuman chapter of WWII. They were initially established in 1940, and by the following year there was already a large network of camps throughout Poland, including one in Kraków itself (in Płaszów suburb). The largest of all was Auschwitz, 60km west of Kraków. Some five million people were put to death in the gas chambers. Over three million Jews – most of Poland's Jewish population – and roughly one million Poles died in the camps.

During Hitler's occupation of Kraków (which lasted five years, four months and 12 days), the city was thoroughly looted by the Nazis but didn't experience major combats or bombing. On its way to Berlin, the Red Army's offensive left many Polish cities in ruins, but miraculously spared Kraków from destruction. Thanks to a manoeuvre by the commander of the Soviet troops, Marshal Ivan Koniev, the Nazis re-treated without a major fight and the city was saved and freed on 18 January 1945 after a swift military operation. As such, Kraków is virtually the only large Polish city that has preserved its historic architecture almost intact.

While Kraków was one of the luckier survivors, most of Poland's territory lay in ruins. Many cities were totally devastated; in Warsaw and Gdańsk, only 15% of the buildings had survived. The country lost about 40% of its national wealth and over six million people – 20% of its prewar population.

Communist Rule

After the liberation, Poland fell under Soviet domination. A provisional communist Polish government was set up in Moscow in 1945, then transferred to Warsaw, and Stalin launched an intensive Sovietisation campaign. Wartime resistance leaders were charged with Nazi collaboration, tried in Moscow and summarily shot or sentenced to arbitrary prison terms. The Polish United Workers' Party (PZPR) was formed to monopolise power, and a Soviet-style constitution was adopted. The Moscow-linked apparatchik, Bolesław Bierut, was placed into presidency.

New Polish borders were established at the Yalta and Potsdam conferences, and the radical boundary changes were followed by population transfers of some 10 million people: Poles were moved into the newly defined Poland while Germans, Ukrainians and Belarusians were resettled outside its boundaries.

Some major cities, such as Wrocław and Gdańsk, changed their ethnic picture altogether. Warsaw, which lost 700,000 people (over half of the city's prewar population), was repopulated with newcomers, significantly weakening its cultural traditions in the process. Kraków lost most of its Jewish population, but otherwise preserved its social fabric largely intact.

In an attempt to break Kraków's traditional intellectual and religious framework, the communist government presented the city with a huge steelworks at Nowa Huta, built just a few kilometres from the historic quarter. The social engineering proved less successful than its unanticipated by-product – an ecological disaster. Monuments which had somehow survived Tatars, Swedes and Nazis plus numerous natural misfortunes have gradually and methodically been eaten away by acid rain and toxic gas.

Stalinist fanaticism subsided fairly soon after Stalin's death in 1953. The powers of the secret police were eroded and some concessions were made to popular demands. The press was liberalised and Polish cultural values were resuscitated. However, the political doctrines, institutions and concepts remained in place over the rule of the two consecutive communist leaders, Władysław Gomułka (1956-70) and Edward Gierek (1970-80).

By the 1970s, the opposition had grown into a significant force. The election of Karol Wojtyła, the archbishop of Kraków, as Pope John Paul II in 1978 and his triumphal visit to his homeland a year later dramatically increased political ferment. When in July 1980 the government announced food-price increases, fervent and well organised strikes and riots broke out and spread like wildfire throughout the country. The government was no longer in a position to use force against the workers. The negotiations in the Lenin Shipyard in Gdańsk in August 1980 ended up with an agreement, and a nationwide independent trade union, Solidarność (Solidarity), was founded and soon gathered 10 million members (60% of the workforce). Lech Wałęsa, who led the Gdańsk strike, was elected chairperson.

The period of a spontaneous and chaotic democracy initiated by Solidarity was cut short by the martial law decreed by General Wojciech Jaruzelski in December 1981. However, the political climate in the region began to change after Gorbachev came into power in the Soviet Union in 1985. Four years later Jaruzelski had to compromise with the opposition and the Church over making a democratic system in Poland.

The 1989 round table agreements resulted in appointing the first noncommunist prime minister in Eastern Europe since WWII, which paved the way to the dominolike collapse of communism throughout the Soviet block. The Polish communist party dissolved itself in January 1990, and later the same year Wałęsa was elected as president in the first fully free election in postwar Eastern Europe. Poland rejoined the family of the old European democracies.

Postcommunist Kraków

A jump from Marx to market changed Kraków's priorities altogether overnight. Unlike during communist rule when Kraków was considered primarily an industrial centre, the new authorities turned their attention toward the city's historical values. They also had to redesign Kraków's model of development, taking into consideration environmental issues.

The communist period had brought a massive territorial and demographic expansion of the city, mostly due to the construction of the Nowa Huta steelworks. The postcommunist government cut down the plant's production and the workforce, and further cuts are planned in the coming years, along with the application of free-of-waste technologies. Partly as a result of Nowa Huta's new policies, Kraków's population remained pretty stable throughout the 1990s, as did the city area.

Half a century of indiscriminate pollution has left the city's architectural fabric with an urgent need of thorough repair work. A master revamping plan, drawn up in 1990, outlined priorities and restoration guidelines for some of the city's 12,000 buildings considered historic monuments. A lot has been done over the past decade, though there's still a long way to go.

Preservation of the historic heritage apart, the new authorities also turned their attention to the city's future architectural shape. By far the biggest project for the coming years is the construction of a new city centre around the main train station. It's now at the planning stage and there are many aspects to be defined, but it is going to change the image of Kraków and influence the life of the city.

GEOGRAPHY

Kraków lies in southern Poland, about 100km north of the Tatra Mountains which border with Slovakia. The city sits at an altitude of 216m. Save for some scattered rocky formations, Kraków's topography is relatively flat, but the terrain around the city is rugged in many areas, particularly towards the south.

The metropolitan area is 327 sq km, of which 35% is arable land and a further 5% is woodland.

The city is bisected by the Vistula (Wisła), Poland's longest river (1047km), which flows east then north through Warsaw to Gdańsk and empties into the Baltic Sea. Most of the city districts, including the historic quarter, are on the northern, left bank of the river.

CLIMATE

Kraków, like most of Poland, has a transitional climate. It is between maritime and continental, characterised by clearly differentiated seasons and changeable weather, with significant differences from day to day, season to season and year to year.

Spring starts in March and is initially cold and windy, later becoming pleasantly warm and often sunny. Summer, which begins in June, is mainly warm but hot at times, with plenty of sunshine interlaced with heavy rains. July is the hottest month. Autumn comes in September and is at first warm and usually sunny, turning cold, damp and foggy in November. Winter goes from December to March and includes short or longer periods of snow. High up in the mountains to the south, snow stays well into May. January and February are the coldest months.

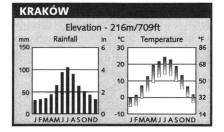

Kraków's average annual rainfall is around 680mm, with the greatest falls in the summer months. The mountainous areas receive more rain (and snow in winter).

ECOLOGY & ENVIRONMENT

The communist regime in Poland embarked on a forced march towards developing heavy industry, particularly coal mining and steel manufacturing, and then hasn't spent a penny on protecting the country's environment. Decades of intensive industrialisation without the most elementary protection have turned rivers into sewers and air into smog.

It wasn't until 1990, after the regime crumbled, that the Ministry of Environmental Protection was founded, which began to develop an environmental policy to try to clean up the mess left by the communists. Today, a decade down the track, Poland's environment is a bit better off yet still in an unenviable state.

Kraków's major air pollutant is the infamous Nowa Huta steelworks which were built in the early 1950s. Hardly ever modernised, this dinosaur of technology has been producing huge levels of sulphur dioxide and particulates for nearly 50 years. Some of the city's architectural monuments have been eaten away by the emissions. People's health is also affected. It wasn't until the mid-1990s that production was cut down and the emissions diminished, yet it still smokes badly.

Another environmental killer, the large aluminium works in the town of Skawina, 14km from Kraków, was closed down in 1981 due to the catastrophic fluor emissions. With a massive increase in motor vehicles over the past decade, transportation is becoming a serious air polluter. Central Kraków's traffic is increasingly gridlocked, and investment in road modernisation is minimal.

The Vistula is heavily polluted both upstream and downstream of Kraków, largely because of big pollutants along the river course and poor waste water treatment, as well as limited alternative natural water supplies. The quality of Kraków's tap water is so bad that many inhabitants don't drink it, opting instead for Oligocene water taken from wells several hundred metres deep. This water has undergone centuries of natural filtration and is potable without any treatment. There are a number of wells in the city accessible to the public.

Treatment of municipal waste is minimal, and practically all the waste ends up in landfills without any separation. Recycling of the waste is unpopular, except for some kinds of recyclable bottles, used for beer and some soft drinks, where you pay a small deposit, refundable in most places that sell them. Large waste bins for glass, plastics and paper have recently appeared at some central locations.

GOVERNMENT & POLITICS

Kraków is governed by the mayor *(prezydent)*, elected for four years by the city council, the members of which are elected locally. Andrzej Gołaś is the current mayor.

Kraków is the capital of Małopolska, one of Poland's 16 provinces *(województwa)*. This administrative division came into force in 1999, replacing the old, 49 province system. The province is ruled by a provincial governor *(wojewoda)*, nominated by the prime minister. Ryszard Masłowski is Małopolska's current governor.

Kraków in Figures

Kraków has today (data from 1999) 750,000 people, 270,000 cars, 580 buses, 490 trams and 3300 taxis. There are about 380 phone numbers and four physicians per 1000 inhabitants. The city has 17 hospitals, 220 pharmacies, 78 post offices, 72 historic churches, 18 cinemas, 13 theatres, 13 universities, 13 consulates and nine sports stadiums.

Kraków is home to 38 museums (counting all museum branches), the largest of which is the National Museum. Altogether they shelter about two million museum pieces, which is approximately a quarter of Poland's museum collections.

Małopolska covers an area of 15,114 sq km (4.8% of Poland's territory) and is populated by 3.2 million people (8.3% of Poland's population).

ECONOMY

Kraków is a significant industrial centre, with the Nowa Huta steelworks being its largest single facility. Before the recent production cuts, the steel mill accounted for nearly half of the national iron and steel output, and employed 35,000 workers. Kraków's well established manufacturing sector features machinery, telecommunications, tobacco, chemical, pharmaceutical, paper and food industries. Over the past decade, there has been a swift development of the service industries, including tourism-related ones.

More than 60% of Poland's GDP is now produced by the private sector, which employs about 60% of the workforce. Like most major urban centres throughout Poland, Kraków has embarked on a thorough privatisation program.

GDP growth was about 5% in 1998 and is expected to remain similarly high in the coming years. The level of unemployment peaked at 17% in mid-1994, but gradually diminished as the economy recovered, and by the end of 1998 was about 10%.

The huge inflation of the early 1990s dropped to 32% in 1994 and came down below 10% in 1998. It's expected to be around 6% in the year 2000. Average monthly wages stood at about US$225 at the end of 1993 and reached around US$375 by mid-1998.

POPULATION & PEOPLE

With the development of Nowa Huta and other new suburbs, Kraków has trebled in population since WWII to about 750,000, to become the country's third largest city after Warsaw and Łódź. The city's ethnic composition is almost entirely homogeneous, with Poles making up 98% of the population. Of the 70,000-strong prewar Jewish community, only around 6000 survived the war. The city's current Jewish population is estimated to be at most 150.

ARTS
Music

Though music has always been an integral part of human life, the first written records mentioning Polish music date only from the 12th century. It was centred around the Church and the court, included both vocal and instrumental forms, followed mostly western patterns and used the Latin language. Folk music certainly contained more native elements but there's not much information about it.

The Renaissance marked some developments in the musical culture but it was not until the Romantic period that Polish music reached its peak. The foremost figure was, without doubt, Frédéric Chopin (1810-49), who crystallised the national style, taking inspiration from folk and court dances and tunes such as *polonez* (polonaise), *mazurek* (mazurka), *oberek* and *kujawiak*. No one else in the history of Polish music has so creatively used folk rhythms for concert pieces and no one else has achieved such international recognition. Chopin has become the very symbol of Polish music.

Overshadowed by Chopin's fame, another composer inspired by folk dances, Stanisław Moniuszko (1819-72), created Polish national opera. Two of his best known operas, *Halka* and *Straszny Dwór*, are staples of the national opera houses. Also put into the shade of Chopin's achievements was Henryk Wieniawski (1835-80), one more of Poland's remarkable 19th century composers, who was also a noted violinist.

The premier musical personality in the first half of the 20th century was Karol Szymanowski (1882-1937). His best known composition, the ballet *Harnasie*, was influenced by folk music from the Tatra Mountains, which he transformed into the contemporary musical idiom.

In the composition of contemporary music, Poland has been up there with the world's best. In the 1950s and 1960s a wealth of talents emerged, among them Witold Lutosławski with his *Musique Funèbre* and *Jeux Vénitiens*, and Krzysztof Penderecki, with his monumental dramatic forms such as *Dies Irae*, *St Luke's Passion*, *Devils of Loudun* and *Ubu Rex*.

Largely eclipsed by the aforementioned masters, another great talent, Henryk Górecki, developed his original musical language. His Symphony No 3 was written in 1976, but it wasn't until the early 1990s that the second recording of this work hit the musical audience worldwide. The phenomenal success of the Third Symphony shed light on the other compositions of Górecki, notably his String Quartets Nos 1 and 2, written for, and exquisitely performed by, the Kronos Quartet.

Another composer whose name has entered international music dictionaries is Zbigniew Preisner, the author of music for Krzysztof Kieślowski's major films, including *Decalogue, The Double Life of Veronique* and *Three Colours*. His first non-film musical piece, *Requiem for my Friend*, dedicated to Kieślowski, saw its much celebrated première in October 1998.

Folk music is no longer common in urban life, but it's still cultivated and propagated by many singers, musicians and bands in rural areas, including the Tatra region south of Kraków.

Jazz took off, underground, in the early 1950s growing around the legendary pianist Krzysztof Komeda who, years later before his tragic death, composed the music to most of the early Roman Polański films. Komeda inspired and influenced many jazz musicians, such as Michał Urbaniak (violin, sax), Zbigniew Namysłowski (sax) and Tomasz Stańko (trumpet), all of whom became pillars of Polish jazz in the 1960s and remain pretty active today. Urbaniak opted to pursue his career in the USA, and today he is the best known Polish jazzman on the international scene.

Of the younger generation, Leszek Możdżer (piano) is possibly the biggest revelation to date. Other young jazz talents to watch out for include Piotr Wojtasik (trumpet), Maciej Sikała (sax), Adam Pierończyk (sax), Cazary Konrad (drums), Piotr Rodowicz (bass) and Kuba Stankiewicz (piano). Warsaw and Kraków are Poland's main jazz centres.

Kraków's Who's Who

Olga Boznańska (1865-1940) – Kraków-born impressionist painter who spent most of her creative life in Paris

Jan Długosz (1415-80) – Poland's most prominent medieval historian and chronicler, author of the comprehensive 12 volume *Historia Polonica*, which is still a major reference work on Polish history up to the author's death

Tadeusz Kantor (1915-90) – founder and director of the world-famous avant-garde *Cricot 2* theatre; also a noted painter

Mikołaj Kopernik (Nicolaus Copernicus, 1473-1543) – famous astronomer, author of the heliocentric theory, who studied at Kraków Academy in 1491-95

Tadeusz Kościuszko (1746-1817) – national hero who distinguished himself in the American War of Independence, then returned to Poland to lead a popular insurrection against Russian troops; despite a victorious battle at Racławice the insurrection was overthrown, which paved the way to the third partition of Poland

Stanisław Lem (born 1921) – Poland's premier science-fiction writer, whose books have been translated into more than 25 languages

Jacek Malczewski (1854-1929) – one of the most distinguished painters of the Young Poland movement, particularly noted for his symbolist works

Jan Matejko (1838-93) – Poland's most remarkable historical painter, memorable for a number of giant canvases depicting milestones in Polish history; also author of the wall paintings in St Mary's Church

Józef Mehoffer (1869-1946) – painter and stained-glass window designer, one of the major representatives of the Young Poland movement

Adam Mickiewicz (1798-1855) – Poland's greatest Romantic poet, spiritually associated with Kraków, though he never succeeded in coming here; his ashes were brought from Paris in 1890 and are now in Wawel Cathedral's crypts

Czesław Miłosz (born 1911) – writer, translator and literary critic, awarded the Nobel prize for literature in 1980; a longtime émigré based in the USA, he returned to Kraków, where he had lived for a short time just after WWII

Sławomir Mrożek (born 1930) – one of Poland's finest dramatists and cartoonists, author of *Tango, Striptease* and *Emigrants*; after a long time as an émigré he returned to Kraków in 1996

Jerzy Nowosielski (born 1923) – one of Poland's most renowned contemporary painters, author of numerous canvases and wall paintings in churches across Poland; many of his works are inspired by the Orthodox Church iconography

Krzysztof Penderecki (born 1933) – one of the world's leading contemporary composers, known for his monumental dramatic forms such *Dies Irae, St Luke's Passion, Devils of Loudun, Paradise Lost, Ubu Rex, Seven Gates of Jerusalem* and *Credo*

FACTS ABOUT KRAKÓW

Kraków's Who's Who

Józef Piłsudski (1867-1935) – founder of the Polish Legions, widely credited for regaining Poland's independence after WWI, then Poland's strong-hand ruler for most of the interwar period

Roman Polański (born 1933) – Paris-born film director and actor of Jewish descent, who lived in Kraków throughout his childhood and youth, including the WWII period when he went through all the horrors of the Podgórze ghetto (from which his mother was deported and died in a gas chamber)

Zbigniew Preisner (born 1955) – composer, author of music for Krzysztof Kieślowski's major films, including *Decalogue, The Double Life of Veronique* and *Three Colours*; his first non-film musical piece was *Requiem for my Friend*, dedicated to Kieślowski

Piotr Skrzynecki (1930-97) – co-founder and longtime leader of the legendary *Piwnica pod Baranami* cabaret

Juliusz Słowacki (1809-49) – one of Poland's greatest Romantic poets; like Mickiewicz, he never had an opportunity to come to Kraków, the city which featured in his work as a symbol of a free homeland; his ashes are now in Wawel Cathedral

Wit Stwosz (Veit Stoss, 1445-1533) – Nuremberg artist who lived in Kraków in 1477-96, and created here some extraordinary sculptural work, including the altarpiece in St Mary's Church, widely regarded as the finest piece of Gothic art in Poland

Karol Szymanowski (1882-1937) – Zakopane-based composer, best known for his ballet *Harnasie*, influenced by the folk music of the Tatra Mountains

Wisława Szymborska (born 1923) – poet, translator and literary critic, awarded the Nobel prize for literature in 1996

Andrzej Wajda (born 1926) – veteran film and theatre director, who began his career in the 1950s and is artistically active to this day; his films include *Ashes and Diamonds, Promised Land, Man of Marble, Man of Iron* and *Danton*

Karol Wojtyła (born 1920) – Kraków archbishop and cardinal who became Pope John Paul II in 1978

Stanisław Wyspiański (1869-1907) – poet, painter, playwright and stage designer, the major spiritual leader of the Young Poland movement. He is the author of *The Wedding*, one of the greatest Polish dramas, and of amazing Art Nouveau stained-glass windows, the best of which are in the Franciscan Church

KRZYSZTOF DYDYŃSKI

Stanisław Wyspiański

Literature

Literature developed after the introduction of Christianity in the 10th century, and for nearly half a millennium consisted mostly of chronicles and political treatises, written almost exclusively in Latin. The oldest surviving document is a chronicle from around the 12th century written by Gall Anonim, a foreigner of unknown origin. Jan Długosz (1415-80) was the most outstanding native historian, and his monumental, 12 volume chronicle (in Latin), narrating Polish history from the very beginnings right up till the author's death, is an invaluable source of information. The oldest text in Polish, the song *Bogurodzica* (Mother of God), was reputedly written in the 13th century and became the national anthem until the 18th century.

During the Renaissance, first the Polish language came into general use, then the invention of printing meant that books became widespread. The first printed text in Poland appeared in Kraków in 1473. During the course of the 16th century Polish largely replaced Latin, and Polish-language literature developed.

It wasn't actually until Romanticism, the period when Poland formally didn't exist, that Polish poetry really blossomed. Two poets, Adam Mickiewicz (1798-1855) and Juliusz Słowacki (1809-49), both associated with Kraków but working in exile, produced some of the greatest masterpieces of Polish poetry ever written. It comes as no surprise that their work is strong in patriotic feelings and prophetic visions.

In the period which followed, the central stage was dominated by two extraordinary historical novelists, Henryk Sienkiewicz (1846-1916) and Władysław Reymont (1867-1925). Both were awarded the Nobel prize in literature. Meanwhile, Kraków saw the birth of one of the greatest Polish dramas, *Wesele* (The Wedding) by Stanisław Wyspiański. Outsiders, however, will probably know better the work of Joseph Conrad (1857-1924). Born in Poland as Józef Konrad Korzeniowski, he left the country in 1874 and, after 20 years travelling the world as a sailor, settled in England and dedicated himself to writing (in English).

The interwar period produced several brilliant avant-garde writers who were only fully understood and appreciated after WWII. They include Bruno Schulz (1892-1942), Witold Gombrowicz (1904-69) and Stanisław Ignacy Witkiewicz, or Witkacy (1885-1939).

An unusual talent in many fields, including painting, literature and photography, Witkacy was not only an originator of unconventional philosophical concepts – the most notable of which was the 'theory of pure form' – but also the creator of the theatre of the absurd long before Eugène Ionesco made it famous. Only in the 1960s were Witkacy's plays, such as *Matka* (Mother), *Szewcy* (Cobblers) and *Nowe Wyzwolenie* (New Deliverance), discovered internationally. Witkacy committed suicide soon after the outbreak of WWII as an expression of his belief in 'catastrophism', the disintegration of civilisation.

The postwar period imposed a choice on many writers between selling out to communism and taking a more independent path. Czesław Miłosz, who himself had to solve this moral dilemma and eventually broke with the regime, gives an analysis of the problem in *Zniewolony Umysł* (The Captive Mind). Miłosz occupies the prime position in Polish postwar literature, and the Nobel prize awarded him in 1980 was a recognition of his achievements. He started his career in the 1930s and expresses himself equally brilliantly in poetry and prose, dividing his time between writing, translating and giving lectures on literature. After a long émigré period abroad, mostly in the USA, he finally returned to live in his beloved Kraków.

Another internationally known émigré, Sławomir Mrożek, is Poland's foremost dramatist, who by means of burlesque and satire parodies sociopolitical nonsense. Author of a dozen exquisite dramas, including *Tango* and *Emigranci* (Emigrants), he too decided to return after 30-odd years in exile to his native Kraków, where he started as a journalist in the 1950s.

Polish postwar literature was honoured for a second time with the Nobel prize in

Wisława Szymborska – 1996 Nobel Prizewinner

Polish postwar literature has twice been awarded the Nobel prize: in 1980 it went to Czesław Miłosz and in 1996 to Wisława Szymborska. While Miłosz, a longtime émigré based in the USA, is familiar to international readers due to his extensive literary output and numerous translations, Szymborska is relatively little known outside Poland, or at least she was until 1996.

A poet, translator and literary critic, Szymborska was born in 1923 in a small village near Poznań. In 1931 her family moved to Kraków, where she studied Polish literature and sociology at the Jagiellonian University in 1945-48, and where she lives to this day. Her early literary works, which she later disclaimed, were products of a climate of socialist realism, the official artistic doctrine in postwar Poland.

It wasn't until around 1955 that censorship subsided and artists began to create with increasing freedom. Her 1957 collection of poems entitled *Wołanie Yeti* (Calling out to Yeti) was probably Szymborska's first autonomous work. Next was *Sól* (Salt) of 1962. She was a dissident in the 1970s, and later, in the period of martial law and its aftermath, she wrote under a pen name for the local underground press and for the magazine *Kultura* published in Paris by Polish émigrés. She has also translated some French poetry into Polish.

Szymborska's literary output is relatively modest – no more than just 10 slim poetry collections – yet it's powerful stuff. The Swedish Academy described her as 'the Mozart of poetry' with 'something of the fury of Beethoven', and awarded her the Nobel prize for 'poetry that with ironic precision allows the historical and biological context to come to light in fragments of human reality'.

The Academy also admitted that 'the stylistic variety in her poetry makes it extremely difficult to translate', which is perhaps one of the reasons why she has been so little known outside Poland. For those intending to sample her work, a good introduction is the volume entitled *View with a Grain of Sand*

1996. This time it was awarded to Wisława Szymborska, a Kraków poet who was little known outside of her motherland. Again, Kraków's longtime dweller, Stanisław Lem (born 1921) is without a doubt Poland's premier science-fiction writer, and his books have been translated into more than 25 languages.

All the authors who were listed in this section have been translated into English.

Architecture

The earliest dwellings were made of perishable materials, and hardly any of them have survived. Stone as a construction material was only introduced in Poland with the coming of Christianity in the 10th century. From then on, durable materials – first stone, then brick – were used, and some of that architectural heritage has been pre-

served to this day. One of Poland's earliest stone constructions is the pre-Romanesque Rotunda of SS Felix and Adauctus, at Kraków's Wawel, dated at around 960-80.

Generally speaking, Kraków, like most of Poland, has followed the main Western European architectural styles with some local variations. The first, the Romanesque style, which dominated from approximately the late 10th century to the mid-13th century, used mainly stone, and was austere, functional and simple. Round-headed arches, semicircular apses and symmetrical layouts were almost universal. The best example of the Romanesque style in Kraków is St Andrew's Church.

The Gothic style made its way into Poland in the first half of the 13th century but it was not until the 14th century that the so-called High Gothic became universally adopted. Elongated, pointed arches and ribbed vaults are characteristic of the style. Brick came into common use replacing stone, and the buildings, particularly churches, tended to reach impressive loftiness and monumental size. Countless Gothic churches, castles, town halls and burghers' houses are left in Poland. In Kraków, the most representative include St Mary's Church, St Catherine's Church, Church of the Holy Cross and Collegium Maius.

In the 16th century a new fashion, from Italy, started to push out Gothic as the dominant style. More delicate and decorative, Renaissance architecture didn't aim for verticality and large volume but focused instead on perfect proportions, a handsome visual appearance and, in contrast to Gothic, almost never allowed brick to go uncovered. Attention was paid to detail and decoration, with bas-reliefs, decorative parapets, galleries, round arches and stucco work. Wawel castle's courtyard and some interiors are among Kraków's finest Renaissance structures.

Baroque appeared on Polish soil in the 17th century and soon became ubiquitous. This lavish, highly decorative style put a strong imprint on existing architecture by adding its sumptuous décor, which is particularly evident in church interiors and the palaces of rich aristocratic families. The most prominent figure of the baroque period in Poland was Tylman van Gameren, a Dutch architect who settled in Poland and designed a number of buildings, including some in Kraków. St Anne's Church (one of Gameren's projects) and the Church of SS Peter and Paul are the city's masterpieces of baroque architecture.

In the 18th century baroque culminated in the French-originated rococo, but it did not make much of a mark on Poland, which by then was swiftly sliding into economic and political chaos.

At the beginning of the 19th century, a complex phase of architectural development, known as historicism, started in Poland. This period featured various revivalist styles such as neo-Renaissance, neo-Gothic and even neo-Romanesque fashions.

The most important of all the 'neo' styles was neoclassicism, which used ancient Greek and Roman elements as an antidote to the overloaded baroque and rococo opulence. Monumental palaces adorned with columned porticoes were erected, as well as churches that looked like Roman pantheons. Neoclassicism left its strongest mark on Warsaw's architecture.

The second half of the 19th century was dominated by eclecticism – the style which profited from all the previous trends – but it didn't produce any architectural gems. More innovative was Art Nouveau, which developed in England, France, Austria and Germany, and made its entrance into Poland (still under partition) at the turn of the 19th century. It left behind some fresh decorative marks on architecture, especially in Kraków and Łódź. After WWI, neoclassicism took over again but soon lost out to new trends such as functionalism, constructivism and Art Deco.

The postwar period started with a heroic effort to reconstruct destroyed towns and cities, and the result, given the level of destruction, is really impressive. The Soviet-born architectural style, socialist realism, was imposed by the regime after the war and lasted up to around 1955. The most spectacular building in this style is the Palace of Culture and Science in Warsaw; in Kraków, the Nowa Huta suburb is the best example. Later on, architecture developed with increasing freedom.

Painting & Sculpture

Almost nothing is left of Romanesque painting and sculpture in Kraków, but the Gothic period has left behind quite a few fine examples of these forms of artistic expression, both of which show outstanding beauty and impeccable realism. They were almost exclusively religious in character, and most of the works were anonymous. Kraków's (and Poland's for that matter) best Gothic piece of sculptural art is Veit Stoss' massive, intricately carved altarpiece in St Mary's Church.

Visual arts in the Renaissance period, which were still largely religious, achieved a mastery in the decoration of church and chapel interiors (such as the Sigismund Chapel in the Wawel Cathedral – again, Poland's best) and bas-reliefs on the façades of houses.

Baroque was not only a matter of ornate forms and luxuriant decoration – it brought expression and motion to the visual arts. Baroque works are distinguished by the dynamic, often dramatic, expression of the figures. It also introduced trompe l'oeil wall-painting, which looks three-dimensional. Finally, baroque was extremely generous in the use of gold as an adornment. Many of Kraków's churches are crammed with baroque works of art, including altarpieces, saints' figures and paintings. Artists were increasingly departing from religious themes, taking as their subjects members of distinguished families, landscapes and historical scenes.

Polish Romanticism produced several painters of significance. The most prominent was the Kraków artist Piotr Michałowski (1800-55).

The second half of the 19th century witnessed a proliferation of monumental historical paintings, best represented by Jan Matejko (1838-93), the greatest artist of the genre, closely associated with Kraków. His works showed the glorious moments of Polish history, presumably in an attempt to strengthen the national spirit during the partitions. Today, they are the pride of Poland's museums. Other Kraków painters of the period who documented Polish history, especially battle scenes, include Artur Grottger (1837-67) and Wojciech Kossak (1856-1942), the latter particularly remembered as co-author of the colossal *Panorama Racławicka*, on display in Wrocław.

In the closing decades of the 19th century Europe saw a strong cultural ferment which resulted in a range of new artistic movements and styles such as impressionism, modernism, symbolism and Art Nouveau. The Polish answer to these new artistic winds was the Młoda Polska (Young Poland) movement – see the boxed text.

Witkiewicz (Witkacy) was the most exceptional figure of the interwar period. A

TAMSIN WILSON

Jan Matejko inspired national spirit.

philosopher, painter, dramatist and photographer, he executed a series of expressionist portraits, as well as a large number of colourful abstract compositions. He was also an inspired and prolific writer (see the earlier section on Literature).

After WWII and up till 1955, the visual arts were dominated by socialist realism, but later they expanded into a variety of forms, trends and techniques. Among the best known Kraków postwar painters are Tadeusz Kantor, renowned mainly for his Cricot 2 Theatre but also very creative in painting, drawing and experimental forms; and Jerzy Nowosielski, whose painting is partly inspired by the iconography of the Orthodox Church and who has also carried out internal decorations in churches.

Other important pillars of Kraków's postwar painting, whose works now adorn museum collections, include Stanisław Rodziński, Juliusz Joniak, Jan Szancenbach, Wiesław Obrzydowski, Zbysław Maciejewski, Włodzimierz Kunz and Stanisław Mikulski. Among the Kraków painters of a younger generation, now mostly in their forties, watch out for the works of Jacek Sroka, Andrzej Kapusta, Romuald Oramus, Michał

Young Poland

Young Poland (Młoda Polska) was an artistic movement which developed in Kraków between around 1890 and the outbreak of WWI. Broadly speaking, it was Poland's response to the artistic revolution which spread throughout Europe in the final decades of the 19th century, cutting off links with conventions and traditions, and introducing new artistic ideas, forms and techniques. Various new styles emerged during that period, including impressionism, Art Nouveau and symbolism, now considered milestones in the world's artistic evolution.

Young Poland profited from all these styles, but was firmly based on the great Polish Romantic traditions full of patriotic visions, explained by the fact that Poland formally didn't exist at that time. Yet, whereas the main subject of Romanticism was the male hero, the centre of attention of Young Poland was the woman. The movement was felt across the full spectrum of forms of artistic expression, including painting, architecture, design, literature, decorative arts, theatre and music.

Kraków at that time was part of the Austro-Hungarian empire, so no wonder the Viennese Sezessionstil (made famous by Gustav Klimt) left a significant imprint on Young Poland's artists. Full of sensuous female figures, flowers and flowing sinuous lines, this highly decorative, colourful style developed across Europe, including England, Germany and France, and is internationally known as Art Nouveau (Secesja in Polish).

One of the leading figures of Young Poland was Stanisław Wyspiański. A painter, dramatist and poet, he's as much known for his literary achievements (including *The Wedding*, one of the greatest Polish dramas), as for his pastel portraits and stained-glass designs. Józef Mehoffer (1869-1946) followed Art Nouveau style in his portraits and stained-glass designs, while Jacek Malczewski (1854-1929) was Poland's best symbolist painter of the era. Olga Boznańska (1865-1940), who lived in Paris for most of her creative period, favoured impressionism in her paintings.

Young Poland is also represented by some more traditional painters, including Aleksander Gierymski (1850-1901), Józef Chełmoński (1849-1914), Leon Wyczółkowski (1852-1936) and Julian Fałat (1853-1929), who preferred to express themselves in conventional forms and never completely gave up realism. This is particularly so in their Polish landscapes, an important part of their work.

Xawery Dunikowski (1875-1964) was Young Poland's most prominent sculptor and monument designer, though his most productive and creative period came much later. In music, Karol Szymanowski (1882-1937) leads the league of the early 20th century composers. Kraków's Young Poland theatre life got an important push in 1893 with the opening of the City Theatre (later renamed the Słowacki Theatre).

Świder, Teresa Żebrowska and Lucyna Patalita, to name just a few.

Graphic artists in postwar Kraków include Mieczysław Weiman, Janina Kraupe-Świderska, Jerzy Panek and Jerzy Otręba. Of a generation of the younger artists, who've already achieved remarkable success in graphic arts, it's worth mentioning Jerzy Jędrysiak, the painter Jacek Sroka, Ryszard Grazda, Andrzej Bębenek, Henryk Ożóg and Jerzy Dmitruk.

Among the prominent creators of modern sculpture in Kraków are Bronisław Chromy, Marian Konieczny and Jerzy Bereś. On their heels are younger Kraków sculptors such as Małgorzata Olkuska, Leszek Oprządek, Wiesław Domański, Józef Murzyn, Paweł Erazmus, Józef Polewka and Piotr Woroniec.

There's a lot of activity among the young generation in painting, sculpture and the graphic arts alike. Their works (as well as

Poster Art

Posters in Poland are taken very seriously and since the 1960s have risen to the level of real art, gaining wide international recognition. There is a museum of posters in Warsaw, and plenty of poster exhibitions from local to international level. Among the great Polish poster artists one cannot avoid mentioning names such as Henryk Tomaszewski, Jan Lenica, Jan Młodożeniec, Franciszek Starowieyski, Roman Cieślewicz and Waldemar Świerzy.

Poster art has found many followers who successfully continue this genre today. The most creative (and arguably most interesting) artists of the younger generation include Mieczysław Górowski, Jerzy Czerniawski, Wiesław Rosocha, Stasys Eidrigevičius, Wiktor Sadowski, Piotr Młodożeniec, Wiesław Wałkuski, Roman Kalarus, Andrzej Pągowski and Wiesław Grzegorczyk. See the Shopping chapter for where to buy posters in Kraków.

those by the artists listed previously) are presented by private commercial art galleries, which also sell them.

Theatre

Although theatre traditions go back to the Middle Ages, theatre in the proper sense of the word didn't develop until the Renaissance period, and initially followed the styles of major centres in France and Italy. By the 17th century the first original Polish plays were being performed on stage. In 1765 the first permanent theatre company was founded in Warsaw and its later director, Wojciech Bogusławski, came to be known as the father of the national theatre. The first professional company in Kraków began in 1781.

Theatre development was hindered during partition. Only the Kraków and Lviv theatres enjoyed relative freedom, but even they were unable to stage the great romantic dramas, which could not be performed until the beginning of the 20th century. By the outbreak of WWI, 10 permanent Polish theatres were operating. The interwar period witnessed a lively theatrical scene with the main centres in Warsaw and Kraków.

After WWII Polish theatre acquired an international reputation. Some of the highest worldwide recognition was gained by the experimental Teatr Laboratorium (Laboratory Theatre) created (in 1965) and led by Jerzy Grotowski in Wrocław. It was dissolved in 1984, and Grotowski concentrated on conducting theatrical classes abroad. Another remarkable international success was Kantor's Cricot 2 Theatre of Kraków, formed in 1956. Kantor died in 1990 and the theatre was dissolved a couple of years later. Of the existing experimental theatres, Gardzienice, based in the village of the same name near Lublin, and the Teatr Witkacego (Witkacy Theatre) in Zakopane, are among the best.

Kraków's most prominent theatre is the Teatr Stary (Old Theatre), easily one of the finest in the country. It's also Kraków's oldest company, and occupies the oldest surviving theatre building in Poland (from 1798). The cream of Poland's theatre directors, including Jerzy Jarocki, Andrzej Wajda and Krystian Lupa, has staged plays here.

Cinema

Kraków was Poland's first city that saw films, in December 1896, just a year after the famous show by the Lumière brothers took place in Paris. Kraków's first purpose-built cinema was opened in 1907.

The first Polish film was shot in 1908, but it was only after WWI that film production began on a larger scale. Until the mid-1930s Polish films were largely banal comedies or adaptations of the more popular novels, and were hardly recognised beyond the country's borders. The biggest Polish contribution to international film in that period was that of the actress Pola Negri, who was born in Poland and made her debut in a Polish film before gaining worldwide fame.

During the first 10 years after WWII, Polish cinematography didn't register many significant achievements apart from some semi-documentaries depicting the cruelties of the war. By contrast, the period which followed (1955-63) was unprecedentedly fruitful, so much so that it's referred to as the Polish School. Begun with the debut of Andrzej Wajda, the school heavily drew on literature and dealt with moral evaluations of the war, and its common denominator was heroism. A dozen remarkable films were made in that period, including Wajda's trilogy: *Pokolenie* (A Generation), *Kanał* (Canal) and *Popiół i Diament* (Ashes and Diamonds). Since then, the tireless Wajda has produced a film every couple of years; the ones which have gained possibly the widest recognition are *Człowiek z Marmuru* (Man of Marble), its sequel, *Człowiek z Żelaza* (Man of Iron) and *Danton*.

In the early 1960s two young talents, Roman Polański and Jerzy Skolimowski, appeared on the scene. The former made only one feature film in Poland, *Nóż w Wodzie* (Knife in the Water), and then decided to continue his career in the west; the latter shot four films, of which the last, *Ręce do Góry* (Hands Up), was kept on the shelf for over 10 years, and he left Poland soon after Polański. Whereas Skolimowski's work abroad hasn't resulted in marvels, Polański has made it to the top. His career includes such memorable films as *Cul-de-Sac*, *Rosemary's Baby*, *Chinatown*, *Macbeth*, *Bitter Moon* and *Death and the Maiden*.

Another ambassador of Polish cinema, Krzysztof Kieślowski, started in 1977 with *Blizna* (Scar) but his first widely acclaimed feature was *Amator* (Amateur). After several mature films, he undertook the challenge of making the *Dekalog* (Decalogue), a 10 part TV series which was broadcast all over the world. He then made another noteworthy production, *The Double Life of Veronique*, and confirmed his extraordinary abilities as a film maker with the trilogy of *Three Colours: Blue/White/Red*. The last project brought him important international film awards and critics' acclaim as one of Europe's best directors. He died during heart surgery in March 1996.

Other important directors who started their careers during the communist times include Krzysztof Zanussi, Andrzej Żuławski and Agnieszka Holland. The post-communist period has witnessed a rash of young directors, but one still waits for talent of the class of Polański or Wajda.

Poland has produced a number of world-class cinematographers, including Janusz Kamiński, awarded an Oscar for his work on Steven Spielberg's *Schindler's List*, shot in Kraków. He continued to work for Spielberg and received another Oscar for *Saving Private Ryan*. Less known but perhaps no less talented are several other Polish cinematographers responsible for various acclaimed Hollywood productions, including Adam Holender *(Midnight Cowboy)*, Andrzej Bartkowiak *(Verdict, Jade)*, Andrzej Sekuła *(Pulp Fiction)* and Piotr Sobociński *(Marvin's Room, Ransom)*.

SOCIETY & CONDUCT

By and large, Poles are more traditional than westerners and there's a palpable difference between the city and the village. While the way of life in urban centres increasingly mimics Western European and, especially, North American patterns, the traditional spiritual culture is still very much in evidence in the remote rural areas. Kraków is more conservative than Warsaw.

Poles are friendly and hospitable and there's even a traditional saying, 'a guest in the house is God in the house'. If you are able to befriend Polish people, they may be extremely open-handed and generous, reflecting another popular unwritten rule, 'get in debt but show your best'.

They don't keep as strictly to the clock as people do in the west. You may have to wait a bit until your friend arrives for an appointed meeting. Likewise, if you are invited to dinner or a party in someone's home, don't be exactly on time.

In greetings, Poles, particularly men, are passionate hand-shakers. Women, too, often shake hands with men, but the man should always wait for the woman to extend her hand first. You may often see the traditional polite way of greeting when a man

Kraków vs Warsaw

Competition or rivalry often comes into play when two national urban centres stand out from all the others. Take for instance Montreal and Toronto, Sydney and Melbourne, or Moscow and St Petersburg. Kraków and Warsaw are no different. Both served as capitals for significant periods and have influenced Polish history as no other cities have. Both have long been major cultural and artistic centres sheltering some of the country's best museums, theatres and orchestras, and both have been home to many illustrious artists, musicians and writers.

However, there are substantial differences, the most palpable of which is their approach to tradition and modernity. Broadly speaking, Kraków is a window to the nation's past in much the same way as Warsaw is a door to its future. While Kraków is the guardian of the national history, Warsaw is Poland's driving force behind its progress. History itself has contributed to the widening of the identity gap between the two cities: whereas Warsaw was completely wrecked during WWII, largely breaking traditional physical and spiritual links, Kraków was Poland's most lucky survivor, coming through the war with only minor structural damage.

The central Warsaw cityscape is marked by a thickening forest of steel-and-glass towers, but you won't find any of these in Kraków, where the skyline is dominated by old church spires. And while Warsaw has Poland's most open gay life (though don't expect it to be a New York or Sydney), you'll need a Sherlock Holmes' skill and stamina to find the gay community in Kraków.

KRZYSZTOF DYDYŃSKI

---

kisses the hand of a woman. Here, again, it's the woman who suggests such a form by a perceptible rise of her hand.

RELIGION

Poland is a strongly religious country and over 80% of the population are practising Roman Catholics. Needless to say, the 'Polish Pope', John Paul II, has strengthened the position of the Church in his motherland.

Since its introduction in 966, the Roman Catholic Church has always been powerful. However, in contrast to the present day, before WWII it had to share power with other creeds, particularly with the Eastern Orthodox Church. Always on the borderline between Rome and Byzantium, Poland has had both faiths present for most of its history.

Following WWII, Poland's borders shifted towards the west, and consequently the Orthodox Church is now present only along a narrow strip on the eastern frontier.

Its adherents number roughly 1% of the country's population, yet it is the second largest creed after Roman Catholicism.

A small bunch of Protestant churches exist mostly in the regions which were German before WWII, particularly in Silesia. They represent at most another 0.5% of the population. The remaining creeds are insignificant: Poland's three mosques serve the tiny Muslim population, and a handful of functioning synagogues hold religious services for the Jewish believers.

Kraków has about 160 Roman Catholic churches and chapels, distributed among 80 parishes. There are 24 monasteries and two abbeys in the city, plus a Theological Academy and 15 church seminaries.

Almost all of Kraków's synagogues survived WWII, but only one is now used for regular religious services. There's one Orthodox church, a few Protestant churches, and three tiny Buddhist communities.

LANGUAGE

Most Poles in Kraków only understand and speak the Polish language. This is generally true for attendants at public services such as shops, post offices, banks, bus and train stations, restaurants and hotels (except for some top-end places). You may even encounter language problems at tourist offices. The same applies for phone emergency lines, including the police, ambulance and fire brigade.

Ideally, everyone who wants to travel in Poland should know some basic Polish. A phrasebook and a small dictionary are essential. See the Language chapter at the back of this book for pronunciation and basic vocabulary.

English and German are the best known foreign languages in Poland, though they're by no means commonly spoken or understood. English may be heard in Kraków among the better educated. German is in large part a heritage of prewar territorial divisions, and is therefore mainly spoken in the regions which were once German, such as Masuria, Pomerania and Silesia.

Facts for the Visitor

WHEN TO GO

Theoretically, any time is a good time to visit Kraków, though you'll find a different picture depending on the season you go. Most visitors arrive in the tourist season, which runs roughly from May to September, that is, from mid-spring to early autumn. Its peak is in July and August, the months of school and university holidays, and also the time when most Polish workers and employees take their annual leave. Accordingly, many city dwellers leave for the mountains, beaches or lakes, but crowds of tourists, both nationals and, particularly, foreigners, turn up in town.

In that period, transport becomes more crowded than usual, and can get booked out in advance. Accommodation may be harder to find and more expensive, but fortunately, student dormitories open as student hostels, which roughly meets the demand for budget lodging. Most theatres are closed in July and August.

If you want to escape the crowds, probably the best time to come is either late spring (mid-May to mid-June) or early autumn (mid-September to mid-October), when tourism is under way but not in full flood. These are pleasantly warm periods, ideal for general sightseeing and outdoor activities, if you plan on some excursions, particularly to the Tatra Mountains.

The rest of the year, from mid-autumn to mid-spring, is colder, darker and perhaps less attractive for visitors, but this doesn't mean that it's a bad time to visit Kraków's sights and enjoy the cultural life which is nearly as active as during the tourist season. Understandably, hiking and other outings that depend on the weather are less popular in this period, except for skiing in the mountains in winter.

ORIENTATION

The great thing about Kraków is that almost all you need is at hand, conveniently squeezed into the small compact area of the Old Town (Stare Miasto). Even consulates, which normally prefer quiet locations outside central areas, have gathered in the heart of Kraków's historic quarter or close to it.

The Old Town, about 800m wide and 1200m long, has the Main Market Square (Rynek Główny) in the middle, and is surrounded by the park ring of the Planty, which was once a moat. On the southern tip of the Old Town sits the Wawel castle, and farther south stretches the historic district of Kazimierz.

The bus and train stations – where you're most likely to arrive – are next to each other on the north-eastern rim of the Old Town. The tourist office is right opposite the train station and you'll find a dozen hotels within a 500m radius. Rynek Główny is just a 10 minute walk from the station.

If you're coming by air, you'll arrive at Balice airport, 15km west of the city centre, linked to each other by city buses and taxis.

MAPS

You don't have to worry about maps before coming. The situation in Poland has improved greatly in recent years, and there are now a number of map publishers which produce country, regional and city maps of good quality, inexpensive and easily available. Maps cost roughly $1 to $3 (all prices are in US$), and you normally buy them in bookshops (see the Shopping chapter for details).

The maps in this book will suffice in most cases for general city sightseeing and excursions, but if you need more detail, or maps for special purposes, there's quite a choice on offer. Local tourist brochures and magazines, some free of charge, usually include a city map of central Kraków, which can be an added help.

TOURIST OFFICES
Local Tourist Offices

The Centrum Informacji Turystycznej KART or the state-run city centre of tourist information (☎ 422 04 71, ☎ 422 60 91) is at ul Pawia 8 opposite the train station. The office is open Monday to Friday from 8 am to 4 pm (from June to September until 6 pm and also on Saturday from 9 am to 1 pm).

Two private travel agencies have their own tourist information desks. The Dexter tourist office (☎ 421 77 06, ☎ 421 30 51, fax 421 30 36), strategically located in the Cloth Hall which stands in the middle of the Rynek Główny, is open Monday to Friday from 9 am to 6 pm, Saturday from 9 am to 1 pm. The Jordan tourist office (☎ 9319, ☎ 421 21 25), ul Długa 9, is open Monday to Friday from 9 am to 6 pm, Saturday and Sunday from 9 am to 3 pm.

Kraków also has a knowledgeable Cultural Information Centre – refer to the Entertainment chapter.

Tourist Offices Abroad

Polish tourist offices abroad include:

Austria
 Polnisches Fremdenverkehrsamt
 (☎ 01-524 71 91, fax 524 71 91 20),
 Mariahilfer Strasse 32-34/102, A-1070 Vienna
Belgium
 Bureau du Tourisme Polonais
 (☎ 02-511 81 69, fax 511 80 05),
 18/24 rue des Colonies, 1000 Brussels
France
 Office National Polonais de Tourisme
 (☎ 01-47 42 07 42, fax 42 66 35 88),
 49 ave de l'Opéra, 75002 Paris
Germany
 Polnisches Fremdenverkehrsamt
 (☎ 030-210 09 211, fax 210 09 214),
 Marburger Strasse 1, 10789 Berlin
Netherlands
 Pools Informatiebureau voor Toerisme
 (☎ 020-625 35 70, fax 623 09 29),
 Leidsestraat 64, 1017 PD Amsterdam
Spain
 Oficina Nacional de Turismo de Polonia
 (☎ 01-541 48 08, fax 541 34 23),
 Plaza de España 18 p 3, Edificio Torre de Madrid, 28008 Madrid
Sweden
 Polska Statens Turistbyra
 (☎ 08-21 60 75, fax 21 04 65),
 Kungsgatan 66, Box 449, S-10128 Stockholm
UK
 Polish National Tourist Office

 (☎ 020-7580 8811, fax 7580 8866),
 1st Fl, Remo House, 310-312 Regent St, London W1R 5AJ
USA
 Polish National Tourist Office
 (☎ 312-236 9013, ☎ 236 9123, fax 236 1125),
 33 Nth Michigan Ave, Ste 224, Chicago, IL 60601
 (☎ 212-338 9412, fax 338 9283),
 275 Madison Ave, Ste 1711, New York, NY 10016

DOCUMENTS
Passport

A valid passport is essential, and it must be stamped with a visa if you need one. Theoretically, the expiry date of your passport shouldn't be less than six months after the date of your departure from Poland. Make sure that your passport has a few blank pages for visas and entry and exit stamps.

Visas

Bilateral conventions allowing visa-free visits have been signed with a number of countries, and by 1999 there were already over 50 countries on the list, including most of Eastern Europe, the Commonwealth of Independent States and the three Baltic republics. Among other countries whose citizens don't need visas for Poland are Argentina, Austria, Belgium, Bolivia, Chile, Costa Rica, Cuba, Cyprus, Denmark, Finland, France, Germany, Greece, Honduras, Iceland, Ireland, Italy, Liechtenstein, Luxembourg, Malta, Monaco, the Netherlands, Nicaragua, Norway, Portugal, South Korea, Spain, Sweden, Switzerland, Uruguay, the UK and the USA. Stays of up to 90 days are allowed, except for Britons who are allowed to stay in Poland without a visa for up to 180 days.

Nationals of other countries should check with one of the Polish consulates and apply for a visa if they need one. Canadians, Australians, New Zealanders, Japanese, South Africans and Israelis still did need a visa as we went to press.

Visas are issued for a period of up to 180 days, and the price is the same regardless of the visa's duration, about $40 to $60, varying from country to country. Some of the consulates may give shorter visas if you

Meander through to Wawel along ul Kanonicza.

An old entry to Jewish apartments on ul Józefa.

Plac Matejki with the Grunwald Monument in the centre commemorating a major medieval victory.

Running east from Rynek Główny is ul Mikołajska, one of the historical steets of the Old Town.

apply by mail. You can stay in Poland during the period specified in the visa, which you have to indicate in the application form. You normally cannot extend your tourist visa once you are in Poland, so ask for a sufficiently long period while applying for it at home. There are also 48-hour transit visas (onward visa required) if you just need to pass through Poland. Visas are generally issued in a few days, with an express same-day service available in some of the consulates if you pay 50% more.

Travel Insurance

Ideally, all travellers should have a travel insurance policy, which will provide some sense of security in the case of a medical emergency or the loss or theft of money or belongings. Even if you never use it, it will probably help you to sleep more peacefully during the trip. It may seem an expensive luxury, but if you can't afford a travel health insurance policy, you probably can't afford medical emergency charges abroad either, if something goes wrong.

If you do need to make a claim on your travel insurance, you must produce a police report detailing the loss or theft (refer to the Dangers & Annoyances section later in this chapter). You also need proof of the value of any items lost or stolen. Purchase receipts are the best, so if you buy a new camera for your trip, for example, hang on to the receipt.

Driving Licence

If you plan on driving in Poland, make sure you bring your driving licence. Your licence from home will normally be sufficient if it bears a photograph, but if not, or if you want to play it absolutely safe, bring an International Driving Licence together with your local one. If you're bringing your own vehicle, car insurance (the so-called Green Card) is required.

Hostel Card

A HI membership card will gain you a 25% discount on prices in some youth hostels. Bring the card with you, or have one issued to you in Poland at any of the provincial branch offices of the Polish Youth Hostel Association (PTSM) in the main cities.

Student Card

If you are a student, bring along your ISIC card. You can also get it in Poland if you have your local student card or any document stating that you're a full-time student. The Almatur Student Bureau (which has offices in most major cities) issues ISIC cards for around $7 (bring a photo). The card gives reductions on museum admissions (normally by 50%), Polferry ferries (20%), LOT domestic flights (10%) and urban transport in Warsaw (50%), plus discounts on international transport tickets. There are no ISIC discounts on domestic trains and buses.

International Health Card

No vaccinations are necessary for Poland, though if you come from an area infected with yellow fever or cholera you may be asked for an International Health Certificate with those inoculations. For your own safety, you are advised to have the vaccination for hepatitis or at least a gamma globulin jab. See the Health section later in this chapter for more information.

Photocopies

Make copies of your important documents such as passport (data pages plus visas), credit cards, airline tickets, travel insurance policy and travellers cheque receipt slips. Take notes of the serial numbers of your cameras, lenses, camcorder, notebook and any other pieces of high-tech stuff you'll be taking on the trip. Make a list of phone numbers of the emergency assistance services (credit cards, insurance, your bank etc). Leave a copy of everything with someone at home and keep another with you, separate from the originals. Slip $50 or $100 into an unlikely place to use as an emergency stash.

It's a good idea to store details of your vital travel documents in Lonely Planet's free online Travel Vault in case you lose the photocopies or can't be bothered with them. Your password-protected Travel Vault is accessible online anywhere in the world – create it at www.ekno.lonelyplanet.com.

EMBASSIES & CONSULATES
Polish Embassies & Consulates
Poland has embassies in the capitals of about 90 countries. The consulates are usually at the same address as the embassy. In some countries there are additional consulates in other cities. The list includes:

Australia
(☎ 02-6273 1208)
7 Turrana St, Yarralumla, ACT 2600
(☎ 02-9363 9816)
10 Trelawney St, Woollahra, NSW 2025
Austria
(☎ 01-877 74 44)
Hietzinger Hauptstrasse 42c, 1130 Vienna XIII
Belarus
(☎ 172-13 32 60)
Rumiancewa 6, 200034 Minsk
Canada
(☎ 613-789 0468)
443 Daly Av, Ottawa 2, ON K1N 6H3
(☎ 514-937 9481)
1500 Avenue des Pins Ouest, Montreal, PQ H3G 1B4
(☎ 416-252 5471)
2603 Lakeshore Blvd West, Toronto, Ont M8V 1G5
Czech Republic
(☎ 02-2422 8722)
Václavské Námestí 49, Nové Mesto, Prague 1
(☎ 069-611 80 74)
ul Blahoslavová 4, 70100 Ostrava 1
France
(☎ 01-45 51 82 22)
5 rue de Talleyrand, 75007 Paris
Germany
(☎ 030-220 25 51)
Unter den Linden 72/74, 10117 Berlin
(☎ 0221-38 70 13)
Leyboldstrasse 74, 50968 Cologne
(☎ 040-631 20 91)
Gründgensstrasse 20, 22309 Hamburg
Hungary
(☎ 01-351 17 25)
Városligeti fasor 16, Budapest
Israel
(☎ 03-524 0186)
16 Soutine St, Tel Aviv 64-684
Lithuania
(☎ 02-709 001)
Smelio gatve 20 A, Vilnius
Netherlands
(☎ 070-360 28 06)
Alexanderstraat 25, 2514 JM The Hague
Russia
(☎ 095-255 0017)
ulitsa Klimashkina 4, Moscow

(☎ (812) 274 4170)
ulitsa Sovietskaya 12/14, St Petersburg
(☎ (0112) 274 035)
ulitsa Kutuzova 43/45, Kaliningrad
Slovakia
(☎ 07-580 34 18)
ul Jancova 8, 81102 Bratislava
Sweden
(☎ 08-764 4800)
Prästgardsgatan 5, 172 32 Sundbyberg, Stockholm
UK
(☎ 020-7580 0475)
73 New Cavendish St, London W1N 7RB
(☎ 0131-552 0301)
2 Kinnear Rd, Edinburgh E3H 5PE
Ukraine
(☎ 044-224 8040)
vulitsya Yaroslaviv 12, 252034 Kiev
(☎ 0322-760 544)
vulitsya Ivana Franko 110, Lviv
USA
(☎ 202-234 3800)
2640 16th St NW, Washington, DC 20009
(☎ 312-337 8166)
1530 North Lake Shore Drive, Chicago, IL 60610
(☎ 212-889 8360)
233 Madison Ave, New York, NY 10016
(☎ 310-442 8500)
12400 Wilshire Blvd, Suite 555, Los Angeles, CA 90025

Consulates in Kraków
All countries which maintain diplomatic relations with Poland have their embassies in Warsaw. Consulates are usually at the same address as the embassies, however some countries have additional consulates in other major Polish cities, including Kraków. They include:

Austria
(☎ 421 97 66) ul Krupnicza 42
France
(☎ 422 18 64) ul Stolarska 15
Germany
(☎ 421 84 73) ul Stolarska 7
Hungary
(☎ 422 56 57) ul Mikołajska 26
Russia
(☎ 422 83 88) ul Westerplatte 11
Ukraine
(☎ 656 23 36) ul Krakowska 41
USA
(☎ 429 66 55) ul Stolarska 9

CUSTOMS

When entering Poland, you're allowed to bring duty-free articles for your personal use while you travel and stay there. They include still, cine and video cameras plus accessories; portable self-powered electronic goods such as personal computer, cassette player and the like, together with accessories; a portable musical instrument; sports and tourist equipment such as bicycle, tent, skis etc; and medicines and medical instruments for your own use. You'll rarely be asked to declare these things.

The duty-free allowance on arrival is up to 250 cigarettes or 50 cigars or 250 grams of pipe tobacco and up to two litres of alcoholic drinks (not allowed for people aged under 17). Narcotics are forbidden and you'd be asking for trouble smuggling them across the border.

Unlimited amounts of foreign currency and travellers cheques can be brought into the country, but only the equivalent of up to 5000 euro can be taken out by a foreigner without a declaration. If you enter with more than 5000 euro and want to take it all back out of Poland, you need to fill in a currency-declaration form upon your arrival and have it stamped by customs officials. You are allowed to import or export Polish currency.

When leaving the country, you can legally take out, free of duty, gifts and souvenirs with a total value not exceeding $100. The export of items manufactured before 9 May 1945 is prohibited, unless you get an authorisation from the Department of Monuments' Protection.

MONEY
Currency

The official Polish currency is the złoty (literally 'gold'), abbreviated to zł. It is divided into 100 units called the grosz, abbreviated to gr. New notes and coins were introduced in 1995, and include five paper bills (10, 20, 50, 100 and 200 złotys) and nine coins (1, 2, 5, 10, 20 and 50 groszy, and 1, 2 and 5 złotys). The bills all feature Polish kings, have different sizes and are easily recognisable.

Exchange Rates

Polish currency is convertible and easy to change either way. The official exchange rate roughly represents the currency's actual value and there's virtually no longer a black market. The złoty's rate of depreciation against hard currencies has slowed down significantly over the past few years, to about 8% per year in 1999.

At the time we went to press the approximate rates were:

country	unit		złoty
Australia	A$1	=	2.66 zł
Canada	C$1	=	2.77 zł
euro	€1	=	4.43 zł
France	10FF	=	0.68 zł
Germany	DM1	=	2.27 zł
Japan	¥100	=	3.87 zł
UK	UK£1	=	6.85 zł
USA	US$1	=	4.11 zł

Exchanging Money

An essential question for many travellers is what to bring: cash, travellers cheques or a credit card. Any of the three forms is OK in Poland, though it's a good idea to bring a combination of two or even three to allow more flexibility. Travelling in Poland is generally safe, so there are no major problems in bringing some hard currency in cash, which is easiest to change. Travellers cheques are safer but harder to change and you get about 1% to 3% less than for cash. Finally, with the recent rash of ATMs, credit cards are becoming the most convenient way to get local currency.

Cash The place to exchange cash is at a *kantor*, a private currency-exchange office. Kantors can be either self-contained offices or just desks in the better hotels, travel agencies, post offices, department stores etc. There are so many of them, that we did not bother to mark them on the maps. They're easy to find, but if you can't spot one, just ask anybody for a kantor.

Kantors change cash only (no travellers cheques) and accept a number of the major world currencies. The most common and thus the most easily changed are the US dollar, the Deutschmark and the pound sterling (in that order). There's no commission on transaction – you get what is written on the board (every kantor has a board displaying the exchange rates of currencies it changes). The whole operation takes a few seconds and there's no paperwork involved. You don't need to present your passport or fill out any forms.

Exchange rates may differ slightly from kantor to kantor (about 1%), so check a few if you're going to change a large amount. Kantors buy and sell foreign currencies, and the difference between the buying and selling rates is usually not larger than 2%.

Most kantors are open on weekdays between roughly 9 am and 6 pm and till around 3 pm on Saturday. Some trade on Saturday afternoon and for a half day on Sunday, and a few stay open 24 hours.

Travellers Cheques Changing them is a bit more time-consuming than changing cash, and you'll get a little less. You can change cheques in a bank or at the American Express counter (☎ 422 91 80) in the Orbis office at Rynek Główny 41, and it's usually more favourable and faster to change them at the latter. It's open weekdays from 8 am to 6 pm, Saturday from 8.30 am to 1 pm (till 3 pm in summer).

Amex staff are efficient, speak English and change most major brands of cheque. The office's exchange rate is normally somewhat lower than that of banks, but, unlike banks, it charges no commission, so you are likely to get more złotys from your transaction.

The best known bank which changes travellers cheques is the Bank Polska Kasa Opieki SA, commonly known as the Bank Pekao, with several offices across town (including a convenient outlet at Rynek Główny 31, open weekdays from 8 am to 7 pm, Saturday from 10 am to 2 pm). It changes most major brands of cheque, of which American Express is the most widely known.

The exchange rate for cheques is roughly similar to that for cash in kantors, but banks charge a commission *(prowizja)* on transactions, which varies from bank to bank (somewhere between 0.5% to 2%). Banks also have a set minimum charge of $1.50 to $3. For example, the Bank Pekao commission on changing cheques into złotys is 1.5% with a minimum charge of $2.

Some banks will also exchange travellers cheques for US cash dollars and usually the

Some Tips About Changing Cash

To avoid hassles exchanging currency, one important thing to remember before you set off from home is that any banknotes you take to Poland must be in good condition, without any marks or seals. Kantors can refuse to accept banknotes which have numbers written on them (a common practice of bank cashiers totalling bundles of notes) even if they are in an otherwise perfect condition.

Kantors that trade on Sunday and at night usually give poor rates – try to avoid these times by changing enough money on Saturday to last you until Monday.

Don't forget to change your extra złotys back to hard currency before you leave Poland, but don't leave it to the last minute as exchange facilities at the land border crossings and airports tend to offer poor rates. If you are leaving from Kraków's Balice airport, change your złotys in a kantor in the centre before reaching the airport. If you are going to Slovakia overland, buy some Slovakian currency in Kraków for your initial expenses.

There are still a few street moneychangers hanging around touristy places (including one on ul Floriańska just off the main square), but it's best to give them a miss. They won't offer you a better rate than that in a kantor, and if one does, it may well indicate that you're dealing with a con man.

commission is lower (eg the Bank Pekao charges 0.5% with a minimum of $1.25). Once you have US cash dollars you can go to any kantor and change them into złotys at the usual kantor's rate.

Banks can be crowded and inefficient; you'll probably have to queue a while and then wait until they complete the paperwork. It may take anything from 10 minutes to an hour. You'll need your passport in any transaction. Some banks may insist on seeing the original receipt from where you bought your travellers cheques.

Credit Cards & ATMs Credit cards are increasingly popular for buying goods and services, though their use is still mostly limited to upmarket establishments. Among the most popular cards accepted in Poland are Visa, MasterCard, American Express, Diners Club, Eurocard and Access.

Credit cards are also useful for getting cash advances from banks, and the procedure is faster than changing travellers cheques. The best card to bring is Visa, because it's honoured by the largest number of banks, including the Bank Pekao.

Still faster and more convenient is to get an advance from an ATM *(bankomat)*. They first appeared in Poland in 1996 and spread like wildfire. Today most major banks have their own bankomats, and there are also a number of ATMs operated by Euronet, the largest ATM network in Poland, with a few dozen outfits across Kraków. Euronet ATMs accept 17 different credit cards, including Visa and MasterCard.

International Transfers A credit card solves the problem of transferring money, provided you are prepared to carry the credit charge or have someone back at home pay your expenses for you. Be aware of your credit limit.

If you don't have a credit card, you can have money sent to you through some of the major banks. If you need money urgently, you can use the Western Union Money Transfer. You will receive the money within 15 minutes from the moment your sender pays it (along with the transaction fee) at any of the 25,000 Western Union agents scattered worldwide. Transaction charges are: $50 for a transfer of $1000; $90 for $2000; and $22 for every additional $500 above $2000.

Western Union's outlets can be found at several major banks, including Prosper Bank at ul Miodowa 11; Bank Depozytowo Kredytowy at ul Szpitalna 15; and the Orbis office at Rynek Główny 41. Information on locations and conditions can be obtained on toll-free ☎ 0800 202 24.

Costs

Though not the bargain it used to be, Kraków is still a cheap place for travellers. Just how cheap, of course, depends largely on what degree of comfort you need, what hotel standards you are used to, what kind of food you eat and the means of transport you use. If, for example, you are accustomed to rental cars and plush hotels, you can spend just about as much as in the west.

However, if you are a budget traveller, a daily average of $25 to $30 should be quite sufficient. This amount would cover accommodation in cheap hotels, food in budget restaurants, and would still leave you a margin for some cultural events, a few beers, excursions around the region and occasional taxis. If you plan on camping or staying in youth hostels, and dining out in cheap self-services, it's feasible to cut this average down to $20 per day, without suffering much pain.

Tipping & Bargaining

Restaurants include service in the price so you just pay what is on the bill. Tipping is up to you and there doesn't seem to be any hard and fast rules about it. In low-priced eateries guests rarely leave a tip, although they might round the total up to the nearest whole figure. In upmarket establishments it's customary to tip 10% of the bill.

Tipping in hotels is essentially restricted to the top-end establishments, which usually have decent room service and porters, and all expect to be tipped. Taxi drivers are normally not tipped, unless you want to reward someone for their efforts.

FACTS FOR THE VISITOR

How Much Will It Cost Me?

Following are sample prices (in US$) you would pay for some goods and services in Kraków:

- 1L of milk – $0.40
- loaf of bread – $0.40
- Big Mac – $1.50
- Big Mac menu (with coke and chips) – $2.20
- breakfast in a milk bar – $2
- a filling meal in a budget eatery – $3 to $5
- dinner in a fine restaurant – $15 to $30
- 1L bottle of mineral water in shop – $0.60
- 0.5L bottle of local beer in shop – $0.50 to $0.75
- 0.5L bottle of local beer in pub – $1 to $1.50
- 0.5L bottle of vodka in shop – $5 to $7
- packet of 20 Polish-made Marlboro cigarettes – $1.50
- night in youth hostel – $4 to $6
- night at camp site (in tent) – $4
- double room in upmarket hotel – $80 to $120
- Kraków's average museum admission ticket – $1 to $2
- cinema ticket – $3 to $4
- concert in Philharmonic – $3 to $6
- local newspaper – $0.30
- *Time* or *Newsweek* – $2.50
- local bus or tram ride – $0.40
- 5km daytime taxi ride in the city – $3
- express train ticket Kraków to Warsaw – $13
- regular air fare Kraków to Warsaw – $125
- 1L of unleaded petrol – $0.75
- Polish-made CD – $10 to $15
- 24-exp Kodak print film – $5
- three fine roses – $6
- three minute local phone call – $0.08
- three minute phone call to Warsaw – $0.40 to $0.80
- three minute phone call to USA – $4
- postcard to USA – $0.40
- an hour logging onto the Internet in a cybercafé – $1.50 to $2
- organised half-day tour to Auschwitz – $27
- return bus or train to Auschwitz – $4 to $6

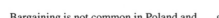

Bargaining is not common in Poland and is limited to informal places such as flea markets, fruit bazaars and street vendors.

Taxes

Value-added tax (VAT) is calculated at three levels: 0% (books, press, some basic food products); 7% (most food); and 22% (hotel accommodation, fine food, petrol, general luxury items). The tax is normally included in the price, so you won't really feel it directly, and in most cases you won't even realise you're paying it.

POST & COMMUNICATIONS

Postal services are operated by the Poczta Polska, while communications facilities are provided by Telekomunikacja Polska. Both

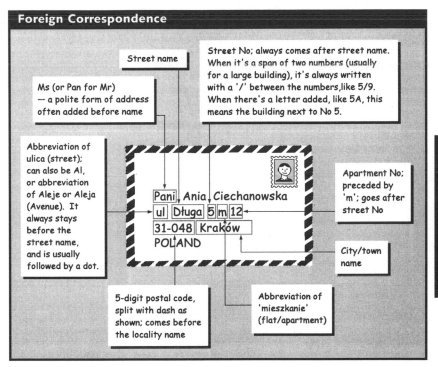

Foreign Correspondence

Street name

Street No; always comes after street name. When it's a span of two numbers (usually for a large building), it's always written with a '/' between the numbers, like 5/9. When there's a letter added, like 5A, this means the building next to No 5.

Ms (or Pan for Mr) — a polite form of address often added before name

Abbreviation of ulica (street); can also be Al, or abbreviation of Aleje or Aleja (Avenue). It always stays before the street name, and is usually followed by a dot.

Apartment No; preceded by 'm'; goes after street No

Pani Ania Ciechanowska
ul Długa 5 m 12
31-048 Kraków
POLAND

City/town name

5-digit postal code, split with dash as shown; comes before the locality name

Abbreviation of 'mieszkanie' (flat/apartment)

these companies usually share one office, called the *poczta* (post office), although recently the Telekomunikacja has been opening its own communications-only offices.

Kraków has a few dozen post offices, of which the Poczta Główna (main post office), ul Westerplatte 20, has the widest range of facilities, including poste restante. It's open weekdays from 7.30 am to 8.30 pm, Saturday from 8 am to 2 pm.

Adjoining the main post office is the Telekomunikacja's telephone centre (open 24 hours), or you can use the more central phone office at Rynek Główny 19 (open till 10 pm). There's also a post/phone office (that has a 24 hour telephone service) at ul Lubicz 4, opposite the central train station.

Sending Mail
Air-mail letters from Kraków take about a week to reach a European destination and

up to two weeks if mailed to most other continents. The rates for a 20g letter are: $0.40 to Europe, $0.45 to the USA and Canada, and $0.50 elsewhere. Packages and parcels don't cost much if sent by surface mail but they can take up to three months to reach their destination. Air-mail packages are expensive, with prices comparable to those in Western Europe.

Receiving Mail
The main post office handles poste restante services. Mail should be addressed care of Poste Restante, Poczta Główna, ul Westerplatte 20, 31-045 Kraków 1, Poland, and can be collected at window No 1. The mail is kept for 14 working days only, then returned to the sender.

Amex customers can use the services of Kraków's Amex office, in which case mail should be addressed care of Poste Restante,

American Express, Rynek Główny 41, 31-013 Kraków, Poland. Mail is kept here for a month.

Telephone

The Polish telephone system is antiquated and unreliable. Modernisation was minimal until the mid-1990s, when the telecommunications progress really took off and some more adequate telephone exchanges have been installed.

Public Phones Public telephones are few and far between by western standards, and not infrequently out of order. If you can't find one that works, go to a post office – each should have at least one functioning public phone. Old phones operate on tokens (*żetony*) which can be bought at the post office. However, these phones have almost disappeared, and may be totally extinct within a few years.

Newly installed telephones only operate on magnetic phonecards, and it's well worth buying one (at the post/communications office) if you think you'll be using public phones. Cards come in three kinds: a 25-unit card ($2), a 50-unit card ($4) and a 100-unit card ($8). One unit represents one three-minute local call. Cards can be used for domestic and international calls. In 1995 Poland introduced toll-free numbers, which begin with 800, for commercial companies and organisations.

Mobile Phones Apart from the regular, cable phone network, there are three cellular phone providers: the analog Centertel and the digital Era and Plus. All three cover most of Poland's territory, including Kraków. Cellular phone numbers begin with ☎ 0501 (Centertel), ☎ 0601 (Plus) and ☎ 0602 (Era), and don't require you to dial the area code.

Mobile phones are quickly becoming popular, both as a status symbol and a more reliable alternative to the jammed stationary lines and scarce and often inoperable public phones. As of late 1998, there were 1.4 million cellular phones in Poland and the number is expected to triple by the end of 2000.

Poland's Phone Area Codes

Telekomunikacja Polska is upgrading the telephone network by applying a uniform seven digit local number system and two-digit area codes. When you are calling long-distance in Poland, you begin with dialling '0', then dial the area code proper and the local phone number. If you call Poland from abroad, don't dial '0' before the area code. Following are area code numbers of Poland's main cities:

Gdańsk	☎ 058
Katowice	☎ 032
Kraków	☎ 012
Lublin	☎ 081
Łódź	☎ 042
Poznań	☎ 061
Warsaw	☎ 022
Wrocław	☎ 071

Domestic Calls Intercity direct dialling is possible to almost anywhere in the country. The cost of the call depends on the distance zone and time of the day. There are three time rates: peak from 8 am to 6 pm; off-peak from 6 to 10 pm; economy from 10 pm to 8 am and all weekend. For example, a three-minute Kraków-Warsaw call will cost $0.80/0.60/0.40 peak/off-peak/economy.

International Calls You can now dial directly to just about anywhere in the world. When dialling direct, a minute will cost around $0.60 to Europe, $1.10 to the USA, Canada and Australia, and $2 to anywhere else. If you place the call through the operator at the post/communications office, the minimum charge is for a three minute call which will cost about $2/4/7, respectively. Every extra minute costs a third more.

To call direct abroad from Poland, dial 00 (the Polish international access code) before the country code of the country you are calling, area code and the local number. To call a telephone number in Kraków from abroad, dial the international access code of the country you're calling from, the country

Country-Direct Collect Calls

Instead of placing a collect call through the local operator in Poland, you can call toll-free directly to the operator in the country you wish to ring, and then make a collect, account or credit-card call. This is possible to most major countries, including:

Australia		☎ 00 800 61 111 61
Canada		☎ 00 800 1 1141 11
France		☎ 00 800 33 111 33
Germany		☎ 00 800 49 111 49
UK		☎ 00 800 44 111 44
USA	AT&T	☎ 00 800 1 1111 11
	MCI	☎ 00 800 1 1121 22

Inquire at a Telekomunikacja Polska office if your country is not listed, though most numbers can be guessed as they follow the same pattern. These calls may cost a fair bit – check with your home phone company before you leave.

code for Poland (☎ 48), the area code for Kraków (☎ 12) and the local phone number.

There's a wide range of local and international phonecards. Lonely Planet's eKno Communication Card (see the insert at the back of this book) is aimed specifically at independent travellers and provides budget international calls, a range of message services, free email and travel information – for local calls you're usually better off with a local card. You can join online at www.ekno.lonelyplanet.com, or by phone from Kraków by dialling ☎ 00800-4511-264. Once you have joined, to use eKno from Kraków, dial ☎ 00800-4511-263.

Check the eKno Web site for joining and access numbers from other countries and updates on super budget local access numbers and new features.

Fax

Faxes can be sent from most large post and communications offices. The service is charged similar to phone calls placed through the operator, with a three minute minimum charge applying.

Email & Internet Access

Though it's still a way behind Western Europe, the Internet is getting popular in Poland and there are a number of service providers. Places that offer public access to the Internet and email have opened in the big cities. Some of these places are cyber-cafés, as commonly understood by this term, but many others are just office-like establishments with computer workstations, put up by computer companies or software shops, which don't necessarily serve coffee and sometimes serve nothing at all.

An hour of surfing the Web or emailing normally costs about $1.50 to $2. Some of the places use dated (and accordingly slow) equipment, but the major problem is insufficient and therefore congested phone lines linking Kraków with the world. The best time to log on is at night, the worst is early afternoon.

Kraków's oldest and best known place is the Cyber Café u Louisa (☎ 421 80 92), set in a vaulted cellar at Rynek Główny 13. It's probably the only venue of its kind in town, where you can read or write emails while having a cigarette and a beer, and listen to live music from the other vaults of the café. If ambience is not so important, you have two dozen other Internet facilities around the town. Places in or near the centre are open daily till 9 or 10 pm and include:

Cafe Internet U Mozilli
  (Map 5; ☎ 429 27 90) ul Św Wawrzyńca 38
Internet Cafe Virtual World
  (Map 3; ☎ 267 63 57) ul Konopnickiej 11
InternetCity.com
  (Map 5; ☎ 429 65 14) ul Dietla 50
Kawiarnia Internetowa Magiel
  (Map 4; ☎ 421 16 51) ul Librowszczyzna 4
Kompit
  (Map 4; ☎ 632 18 96) ul Batorego 20
Looz Internet Café
  (Map 4; ☎ 428 42 10) ul Mikołajska 13
Telekomunikacja Polska
  (Map 4; ☎ 429 17 11) Rynek Główny 19

INTERNET RESOURCES

There are quite a few web sites concerning Poland, and the number is growing. Some of the useful sources of general and tourist information on Poland, including Kraków, are:

www.explore-poland.pl
www.polandtour.org
www.infotur.pl
www.insidepoland.pl
www.polishworld.com
www.gopoland.com

The Lonely Planet Web site has up-to-the-minute travel information, as well as a Poland profile (www.lonelyplanet.com).

BOOKS
Lonely Planet
If you're planning a wider journey than just Kraków, consider taking Lonely Planet's

---

Kraków Online

There are hundreds of Web sites concerning Kraków, and you can look for them by searching 'krakow', 'cracow' or a more specific entry. The following are just a handful of useful sites, all of which have an English-language edition:

www.karnet.krakow2000.pl
    Kraków's cultural information
www.dexter.com.pl
    Dexter travel agency and tourist office
www.inyourpocket.com
    In Your Pocket guidebooks, including the one on Kraków
www.inter.com.pl/Krakow
    Kraków: What, Where, When tourist magazine
www.wawel.krakow.pl
    Wawel castle and cathedral
www.uj.edu.pl
    Jagiellonian University
www.hotelspoland.com
www.poltravel.com
www.meteor.ipl.net
    all three sites cover accommodation in Poland, including Kraków
www.restauracje.krakow.pl
    places to eat and drink in Kraków

Poland, or the wider-ranging *Eastern Europe* or *Central Europe*, depending on which region you're going to travel around. Also note that Lonely Planet has individual guidebooks to most European countries, including some of Poland's neighbours. See the back of this book for a complete rundown.

Guidebooks
You will probably not find many guidebooks on Kraków in your local travel bookshop at home, but there's quite a choice of foreign-language books in Poland itself. Polish publishers have noticed the increasing number of western tourists, and consequently, have rushed to print English and/or German editions of the originally Polish-language guidebooks. Warsaw and Kraków have the best coverage. One of the most complete is *Kraków – The Guide* produced by Pascal, Polish counterpart of Lonely Planet.

First published in July 1999, the thin, booklet-sized *Kraków In Your Pocket* is, admirably, a mine of useful information, covering just about every practical detail on the town you would possibly need to know. Planned to be updated and published five times per year, it's well worth its $1.50 price and is readily available across the city.

History & Politics
God's Playground: A History of Poland by Norman Davies is one of the best accounts of Polish history ever published. This two volume work is beautifully written, very readable and has at the same time a rare analytical depth, which makes it a perfect key to understanding a thousand years of the Polish nation.

The Heart of Europe: A Short History of Poland by Norman Davies is a more condensed account, with a greater emphasis on the 20th century. This is also an excellent work, highly recommended.

The Polish Way: A Thousand-year History of the Poles and their Culture by Adam Zamoyski is one of the best accounts of the culture of Poland from its birth to the recent past. Fully illustrated and exquisitely written, the book is an excellent introduction to both history and the arts.

Jews in Poland: A Documentary History by Iwo Cyprian Pogonowski (Hippocrene Books, New York) provides a comprehensive record of half a millennium of Polish-Jewish relations in the country which until WWII had been the major centre of Jewish culture in Europe.

The theme of the Holocaust has quite an extensive bibliography, including *If this is a Man* and *The Drowned and the Saved*, both by Primo Levi, an Italian Jew who survived Auschwitz. You've probably seen Steven Spielberg's film *Schindler's List*, but it may be interesting to read Thomas Keneally's *Schindler's Ark,* the book the film was based on.

NEWSPAPERS & MAGAZINES

Poland's first paper, *Merkuriusz Polski*, began in Kraków in 1661, but was moved to Warsaw and closed down soon after that. Kraków's first regular daily newspaper, *Gazeta Krakowska*, appeared in 1796 (a year after Poland's final partition), and made it through the difficult period for more than 50 years. During the Nazi occupation, Kraków, along with Warsaw, was a major centre of the underground press, with 158 titles appearing in the city. Save for some scientific publications, none of the war or prewar titles was continued after the war, but many new titles were founded, some remaining quite independent despite communist censorship. The picture got far more diversified after the collapse of communism, and today Kraków has Poland's liveliest press life after Warsaw.

The Warsaw-based *Gazeta Wyborcza* was the first independent daily in postwar Eastern Europe and is now the major national paper, with a daily circulation of about 460,000. It has several regional editions, including one concerning Kraków. More integrally Cracovian is the *Tygodnik Powszechny*, a long-lived opinion-forming Catholic weekly paper, focusing on socio-cultural issues. Also firmly associated with Kraków is *Przekrój*, an illustrated weekly magazine that is lighter in content.

The major Polish publication in English is *The Warsaw Voice* – a well-edited and interesting weekly, costing $1.50. Despite its name suggesting a narrow city profile, it actually covers country-wide politics, business and culture, making it a good insight into Polish current affairs.

Major European and US newspapers and magazines are available locally with increasing ease. Traditionally, *Time* and *Newsweek* have been most widely distributed. The best places to look for foreign press (and *The Warsaw Voice*) are EMPiK stores, foreign-language bookshops and the newsstands in the lobbies of the upmarket hotels. See the Shopping chapter for details.

Tourist Magazines

The English-language tourist press has really developed and includes two useful practical monthly magazines: *Welcome to Cracow* and *Kraków: What, Where, When*. They can be picked up free of charge from tourist offices, some upmarket hotels, restaurants and travel agencies.

There's also the helpful *Cracow etc* monthly magazine, which you can buy for $1.50 from some bookshops, better hotels and newsagencies.

RADIO & TV

The state-run Polish Radio (Polskie Radio), founded in 1927, is the main broadcaster. It operates on the AM long and medium-wave bands and on FM, and is received in every corner of the country. In early 1994, two previously local private broadcasters became nationwide networks: the Warsaw-based Radio Zet and the Kraków-based RFM. Plenty of other private competitors now operate on FM. Apart from the headline news in English broadcast by some of the private stations, all programs are in Polish.

Poland has two state-owned TV channels – the general program I and the more education and culture-focused program II – and the private venture called PolSat. All three are country-wide and have commercial advertisements (up to 8% of transmission time). These three apart, there are several regional channels.

TV in Kraków began in 1957, and five TV sets were registered that year. Thirty years later, the city already had 226,000 TV sets. In 1966 program II reached Kraków and in the 1970s colour TV began on a larger scale.

In the 1990s, satellite TV boomed, allowing Poles to have direct access to western media. Rough estimates indicate that Poland owns more satellite dishes than any other country in Europe except for France and the UK. The indiscriminate installation of dishes and unauthorised reception of diverse broadcasting networks have been under scrutiny, meaning that Poland has entered the era of pay TV. There are already a number of coded cable TV channels and a queue of operators waiting for licences. Most better hotels have either satellite or cable TV.

VIDEO SYSTEMS

If you want to record or buy video tapes to play back home, you won't get a picture if the image registration system is different. The French SECAM used to be the standard image registration system in communist Poland, but it has been replaced by PAL, the same as in most of Western Europe. Most video equipment entering the market is set up for PAL and NTSC (the latter is used in North America and Japan).

PHOTOGRAPHY & VIDEO

Except for the usual restrictions on photographing military, industrial, transport and telecommunications installations, you can take snapshots or videos of just about anything. Nobody usually minds you taking photos of church interiors, but such places are usually pretty dim and a tripod or a flash may be necessary. Many museums don't allow photography inside, or will charge extra (sometimes a lot) for the permit.

Film & Equipment

Kodak is the most popular film in Poland, followed by Fuji and Agfa. You can buy both slide and negative film in several common speeds. For those who are more demanding, high quality Ilford B&W films are available as well as Fujichrome professional series films including Velvia and Provia. Sample prices of films are: a roll of Kodacolor about $5; Fujichrome 100 around $7; Velvia about $10. These prices are for a roll of 36 exposures and do not include processing.

As for processing, you can easily have your prints done, often within an hour, in any of the numerous photo minilabs. There's also an increasing number of laboratories which handle E6 slide processing, but not all seem to do a good job. Kraków's most reputable place for processing slide film is the Foto Studio (☎ 421 70 00), Plac Matejki 9.

You can buy Nikon, Canon, Minolta and other popular Japanese cameras, but the choice may be limited and the prices rather high. Bring along your own reliable gear. Getting your camera repaired in Poland can be a problem if you have an uncommon make and any original spare parts are necessary. See the Shopping chapter for where to buy photo equipment and film in Kraków.

Video

VHS is the standard format for recording from TV and viewing rented films at home. As is the case elsewhere in the world, Video 8mm is now the favourite system used by amateurs shooting their own videos. Equipment for both systems is available, but the variety is limited, and it's expensive.

Poland is sufficiently safe for a tourist to carry a video camera and there are a lot of sights and events worth capturing on tape. If you decide to bring a camera, don't forget to bring along a conversion plug to fit electric sockets (two-round-pin type) if you have a different system.

TIME

All of Poland lies within the same time zone, GMT/UTC+1. When it is noon in Kraków, it's also noon in Berlin, Budapest, Paris, Prague and Stockholm, 6 am in New York and Toronto, 3 am in San Francisco, 8 pm in Tokyo, 9 pm in Sydney and 11 pm in Auckland. Poland pushes the clocks forward an hour in late March and back again in late September.

A 24 hour clock is applied in Poland for official purposes, including all transport schedules. In everyday conversations, however, people commonly use the 2 x 12 hour system, and if necessary add 'in the morning', 'in the afternoon' or 'at night'.

ELECTRICITY

Electricity is 220V, 50Hz. Plugs with two round pins are used, the same as in the rest of continental Europe. If you have a different plug, bring an adaptor, as they are difficult to find locally. North American appliances will also need a transformer if they don't have built-in voltage adjustment.

WEIGHTS & MEASURES

Poland uses the metric system. There's a conversion table at the back of this book.

LAUNDRY

Dry cleaners *(pralnia chemiczna)* are in sufficient supply, and will clean your clothes efficiently in one day, but they are not that cheap – cleaning a shirt or a pair of trousers will cost $2 each. Kraków's central facilities include those at ul Zwierzyniecka 6, Wielopole 28 and Długa 17. Top-class hotels also offer dry cleaning services and are even more expensive.

Laundrettes are almost unheard of so far in Poland. Kraków has just one, the Pralkomat (☎ 648 55 74), Osiedle Złotego Wieku 83 in Nowa Huta. It's open weekdays from 8 am to 10 pm, Saturday from 8 am to 9 pm, and Sunday from 11 am to 7 pm. Washing and drying a 7kg load will cost about $2.50.

The Hotel Studencki Piast (Map 3; ☎ 637 49 33), ul Piastowska 47, has a cheap laundry which offers service washing.

TOILETS

Self-contained public toilets are few and far between, but there are two in the Planty (at ul Sienna and ul Franciszkańska) and one strategically situated in the Cloth Hall on the main square. It's hugely popular and almost an institution. If you're really desperate and some distance from the listed facilities, look for a restaurant or café. A train station is another emergency option.

The use of a public toilet (including those in restaurants and the train station) is almost never free; it costs from $0.10 to $0.50, and the price doesn't necessarily reflect the cleanliness of the establishment. Charges are pasted on the door and collected by toilet attendants sitting at the door, who will give you a piece of toilet paper. It's a good idea to carry a roll of paper, just in case you need to use a free toilet (at museums, offices, universities, cinemas and McDonald's), which rarely have any paper left.

It may be helpful to know that the toilet is labelled 'WC', 'Szalet' or 'Toaleta'. The gents will be labelled 'Dla Panów' or 'Męski' and/or marked with a triangle, and the ladies will be labelled 'Dla Pań' or 'Damski' and/or marked with a circle.

LEFT LUGGAGE

Like all the large train stations throughout Poland, Kraków's main station has its left luggage facilities *(przechowalnia bagażu)*, where you can store your luggage for up to 10 days. There's a basic storage charge of $1 per item for the first 24 hours and $0.50 for each consecutive 24 hour period or part of it. This aside, you need to pay 1% of the declared value of the luggage as insurance, and the staff will automatically charge a minimum of $0.50 to $1 per backpack, regardless of whether you want to insure your bags or not.

There are two round-the-clock left luggage outputs at the station: in the main building (which is closed from 11pm to 5 am but there's an access from the platform) and at the entrance to the passageway running under the railways.

If you've put your baggage in storage, be sure to arrive at a reasonable time before your departure to allow time for some queuing and paperwork. You pay the charge when you pick your luggage up, not when you deposit it.

There's a cheaper left luggage facility in the Dom Turysty PTTK, ul Westerplatte 15/16. It's open from 7 am to 10 pm, but you can pick up your gear any time at night. Some hotels may keep their guests' luggage while they travel around the region.

HEALTH

Poland is not the most disease-ridden place on earth, but sanitary conditions still leave something to be desired and heavy pollution contaminates the water and air. The medical service and the availability of medications are not as good as in the west.

The public health service is in trouble: public hospital conditions are bad and medical equipment is out-dated and insufficient. Private clinics have mushroomed and they are usually better but more expensive.

Care in what you eat and drink is the principal health rule. Stomach upsets are the most likely travel health problem but the majority of these will be relatively minor. If possible, try to avoid drinking unboiled tap water; it is heavily chlorinated and tastes awful. Instead, stick to bottled water; it's readily available in shops and supermarkets. Many locals don't use tap water for drinking either, opting instead for Oligocene water from underground wells, or bottled water.

Health Insurance

A travel insurance policy that covers medical treatment abroad is a good idea. The international student travel policies handled by STA or other student travel organisations are usually good value. Check to see if the policy covers ambulances or an emergency flight home. You may prefer a policy which pays doctors or hospitals direct rather than you having to pay on the spot and claim later. If you have to claim later, make sure you keep all documentation.

Immunisations

No vaccinations are required for Poland, but you are advised to get vaccinated against hepatitis A or at least get a gamma globulin jab. Due to poor sanitation, hepatitis A is still a problem in Poland.

Pharmacies

Most minor health problems, such as mild diarrhoea, cold, cough, pain, small cuts and wounds etc, can be solved by just applying a proper remedy which you can buy in a pharmacy (apteka). They have qualified staff, some of whom speak English and may help

> ## Water
>
> The number one rule is 'be careful of the water' and especially ice. If you don't know for certain that the water is safe, assume the worst. Reputable brands of bottled water or soft drinks are fine, but only use water from containers with a serrated seal – not tops or corks. Take care with fruit juice, particularly if water may have been added. Milk should be treated with suspicion, though boiled milk is fine if it is kept hygienically. Tea or coffee should also be OK, since the water should have been boiled.

you with advice on buying the right medication and treating wounds. You may also need pharmacies for buying condoms, tampons and syringes (condoms and tampons are also available in supermarkets).

Kraków has 220 pharmacies, including one at Rynek Główny 13, and more in the adjacent streets. There's always one pharmacy in every suburb of the city that takes its turn to stay open the whole night. They are listed in the local press.

Medical Services

In the event of a more serious illness or injury you should seek qualified medical help promptly. Your consulate may recommend doctors or clinics, or try Kraków's US consulate department of citizen services (☎ 429 66 55), which can provide a list of doctors speaking English.

Profimed (☎ 421 79 97), Rynek Główny 6, has private doctors including different specialists. Medicover (☎ 422 76 33), ul Krótka 1, has 24 hour English-speaking medical services. Dent America (☎ 421 89 48), Plac Szczepański 3, is a dual Polish-American dental clinic. The Falck (☎ 96 75), ul Racławicka 26, attends house calls and has its own ambulance service.

If nothing else works, ask anybody for the nearest przychodnia or out-patient clinic. These clinics have physicians of various specialities and are the places Poles go when they get ill. Charges are relatively small.

The city ambulance emergency phone number is ☎ 999, but don't expect the operator to speak English. Ask any Pole around to call it for you. See the Language chapter at the end of the book for some basic emergency words and phrases.

WOMEN TRAVELLERS
Travel for women in Poland is pretty much hassle free except for occasional encounters with local drunken males. Harassment of this kind is not usually dangerous, but can be annoying. Steer clear of the drunks and avoid places considered male territory, particularly cheap drink bars.

GAY & LESBIAN TRAVELLERS
Homosexuality isn't illegal in Poland, but the overwhelmingly Catholic society tends to deny and suppress it. To be openly gay in Poland can often limit vocational and social opportunities and may cause family ostracism. Consequently, few gays, and still fewer lesbians, voice their attitudes in a family or workplace forum, opting instead for pursuing their lifestyles with discretion.

The Polish gay and lesbian movement is still very much underground and pretty faint. Warsaw has the largest gay and lesbian community and possibly the most open gay life, yet it's in the stone age by western standards. Kraków is still way behind, probably the dinosaur age.

There's no gay and lesbian organisation, office or even a contact phone number in Kraków, just a few places where they go – see the Entertainment chapter.

DISABLED TRAVELLERS
Kraków, like the rest of Poland, offers very little to people with disabilities. Wheelchair ramps are available only at a few upmarket hotels and restaurants, and public transport will be a challenge for anyone with mobility problems. Hardly any office, museum or bank provides special facilities for disabled travellers, and wheelchair-accessible toilets are few and far between. Only quite recently there has been some more determined efforts to develop the infrastructure for handicapped people.

SENIOR TRAVELLERS
There are very few discounts for senior Poles and still fewer for senior visitors. Senior travellers (both nationals and foreigners) can expect a 20% reduction on LOT domestic flights and the Baltic ferries but that's about it.

Up till now, there have been no discounts for senior citizens on train and bus fares, or on accommodation rates and cinema or theatre tickets, though this may be slowly changing. Legally, senior Poles get discounts on their admission fees to museums and other sights, but this doesn't apply to foreigners.

KRAKÓW FOR CHILDREN
Few foreigners travel with their children in Poland, but if you do plan on taking your offspring, there are no particular problems. Poles are generally family orientated and children enjoy privileges on local transport, accommodation and entertainment. Age limits for particular freebies or discounts vary from place to place, but are not often rigidly enforced. Basic supplies (including disposable nappies and baby food) are readily available in the supermarkets and pharmacies, and there are quite a few speciality shops devoted to children's clothes, shoes and toys.

International Cultural Centre

The Międzynarodowe Centrum Kultury deals with issues of international cultural heritage and its protection, focusing essentially on Central Europe's multiculturalism. The centre's specific activities include educational programs, seminars and conferences – some of which are open to the general public – which are held in its newly built conference centre on the ground level.

The centre operates a gallery (1st floor) staging temporary exhibitions presenting some of the prominent events of European art. There's also a library, and a bookshop selling publications and books published by the centre.

Jagiellonian University – Poland's Alma Mater

The university was founded by King Kazimierz Wielki in 1364, originally under the name of the Kraków Academy. It was Central Europe's second university, after the one in Prague (founded in 1348), and had initially three faculties: medicine, law and philosophy. It's not exactly known where it was located, with theories placing its seat at Wawel, Kazimierz or the Old Town. It didn't enjoy great fame in those days anyway; following the king's death in 1370, the university declined and was nearly closed down altogether.

It wasn't until 1400 that Poland's new ruler, King Władysław Jagiełło, refounded the academy and introduced far-reaching reforms to boost its progress. Indeed, the university soon prospered and its reputation and fame spread far beyond Poland's borders. During the 15th century, 45% of its students were foreigners.

In the 18th century the university, like the whole of Poland, declined. Following Poland's final partition of 1795, the academy saw hard days, yet it was the only Polish institution of higher education where Poles were allowed to study. So it became a focus of education for the whole of Poland, then formally a non-existent country. In 1817 the school was renamed to honour the dynasty responsible for its rebirth and development, and the name, Jagiellonian University (Uniwersytet Jagielloński, commonly referred to as UJ), has stayed to this day.

Following Kraków's occupation during WWII, the Nazis arrested 140 UJ professors and scholars, most of whom were later murdered in Sachsenhausen concentration camp. Despite this horror and the official closing down imposed by the Nazis, the university conducted clandestine teaching, and in 1944 alone it had 900 students.

After the war the university expanded and established new faculties. It now has 33 faculties and various research centres scattered all over the city, though its core remains in Kraków's heart. It employs about 380 professors and teaches 27,200 students. The much celebrated 600th anniversary of the academy's refounding is to be held throughout the year 2000.

KRZYSZTOF DYDYŃSKI

Collegium Novum at Jagiellonian University

UNIVERSITIES

Kraków's (and Poland's for that matter) oldest and most distinguished university is the Jagiellonian University, founded as the Kraków Academy in 1364. This apart, Kraków has twelve major institutions of higher education, including the Academy of Fine Arts, the Academy of Music, Kraków's University of Technology, the Theatre High School, Academy of Agriculture, Trade High School and Academy of Economics.

Alfresco cafés in Kazimierz, a suburb with a colourful history, just a short walk from Rynek Główny.

The Cloth Hall was a centre for the cloth trade in the 14th century. Its arcades were added later.

Houses in Rynek Główny have amazing architectural features, that the pigeons find very useful.

Find the Frog in this house designed by Talowski.

Courtyard on beautiful ul Kanonicza.

Centre of Japanese Art & Technology 'Manggha'

This centre was the brainchild of the Polish film director Andrzej Wajda, who donated towards it the whole of the US$340,000 Kyoto Prize money he received from the Inamori Foundation in 1987 for his artistic achievements. The building was designed by the Japanese architect Arata Isozaki, and the centre was opened in 1994.

The centre's main aim is to exhibit the Japanese art collection of historic weapons, ceramics, fabrics, scrolls and woodcuts. Numbering about 6000 pieces, this valuable collection was assembled by Feliks Jasieński (1861-1929), an avid traveller, art collector, literary critic and essayist, known by his pen name of Manggha (which is where the centre's name comes from). He donated the collection to Kraków's National Museum in 1920, but it had no facilities to exhibit it until the centre was built. Part of the collection is now finally presented on permanent display in the centre's exhibition rooms.

The centre also has a multifunctional high-tech auditorium where events presenting Japanese culture (film, theatre, traditional music) are held. The centre's café serves a Japanese set meal (on weekdays from 1 to 4 pm) – actually the only place in Kraków to serve Japanese cuisine so far.

CULTURAL CENTRES

Cultural centres in Kraków (shown on Maps 4 and 5) include:

British Council
  (☎ 422 94 55) Rynek Główny 26
Centre of Japanese Art & Technology 'Manggha'
  (☎ 267 27 03, fax 267 40 79)
  ul Konopnickiej 26
French Institute
  (☎ 422 09 82) ul Św Jana 15
Goethe Institute (German)
  (☎ 422 69 02, fax 422 69 46) Rynek Główny 20
International Cultural Centre
  (☎ 421 86 01, fax 421 85 71) Rynek Główny 25
Italian Institute of Culture
  (☎ 421 89 46) ul Grodzka 49
Jewish Cultural Centre
  (☎ 423 55 95, fax 423 50 34) ul Meiselsa 17

DANGERS & ANNOYANCES

Kraków, like all of Poland, is a relatively safe place to travel in, even though there has been a steady increase in crime since the fall of communism. As in all cities around the world, petty theft, pickpocketing, purse snatching and other such things exist in Kraków, though they are not common by any definition.

You've obviously heard it so many times that your money is safest next to your skin (eg in a money belt) regardless of whether you are in New York, New Delhi or New Zealand, and Kraków is no exception. By the same token, your brand-new Nikon slung carelessly over your shoulder, your thick wallet half outside your back pocket or your flashing gold earings may attract someone's attention even in the safest of cities. It's best just to use common sense and keep your eyes open.

Don't venture into rundown areas and dubious-looking suburbs or desolate parks, especially after dark. Use taxis if you feel uncertain about an area. Watch out for groups of suspicious characters hanging around markets, shady bars and bus or train stations, and stay away from them.

Keep an eye on your pockets and your bag in crowded places such as markets and city buses and trams. Beware of short-changing at train stations, in taxis, restaurants etc. Always have some small bills and coins to make getting change easier. Hotels are generally safe, though it's better not to leave valuables in your room; in most places you can deposit them at the reception desk.

Break-ins to cars have become a problem (see the Car & Motorcycle section in the Getting Around chapter). Theft and robbery in trains have also been on the increase – see Train in the Getting There & Away and Getting Around chapters.

Reporting Theft & Loss

It's probably best to contact your embassy or consulate first, especially if you've lost your passport. You then need to report the theft or loss to the police. They will give you a copy of the statement which serves as a temporary identity document; if you have insurance, you'll need to present it to your insurer in order to make a claim.

English-speaking police are rare, so it is best to take along an interpreter if you are able to. Don't expect your things to be found, for the police are unlikely to do anything.

General Annoyances

Heavy drinking is unfortunately a way of life in Poland and drunks may at times be disturbing. Poles smoke a lot, and the anti-tobacco campaign hasn't been as thorough or successful as in some western countries. Polish cigarettes are of low quality and the smoke they produce is hardly tolerable for anyone unused to them, let alone a non-smoker.

Slow and impolite service in shops, offices and restaurants is slowly being eradicated by the competitive market economy, though you can still occasionally experience it. Cheating is not common but there are some areas, especially those connected with foreign tourism, where you should be alert.

Travellers looking racially quite different, eg of African or Asian background, may attract some stares from the locals and they may occasionally encounter low-level discrimination.

Emergency

The nationwide toll-free 24 hour emergency phone numbers include:

Police	☎ 997
Fire Brigade	☎ 998
Ambulance	☎ 999
Roadside Assistance	☎ 981

The attendants of any of these services are unlikely to speak English, so try to get a local to call on your behalf.

LEGAL MATTERS

Foreigners in Poland, as elsewhere, are subject to the laws of the host country. While your embassy or consulate is the best stop in any emergency, bear in mind that there are some things it cannot do for you. These include getting local laws or regulations waived because you're a foreigner, investigating a crime, providing legal advice or representation in civil or criminal cases, getting you out of jail, and lending you money. A consul can, however, issue emergency passports, contact relatives and friends, advise on how to transfer funds, provide lists of reliable local doctors, lawyers and interpreters, and visit you if you've been arrested or jailed.

It's an unwritten rule that you should carry your passport at all times, in as much the same way as Poles should carry their identity document *(dowód osobisty)*. Document checks are rare these days, but if you can't prove your identity to the police, you may end up at the police station for lengthy interrogations.

BUSINESS HOURS

Most grocery shops are open on weekdays from 7 or 8 am to 6 or 7 pm and for half a day on Saturday. Delicatessens and supermarkets usually stay open longer, until 8 or 9 pm, and there's at least one food shop in every suburb which is open 24 hours. All such night shops have a section selling beer, wine and spirits, which is what keeps them going. General stores (selling clothing, books, stationery, household appliances, photo and sports stuff etc) normally open at 10 or 11 am and close at 6 or 7 pm (at 2 or 3 pm on Saturday). The office working day is theoretically eight hours long, Monday to Friday, and there's usually no lunch-time break, but attendance to the public may be limited to a shorter period.

The opening hours of museums and other tourist sights vary greatly from place to place. The overwhelming majority of museums are open on Sunday but closed on Monday; most of them also stay closed on the day following a public holiday. Some museums may close an hour or two earlier in the off season. Museums usually stop selling tickets half an hour before their official closing time.

Churches are a bigger puzzle. Some major churches in the city centre are open all day long. Most small churches in the centre and, particularly, in the suburbs are locked except during mass, which may be held only once a day, early in the morning or late in the afternoon. There's usually a board near the church's entrance which lists · masses held on Sunday *(niedziela)* and other days of the week *(dni powszednie)*.

PUBLIC HOLIDAYS

Official public holidays in Poland include New Year's Day (1 January), Easter Monday (March or April), Labour Day (1 May), Constitution Day (3 May), Corpus Christi (May or June), Assumption Day (15 August), All Saints' Day (1 November), Independence Day (11 November), and Christmas (25 and 26 December).

SPECIAL EVENTS

Kraków has arguably the richest cycle of annual events in Poland, and there's almost always something going on. The Cultural Information Centre (see the Entertainment chapter) will give you full program details. Apart from the city festivals, some of which are listed below, note that there are some important events near Kraków, particularly the famous Passion Play on Maundy Thursday and Good Friday during Easter week in Kalwaria Zebrzydowska, a small town 33km south-west of Kraków.

In the year 2000, Kraków is a European City of Culture (along with Avignon, Bergen, Bologne, Brussels, Helsinki, Prague, Reykjavik and Santiago de Compostela). Expect plenty of events, including new festivals dedicated to Stanisław Wyspiański and Tadeusz Kantor. 'Spirituality' is the main theme chosen by the city for its Kraków 2000 Festival. Check the Web site at www.krakow2000.pl for a full program.

On the next pages are some of Kraków's major regular annual events (some of which are to be part of the Kraków 2000 Festival).

Chopin Open

Tired of Chopin piano pieces? No worries, here comes the refreshing Chopin Open, a new festival-competition which started in June 1999. According to its conditions, participants can play 'all the instruments except for the piano'.

The inaugural event brought together a rare gathering of individuals 'playing' just about anything that produced a sound. The 'instruments' used by the competitors included ocarinas, Scottish bagpipes, hand saws, bottles, a rubber monkey, hair combs, tree leaves, a razor and a colour photocopier. The interpretations were so free-spirited that the jury (which included a psychiatrist) had to employ a pianist to play a fragment of the original piece as a reference before the competitor played it.

One of the prizes was a coffee maker presented to the winner with a recommendation of a 'possible use in the next competition'.

It was a lot of fun, and all for free. It should be followed by further editions including a grand finale around the anniversary of Chopin's birthday (22 February). Look out for news – if you spot a poster depicting Chopin playing panpipes or congas, read it closely as it might be an ad for the event.

MARTIN HARRIS

January & February
Shanties – Festival of Sailors' Songs

Curiously, Poland's largest and oldest shanties festival is held (since 1980) near the mountains rather than close to the sea, and in winter! It goes for four days in late February and attracts an increasing number of foreign guests

March & April
International Festival of Avant-garde Theatres

Organised by the Rotunda Student Cultural Centre in late March, this 25-year-old festival draws in a mosaic of alternative theatres

Ludwig van Beethoven Easter Festival

Held during Easter week, this young (inaugurated in 1997) but already prestigious event features distinguished international soloists and orchestras performing works by various classical composers, not only by Beethoven

Organ Music Festival

With a tradition of 35 years, this one-week festival, in March or April, gives you a chance to listen to organ recitals, which take place in several city churches

May & June
Kraków Spring Ballet

Running throughout May and June with regular performances in Słowacki Theatre, the festival witnesses a mix of classical and modern ballet by local and international groups

Student Song Festival

Held in early May, this is Poland's most important student festival dating from the mid-1960s, and includes open-air free concerts staged on the main square; it attracts big stars (who were once here as students) and discovers new faces who some day may be big stars

Juvenalia

A student carnival, in May, when students get symbolic keys to the town's gates and 'take power' over the city for four days and three nights, with street dancing, fancy dress parades, masquerades and lots of overall fun.

Polish and International Short Film Festival

Held in late May and early June, annually since the mid-1960s, this is the most prestigious event of its kind in this part of Europe

Lajkonik Pageant

The pageant, headed by the legendary figure of Lajkonik, parades from Zwierzyniec to the main square, a week after Corpus Christi (May or June)

Jewish Culture Festival

This week-long festival, beginning in late June, features a variety of cultural events including theatre, film, concerts and art exhibitions; reputedly the biggest festival of its kind in Europe, it concludes with a grand open-air *klezmer* music concert on Szeroka Street; the festival is planned to be extended to two weeks

July & August
Organ Recitals

The recitals are held in the Benedictine Abbey in Tyniec, on every Sunday from late June to late August; there are also organ recitals in July and August in St Mary's Church, Carmelite Church and Pauline Church

International Festival of Street Theatre

A dozen (or more) street theatres take over the main square for several days in early July; big fan and lots of fireworks for free!

Summer Festival of Early Music

Held during the first half of July in various locations around the town (mostly in churches), this young festival features a varied program including anything from Gregorian chants to organ recitals

Summer Festival of Opera & Operetta

Running nightly for two weeks of July in the Słowacki Theatre, the event includes a balanced mix of works by great composers from early to contemporary times

Summer Jazz Festival

On nightly for the whole of July in Piwnica pod Baranami, the festival hosts the cream of national jazz musicians (plus some foreign guests), giving a good picture of what's on in Polish jazz

Old Jazz in Kraków

Unlike the Summer Jazz Festival which features mostly modern jazz, the Old Jazz focuses on traditional jazz forms such as Dixieland and swing; it's held throughout July and August and includes open-air weekend concerts staged at Rynek Główny and the Planty

Wawel Jazz Festival

Inaugurated in late July 1999, this brand-new festival hosted some of the biggest names on the international jazz scene, who performed in the open-air of the outer courtyard of Wawel; a good start for yet another attractive regular event on Kraków's busy summertime artistic schedule

Music in Old Kraków – International Festival

Celebrating its 25th anniversary in 2000, this is one of Kraków's most important musical events, going for the last two weeks of August; it spans five centuries of musical tradition, from medieval to contemporary, presented in concert halls, churches and other historic interiors across the city; it is often performed by top international virtuosos

Lajkonik – Kraków's Legendary Figure

Lajkonik is a fairy-tale figure looking like a Tatar riding a little horse, decked out in embroidered garments. It comes to life on the Thursday seven days after Corpus Christi, and heads a joyful pageant from the Premonstratensian Convent in the suburb of Zwierzyniec to the Rynek Główny. Lajkonik is performed by a disguised man, and the person who currently does it has already played this role for over a decade.

The pageant, accompanied by a musical band, takes at least six hours to complete the trip, while Lajkonik takes to dancing, jumping and running, greets the passers-by, pops into cafés en route, collects donations, and strikes people with his mace which is said to bring them good luck. Once the pageant reaches the main square, Lajkonik is greeted by the city mayor and presented with a symbolic ransom and a goblet of wine.

The event is believed to stem from the Tatar invasions of the 13th century: legend has it that the headman of the local raftsmen defeated a Tatar khan, then put his robes on and triumphantly rode into the city. There are no historical records linking the feast to the Tatar raids, but what is known is that the Lajkonik festivities have taken place for two hundred years.

The horse's structure and garb used in the event were designed by Stanisław Wyspiański in 1904 and the original is kept in the Historical Museum of Kraków. It consists of a wooden frame covered with leather and caparison, embroidered with nearly 1000 pearls and coral beads. The whole outfit weighs about 40kg. There are plans to make it a bit lighter by using modern technology.

MARTIN HARRIS

September & October
International Triennial of Graphic Arts
Held every three years during September and October (the next one comes in 2000), this prestigious event with long traditions features works by some of the best graphic artists from all over the world

All Souls' Day Jazz Festival
With its 45-year-long history, this is Eastern Europe's oldest jazz festival, taking place at the end of October in the city jazz clubs; it traditionally ends with a Jazz Mass held in the Dominican Church, in memory of musicians who have passed away

November & December
Audio Art Festival
This young but dynamically developing avant-garde festival, the only one of its kind in Poland, gathers together composers, visual artists, performers, designers of sound installations, inventors of new instruments etc; the festival's main events are in November

Competition of Nativity Scenes
The Szopki competition is held on the main square beside the statue of Adam Mickiewicz on the first Thursday of December

Silent Film Festival
Reputedly one of the few events of its kind in the world, this one-week festival, held around mid-December, gives you a rare opportunity to see the films of a bygone era, which are otherwise kept out of the public view deep in the vaults of the National Film Archives; an added bonus is the accompanying music performed live by local pianists and jazz bands, often composed by local musicians specifically for this unique occasion

Kraków's Szopki – The Art of Nativity Scenes

A sort of Nativity scene, but very different from those elsewhere in the world, Kraków's *szopki* are elaborate constructions built in an architectural, usually church-like, form. They are made in astonishing detail from cardboard, wood, tinfoil and the like, and sometimes even mechanised. They sparkle with all the colours of the rainbow, and often feature circuits of multi-coloured electric lights. They range wildly in size: the smallest can easily fit in a matchbox, while the largest are towers a few metres high.

Kraków's szopki have taken their roots from the traditional Nativity scenes displayed for centuries in churches countrywide during the Christmas period. These tableaux of Christ's Nativity vary widely from church to church, but are usually compositions of figurines placed in a countryside-type landscape, their central feature being the infant Jesus in a crib surrounded by the holy family.

For some reason, Kraków's artisans turned more attention to architecture rather than to Biblical personalities, often incorporating elements and details from existing city buildings, thus creating a distinctive local style. In the course of time, the traditional crèche scene has become just a small part of the whole composition, now over-whelmed by spires and parapets, domes, windows, turrets and other architectural paraphernalia.

Kraków's Nativity scenes evolved during the 19th century and by 1900 there was a well established distinctive local genre and a separate guild of szopki-makers in the city. The fashion for the szopki diminished after WWI, but various actions were undertaken to save the tradition. The most effective of these was the contest for the most beautiful Nativity scene, first organised in 1937. As many as 86 specimens competed for the title that year.

The competition continues to be held annually at the foot of the Mickiewicz statue, as it was from the beginning, and these days it can attract up to 200 szopki. The competitors begin to arrive with their szopki by 8 am or so, and at noon they all head for the Historical Museum of Kraków, where the szopki are judged by the jury. The prizewinning specimens are put on display till mid-February at a special exhibition held by the museum.

Some amazing historic szopki, the oldest of which date from the times of WWI, are on display in the Ethnographic Museum.

TAMSIN WILSON

WORK

Travellers looking for paid work on the spot in Poland will probably be disappointed. First of all, to work legally you need a work visa, and getting one involves complex and lengthy paperwork. Secondly, wages are low in Poland (an average monthly salary is about $400), so unless you are a highly qualified specialist in some area it's not a great deal in financial terms. Lastly, forget about casual manual jobs as there are armies of 'tourists' from beyond Poland's eastern border, who are eager to work for much less than you would ever expect to be paid.

Qualified English teachers have perhaps the best chance of getting a job – try the English-teaching institutions, the linguistic departments at universities and private language schools. If you don't have bona fide teaching credentials, they may still want to employ you, or at least you will be able to arrange some informal agreements, like giving private language lessons.

Another possible area of informal work is busking, but Kraków these days has heaps of buskers, especially musicians, performing virtually at sound distance from each other.

If you are seriously thinking about a long-term legal work contract in Kraków (or anywhere else in Poland), it's best to start well ahead, in your home country, by inquiring at your local Polish consulate about job options in your professional field, then contacting the relevant institutions in Poland. Your country's consulate in Poland may also be helpful in providing some orientation guidelines and information, as can the following Kraków-based chambers of commerce:

American Chamber of Commerce
  (☎ 423 83 67) ul Zapolskiej 38
Austrian Commerce Office
  (☎ 421 10 00) ul Grodzka 1
British Chamber of Commerce
  (☎ 421 56 56) ul Św Anny 9

Use the Internet to get into Polish business circles. In the end, you'll probably still need to come to Poland to finalise your job arrangements with your potential employers, but you can make things much easier by establishing as many connections as you can beforehand.

Getting There & Away

AIR

Kraków is not exactly the busiest air hub in this part of the world. Apart from domestic links with Warsaw, it only has regular direct connections with Frankfurt, London, Paris, Rome, Vienna and Zurich. So to fly to Kraków, you need to fly first to one of these cities, or go through Warsaw. You may also consider flying no farther than Warsaw then taking a 2¾ hour train trip to Kraków.

Prices in this chapter are in US$, unless otherwise stated.

Kraków's Airport

Kraków's airport is in Balice, about 15km west of the city centre, and linked to it by local buses (see the Getting Around chapter for details on airport transport). It's a small and unhurried place, so don't be shocked if coming from, say, Amsterdam's Schiphol, London's Heathrow or Paris' Charles de Gaulle. The modest terminal has a few facilities, including a newsagency, public phones and a bank which gives ridiculously low rates (it's advisable to change here only enough money to get to the centre).

Departure Tax

There's an international airport departure tax of $10, payable when you buy your ticket. There's no airport tax on domestic flights.

Other Parts of Poland

Kraków's only direct domestic air links are with Warsaw (three or four flights daily), with connections to other Polish cities, including Gdańsk, Poznań, Szczecin and Wrocław. Connections are not always timely – you may need to wait several hours in Warsaw. All flights are serviced by LOT Polish Airlines, Poland's only commercial carrier. On domestic routes, LOT uses mainly the French-Italian ATR 72 turbo aircraft. Occupancy is low and cancellation or suspension of LOT flights is a fact of life.

The regular one-way Kraków-Warsaw fare is around $125. Any combined flight via Warsaw (eg Kraków-Gdańsk) will cost around $150. Tickets can be booked and bought at any LOT and Orbis office across the country and from some travel agencies. In Kraków, inquire at the LOT office (☎ 411 67 00) at ul Basztowa 15 or the Orbis office (☎ 422 40 35) at Rynek Główny 41.

People over 60 years of age (both locals and foreigners) pay 80% of the full fare on all domestic flights. Foreign students holding an ISIC card get a 10% discount. There are attractive stand-by fares (about 25% of the regular fare) for people under 20 and students under 26; tickets have to be bought right before scheduled departure. There are also some promotional fares on some flights in some periods (eg early or late flights, selected weekend flights etc); they can be just a third of the ordinary fares and are applicable to everybody.

Most domestic airports are a manageable distance – 10km to 20km – from city centres and are linked to them by public transport. Only Szczecin and Katowice airports are farther out. You must check in at least 30 minutes before departure. Have your passport at hand; you'll be asked to show it.

The UK

LOT has London-Kraków direct flights a few days a week all year long (with an additional flight in summer). Alternatively, you can fly via Warsaw (both British Airways and LOT operate the London-Warsaw route once daily, with more LOT flights in summer). LOT also services Manchester-Warsaw flights a few days a week in summer, with connections to Kraków.

Regular fares on all these flights are expensive, but fortunately, the travel market is very busy in London and there are countless agents competing to offer cheap rates. STA Travel, Council Travel and Campus Travel may offer competitive deals for both students and nonstudents. The London offices of the three agencies are:

STA Travel
　(☎ 020-7937 9962) 74 Old Brompton Rd,
　London SW7 3LQ
Council Travel
　(☎ 020-7437 7767) 28A Poland St, London W1
Campus Travel
　(☎ 020-7730 8111) 52 Grosvenor Gardens,
　London SW1 0AG

It's also worthwhile checking travel agencies specialising in Eastern Europe, which offer transportation tickets (air, train, bus) as well as organised tours. Useful agencies, some of which focus specifically on Poland, include:

Fregata Travel
　(☎ 020-7734 5101, ☎ 7451 7000)
　100 Dean St, London W1
　(☎ 0161-226 7227) 117A Withington Rd,
　Manchester M16
New Millennium
　(☎ 0121-711 2232) 20 Hill St, Solihull,
　Birmingham B91 3TB
Polish Travel Centre
　(☎ 020-8741 5541) 246 King St, London
　W6 0RF
Polorbis
　(☎ 020-7636 2217) 82 Mortimer St, London W1
Tazab Travel
　(☎ 020-7373 1186) 273 Old Brompton Rd,
　London SW5
Travelines
　(☎ 020-8748 9609) 246A King St,
　Hammersmith, London W6 0RA
　(☎ 020-7828 9008) Victoria Station

Expect a London-Warsaw or London-Kraków return ticket to cost somewhere between £180 and £250, but it can well be cheaper if you are under the age of 26.

Continental Europe

There are a number of flights to Warsaw from all major European capitals, and most have connections to Kraków. There are also direct flights from Frankfurt, Paris, Rome, Vienna and Zurich. The closer to Poland you are, the more attractive the train and coach options become as they guarantee a considerable saving over the cost of an air fare.

The USA & Canada

There are direct nonstop LOT flights from New York, Chicago and Toronto to War-

saw, and there may also be some scheduled or charter flights from these three cities direct to Kraków, but they are not necessarily the cheapest. Inquire at LOT on toll-free ☎ 800-223 0593 in the USA, ☎ 800-668 5928 in Canada.

Agents often use indirect connections with other carriers such as British Airways, Lufthansa, Swissair, KLM or Air France. Not only may these work out cheaper, but they can also let you break the journey in Western Europe for the same price or a little extra – a bonus if you want to stop en route in London, Paris or Amsterdam.

In the USA, two reputable discount travel agencies are STA Travel (toll-free ☎ 800-777 0112, ☎ 800-781 4040) with a Web site at www.sta-travel.com and Council Travel (toll-free ☎ 800-226 8624) with a Web site at www.counciltravel.com. Canada's leading bargain ticket agency is Travel CUTS (☎ 800-667 2887) with a Web site at www.travelcuts.com. All have offices throughout their respective countries.

Expect return air fares to Poland to start at around $600 from the USA and C$1000 from Canada. If money is more of a concern to you than comfort or time, fly with any of several hotly competing airlines to one of the main European destinations such as London or Amsterdam, and then continue overland by bus. Also check the air fare to Berlin, which may be a reasonable compromise.

Australia & New Zealand

There are no direct scheduled flights between Australasia and Poland, so any journey will involve a change of flight and, possibly, of carrier as well. From Australia, you can fly to Bangkok, from where LOT will take you direct to Warsaw. LOT flies once or twice a week between Warsaw and Bangkok and has arrangements with other carriers, principally Qantas, which take passengers to and from various Australian cities. The return fare from Sydney/ Melbourne to Warsaw/Kraków will cost somewhere between A$1600 and A$2200, depending on the season.

Alternatively, you can fly with a major European carrier such as British Airways,

Baggage Allowance This will be written on your ticket and usually includes one 20kg item that will go in the hold, plus one item of hand luggage.

Bucket Shops These are unbonded travel agencies that specialise in discounted airline tickets.

Bumped Just because you have a confirmed seat doesn't mean you're going to get on the plane (see Overbooking).

Cancellation Penalties If you have to cancel or change a discounted ticket, there are often heavy penalties involved; insurance can sometimes be taken out against these penalties. Some airlines impose penalties on regular tickets as well, particularly against 'no-show' passengers.

Check-In Airlines ask you to check in a certain time ahead of the flight departure (usually one to two hours on international flights). If you fail to check in on time and the flight is over-booked, the airline can cancel your booking and give your seat to somebody else.

Confirmation Having a ticket written out with the flight and date you want doesn't mean you have a seat until the agent has checked with the airline that your status is 'OK' or confirmed. Meanwhile you could just be 'on request'.

Courier Fares Businesses often need to send urgent documents or freight securely and quickly. Courier companies hire people to accompany the package through customs and, in return, offer a discount ticket which is sometimes a phenomenal bargain. In effect, what the companies do is ship their freight as your luggage on regular commercial flights. This is a legitimate operation, but there are two shortcomings – the short turnaround time of the ticket (usually not longer than a month) and the limitation on your luggage allowance. You may have to surrender all your allowance and take only carry-on luggage.

Full Fares Airlines traditionally offer 1st class (coded F), business class (coded J) and economy class (coded Y) tickets. These days there are so many promotional and discounted fares available that few passengers pay full economy fare.

ITX An ITX, or 'independent inclusive tour excursion', is often available on tickets to popular holiday destinations. Officially it's a package deal combined with hotel accommodation, but many agents will sell you one of these for the flight only and give you phoney hotel vouchers in the unlikely event that you're challenged at the airport.

Lost Tickets If you lose your airline ticket an airline will usually treat it like a travellers cheque and, after inquiries, issue you with another one. Legally, however, an airline is entitled to treat it like cash and if you lose it then it's gone forever. Take good care of your tickets.

MCO An MCO, or 'miscellaneous charge order', is a voucher that looks like an airline ticket but carries no destination or date. It can be exchanged through any International Association of Travel Agents (IATA) airline for a ticket on a specific flight. It's a useful alternative to an onward ticket in those countries that demand one, and is more flexible than an ordinary ticket if you're unsure of your route.

No-Shows No-shows are passengers who fail to show up for their flight. Full-fare passengers who fail to turn up are sometimes entitled to travel on a later flight. The rest are penalised (see Cancellation Penalties).

Air Travel Glossary

On Request This is an unconfirmed booking for a flight.

Onward Tickets An entry requirement for many countries is that you have a ticket out of the country. If you're unsure of your next move, the easiest solution is to buy the cheapest onward ticket to a neighbouring country or a ticket from a reliable airline which can later be refunded if you do not use it.

Open Jaw Tickets These are return tickets where you fly out to one place but return from another. If available, this can save you backtracking to your arrival point.

Overbooking Airlines hate to fly empty seats and since every flight has some passengers who fail to show up, airlines often book more passengers than they have seats. Usually excess passengers make up for the no-shows, but occasionally somebody gets 'bumped' onto the next available flight. Guess who it is most likely to be? The passengers who check in late.

Point-to-Point Tickets These are discount tickets that can be bought on some routes in return for passengers waiving their rights to a stopover.

Promotional Fares These are officially discounted fares, available from travel agencies or direct from the airline.

Reconfirmation If you don't reconfirm your flight at least 72 hours prior to departure, the airline may delete your name from the passenger list. Ring to find out if your airline requires reconfirmation.

Restrictions Discounted tickets often have various restrictions on them – such as needing to be paid for in advance and incurring a penalty to be altered. Others are restrictions on the minimum and maximum period you must be away, such as a minimum of 14 days or a maximum of one year.

Round-the-World Tickets RTW tickets give you a limited period (usually a year) in which to circumnavigate the globe. You can go anywhere the carrying airlines go, as long as you don't backtrack. The number of stopovers or total number of separate flights is decided before you set off and they usually cost a bit more than a basic return flight.

Stand-by This is a discounted ticket where you only fly if there is a seat free at the last moment. Stand-by fares are usually available only on domestic routes.

Transferred Tickets Airline tickets cannot be transferred from one person to another. Travellers sometimes try to sell the return half of their ticket, but officials can ask you to prove that you are the person named on the ticket. This is less likely to happen on domestic flights, but on an international flight tickets are compared with passports.

Travel Agencies Travel agencies vary widely and you should choose one that suits your needs. Some simply handle tours, while full-service agencies handle everything from tours and tickets to car rental and hotel bookings. If all you want is a ticket at the lowest possible price, then go to an agency specialising in discounted fares.

Travel Periods Ticket prices vary with the time of year. There is a low (off-peak) season and a high (peak) season, and often a low-shoulder season and a high-shoulder season as well. Usually the fare depends on your outward flight – if, say, you depart in the high season and return in the low season, you pay the high-season fare.

GETTING THERE & AWAY

Lufthansa or KLM, to London, Frankfurt or Amsterdam, respectively, from where the same airline or one of its associates will take you to Warsaw and, in some cases, to Kraków. These air fares are marginally higher than those of LOT – say, between A$1700 and A$2300.

From New Zealand, you can fly through Australia or South-East Asia, but flights routed through the USA may work out cheaper. A round-the-world ticket could be cheaper still.

STA Travel and Flight Centre are major dealers in cheap air fares, each with offices throughout Australia and New Zealand. If you consider flying with LOT, the best specialists in these flights are travel agencies run by Polish émigrés. Of these, Magna Carta Travel is possibly the largest, with offices in Sydney (☎ 02-9746 9964), Melbourne (☎ 03-9523 6981) and other major Australian cities.

TRAIN

Kraków is relatively well connected by train to the rest of Poland and beyond. It has regular services throughout the country and direct connections with the capitals of the neighbouring countries. All international rail traffic (and most domestic traffic) is handled by the central train station, Kraków Główny, on the north-eastern outskirts of the Old Town. The station sports a range of facilities, including a restaurant, snack bars, newsstands, a left-luggage room, a bank, an ATM and toilets. The post office is just opposite the entrance.

Other Parts of Poland

Poland's 27,000km railway network is administered by the Polish State Railways, commonly known as PKP. Services include EuroCity (EC), InterCity (IC), express (Ex), fast and ordinary. Almost all trains have seats in two classes – 1st class (pierwsza klasa) and 2nd class (druga klasa) – and some night trains carry cars with couchettes (kuszetki) or sleepers (miejsca sypialne).

Tickets (bilety) can be purchased up to 30 days ahead, at train stations or Orbis offices. On some trains (including express

---

One Ticket Please ...

As cashiers rarely speak English, the easiest way to buy a train ticket is to have all relevant details written down on a piece of paper. These should include the destination, the departure time and the class (pierwsza klasa or druga klasa). If seat reservation is compulsory on your train, you'll automatically be sold a reserved seat ticket (miejscówka); if it's optional, you must state whether you want a miejscówka or not. Make sure to ask for a seat in a nonsmoking compartment (dla niepalących) unless you don't mind being exposed to a heavy smell and clouds of cigarette smoke (or carry a mask). If you want a seat by the window, add przy oknie.

---

and fast) you also buy a reserved seat (miejscówka), which can be optional or compulsory. Most large stations have been computerised, so buying tickets is now less of a hassle than it used to be, but queuing is still a way of life – try to be at the station at least half an hour before the departure, or buy your ticket in advance.

Domestic fares are still low: travel in 2nd class by ordinary train costs about $3.50/6 per 100/300km. Fast-train tickets cost 50% more than those for ordinary trains, and an express train costs 33% more than a fast train (ie twice as much as an ordinary train). EC and IC trains are marginally more expensive than express trains. First class costs 50% more than 2nd class. A reserved seat ticket costs an additional $1.50 ($3 on IC trains) regardless of distance. There are no discounts for ISIC cardholders on domestic trains, even though there are reduced fares for Polish students.

If you plan to travel a lot in Poland, consider buying an internal Polrail Pass offered by PKP, which allows unlimited travel on the entire domestic rail network. The pass has a duration of eight days ($78/114 2nd/1st class), 15 days ($90/132), 21 days ($102/156) or 30 days ($132/192). Persons aged under 26 years can buy a 'Junior' pass for about 25% less. Seat reservation fees are included. The pass is available through Rail Europe or Orbis/Polorbis offices abroad, and it also can be bought in Poland (from Orbis offices and train stations).

Kraków Główny central station handles trains throughout the region as well as to/from most major cities across Poland. Fares listed below are for 2nd class travel.

There are five InterCity trains a day to Warsaw (297km; $14 including the compulsory seat reservation; 2¾ hours), plus half a dozen express trains ($13; 2¾ hours).

A dozen fast trains a day depart to Wrocław (268km; $8; five hours) and similar number to Rzeszów (158km; $6; 2½ hours). There are also services to Częstochowa (132km), Zakopane (147km) and Oświęcim (Auschwitz; 60km) – see the sections in the Excursions chapter for details.

Tickets and couchettes can be booked directly from Kraków Główny station or from the Orbis office at Rynek Główny 41.

Other Countries

There are one or two direct trains daily between Kraków and Berlin, Bratislava, Bucharest, Budapest, Dresden, Frankfurt/Main, Kyiv, Leipzig, Odesa, Prague and Vienna. There are more international trains calling at Warsaw (including direct trains from Brussels, Cologne, Moscow and St Petersburg), so you can use it as a bridge.

Various European rail discount fares and passes, including Inter-Rail and Eurotrain, are valid on Polish trains and may be good value for getting to/from Poland. Travel within Poland, however, will probably be cheaper using local fares or a Polrail Pass (see earlier in this section) than with an international pass.

International trains to Poland, as to other Central European countries, have become targeted by thieves. Keep a grip on your bags, particularly on the Berlin-Warsaw overnight trains, which are notorious for gangs of thieves, who unlock compartments and rob the sleeping passengers. There have also been reports of armed assaults in these trains. You should also be on guard in the Berlin-Kraków, Prague-Warsaw and Prague-Kraków trains, though theft here hasn't reached alarming proportions so far.

BUS

The Main Bus Terminal (Dworzec Główny PKS), next to Kraków Główny train station, handles most domestic bus transport. There's also a small square without facilities at the eastern outlet of the passageway under the rail tracks, grandiloquently named Eastern Bus Terminal (Dworzec Wschodni PKS), from where some buses to Oświęcim depart. International buses depart from either terminal, although some may leave from the offices of the travel agencies which run them.

Other Parts of Poland

Bus travel in Poland is a little cheaper than train travel, but slower and less regular on most long-distance routes. Within the region, though, it's often more convenient. Most domestic bus transport is serviced by the state bus company, PKS, which was previously the only operator, but now faces increasing competition. A number of small private companies run vans, minibuses and buses on mostly short-distance regional routes, and Polski Express services several major long-distance routes, including Kraków-Warsaw (via Kielce and Radom or Katowice and Łódź).

PKS provides a local ordinary service ($2.50 per 100km) and the 25% more expensive fast service. The only place to buy PKS tickets is the terminal itself; Orbis doesn't handle this service. Tickets on long routes serviced by fast buses can be bought up to 30 days in advance but those for short, local routes are only available the same day. There are no student concessions on PKS buses.

From Kraków, travel by bus is particularly advisable to Zakopane (104km) as it's shorter and faster than by train. Fast PKS buses go there every hour ($3.50; 2½ hours). A private company runs nine buses a day to Zakopane, which are faster and cheaper again ($3); tickets are available from Waweltur at ul Pawia 8. Buy your ticket in advance.

There are two convenient morning departures to Częstochowa (119km), nine buses a day to Oświęcim (64km) and eight to Cieszyn (Czech border, 121km). You can also go by bus to Kalwaria Zebrzydowska (33km) and Ojców (22km). To other destinations, it is better to go by train.

Other Countries

Bus is the cheapest means of public transport to Poland from most of Europe. There are a few reputable international bus companies servicing Poland, of which Eurolines is possibly the best known, plus a number of bus carriers run by Polish émigrés. In recent years there's been a revolution in this business in Poland, with countless small private operators offering services from Warsaw, Kraków and other Polish cities to just about anywhere in Europe.

There are plenty of international bus routes originating in Kraków, going to Amsterdam ($75), Berlin ($40), Budapest ($30), London ($80), Munich ($60), Paris ($80), Rome ($75), Vienna ($28) and dozens of other destinations. Information and tickets are available from a number of travel agencies throughout the town, including Sindbad (☎ 421 02 40) in the main bus terminal.

CAR & MOTORCYCLE

Travellers bringing their vehicles to Poland need their driving licence, vehicle registration and insurance policy. Normally your domestic licence will do if it bears your photograph, but if not, bring an International Driving Permit as well. If you are arriving in someone else's car, bring a notarised letter from the owner saying you're allowed to drive it. A certificate of insurance, commonly known as a Green Card, is available from your insurer. If you haven't bought it at home, you'll be required to buy one at the border, but not all border crossings provide this facility.

Roads

Poland has a dense network of paved roads that total 220,000km. The massive increase in traffic over recent years, along with extreme climatic conditions, have led to deterioration in road surfaces, so some are better than others.

There are only a few motorways in the proper sense of the word, but an array of two and four-lane highways crisscross the country; some of these roads can be crowded. Secondary roads are narrower but they usually carry less traffic and are OK for leisurely travel.

Road Rules

As in the rest of continental Europe, you drive on the right-hand side of the road in Poland. Traffic coming from the right has priority unless indicated otherwise by signposts. Seat belts must be worn by the driver and all the passengers at all times. This applies to passengers in taxis as well. From October to February, car lights must be on at all times while driving, even on sunny days. Motorbikes must have lights on at all times throughout the year.

Unless signs state otherwise, cars and motorbikes can be parked on pavements, as long as a minimum 1.5m-wide walkway is left for pedestrians. Parking in the opposite direction to the flow of traffic is allowed. The permitted blood alcohol level is 0.02%, so it's best not to drink at all before driving. Motorcyclists should note that both rider and passenger must wear crash helmets.

Speed limits are 60km/h in built-up areas, 90km/h on country roads, 100km/h on two-lane express highways, 110km/h on four-lane express highways and 130km/h on motorways. Traffic signs may override the general rules and impose sometimes ridiculously low speed limits, but don't ignore them as these are favourite spots for the police to raise revenue with well hidden radar speed traps.

In the cities, special care should be taken when crossing the tramway track, particularly while turning left and on roundabouts; in both cases you have to give way to trams. If you see a tram halting at a stop in the middle of the street, you are obliged to stop behind it and let all passengers get off and on. However, if there's a pedestrian island, you don't have to stop.

Petrol

Petrol is now readily available at hundreds of gas stations, which have mushroomed in the cities and countryside throughout Poland. They sell several kinds and grades of petrol, including the 94-octane leaded ($0.75 per litre), 95-octane unleaded ($0.75), 98-octane unleaded ($0.80) and diesel ($0.65). A rise in petrol prices is planned for 2000. Many stations located along main roads and in the large cities are open round the clock.

Bringing Your Own Vehicle

If you bring your own vehicle to Poland, you'll find that life is easier if it's not brand-new or a fancy model. A more modest vehicle won't draw curious crowds – or gangs of thieves. The shabbier your car looks, the better. Don't wash it too often.

There's a network of garages that specialise in fixing western cars (though not many for motorcycles), but they mostly deal with older, traditional models with mechanical technology. The more electronics and computer-controlled bits in your car, the more problems you'll face having something fixed, and the more it will cost.

Bring along a good insurance policy from a reliable company for both the car and your possessions. Car theft is well established in Poland, with several gangs operating in the large cities. Some of them cooperate with Russians in smuggling stolen vehicles across the eastern border, never to be seen again.

Even if the car itself doesn't get stolen, you might lose some of its accessories, most likely the radio/cassette player, as well as any personal belongings you've left there. Hide your gear, if you must leave it inside; try to make the car look empty. Preferably, take your luggage to your hotel. If possible, always park your car in a guarded car park *(parking strzeżony)*. If your hotel doesn't have its own, the staff will tell you where the nearest one is, probably within walking distance. The cost per night shouldn't be more than $10.

Drive carefully on country roads, particularly at night. There are still a lot of horse-drawn carts on Polish roads, and the farther off the main routes you wander, the more carts, tractors and other agricultural machinery you'll encounter. They are lit poorly or not at all. The same applies to bicycles – you'll hardly ever see a properly lit bike. Pedestrians are another problem, of whom drunks staggering along the middle of the road are the biggest danger.

BICYCLE

The Polish countryside is not a bad place for cycling. Most of the country is fairly flat, so riding is easy and any ordinary bike is OK, but if you plan on travelling in the mountainous regions south of Kraków, you'll do better with a multispeed bike. Camping equipment isn't essential, as hotels and hostels are usually no more than an easy day's ride apart.

Major roads can carry pretty heavy traffic and are best avoided. Instead, you can easily plan your route along secondary and other minor roads, which are less crowded and in fair shape, and you'll have a chance to see villages and small towns which are bypassed by main arteries.

On a less optimistic note, cities are not pleasant for cyclists, as separate bike tracks are almost nonexistent, and some car drivers are not particularly polite to cyclists. Furthermore, city roads are often in poor shape, and cobbled streets are not uncommon.

Hotel staff will usually let you put your bike indoors for the night, sometimes in your room; it's often better to leave it in the hotel during the day as well, and get around city sights on foot or by public transport. Bikes, especially western ones, are attractive to thieves, so it's a good idea to carry a solid lock and chain, for the frame and both wheels, and always use them when you leave the bike outdoors.

HITCHING

Hitchhiking *(autostop)* is never entirely safe anywhere in the world. Travellers who decide to hitch should understand that they are taking a small but potentially serious risk. Those who choose to hitch will be safer if they travel in pairs, and let someone know where they are planning to go.

GETTING THERE & AWAY

That said, hitching does take place in Poland, though it's not very popular. Car drivers rarely stop to pick up hitchhikers, and large commercial vehicles (which are easier to wave down) expect to be paid the equivalent of a bus fare.

ORGANISED TOURS

A number of tours to Poland can be arranged from abroad. Orbis, Poland's largest travel agency, has traditionally been the major operator and is still some distance ahead of the other Polish companies based abroad. It offers packages, usually one to two weeks long, from sightseeing around the historic cities to skiing or horse-riding holidays. Travel agencies run by Polish émigrés who deal with transportation tickets also have a selection of packages. Some of the other US and UK-based tour operators which include Poland in their programs are specified below.

The USA

Affordable Poland (☎ 800-801 1055, fax 408-871 8421), 1600 Saratoga Ave, Suite 609, San Jose, CA 95129, specialises exclusively in Poland. The agency has standard and deluxe tours covering Poland's highlights, and offers a range of independent packages, so you can build your own tour and explore destinations of your choice at your own pace.

Walking Softly Adventures (☎ 888-743 0723, ☎ 503-788 9017, fax 503-788 0463, email info@wsadventures.com), PO Box 86273, Portland, OR 97286, runs hiking tours in European mountains, including the Tatras. Its 16-day Tatra Trails packages include a few days in Kraków and cost about $2500 (flights apart). Visit their Web site on www.wsadventures.com.

American Travel Abroad (AMTA) organises tours with fixed dates around Poland and Central Europe. The agency has two offices in the USA: 250 West 57th St, New York, NY 10107 (☎ 212-586 5230 or toll-free ☎ 800-228 0877); and 4801 West Peterson Ave, Chicago, IL 60646 (☎ 773-725 9500 or toll-free ☎ 800-342 5315). AMTA has its main office in Warsaw (☎ 022-825 35 17).

American-International Homestays (toll-free ☎ 800-876 2048, ☎ 303-642 3088, fax 303-642 3365, email ash@igc.apc.org), 2823 Jay Rd, Boulder, CO 80301; PO Box 1754, Nederland, CO 80466, organises multi-city tours with accommodation in private homes, known as homestays. The 17 day Prague-Budapest-Kraków program costs around $2500 from New York. The company also arranges ordinary B&B accommodation.

The UK

Martin Randall Travel (☎ 020-8742 3355), 10 Barley Mow Passage, Chiswick, London W4 4PH, has tours to Poland, including a 10 day 'Monasteries, Mansions and Country Towns' tour, which covers Warsaw, Kraków and the south and east of the country; and the Amber Route, which goes to Gdańsk and the Baltic coast.

Exodus Expeditions (☎ 020-8675 5550), 9 Weir Rd, London SW12 0LT, has a 14 day 'Historic Poland' tour, which includes Warsaw, Kraków, Gdańsk and Białowieża National Park. Exodus also offers a 14 day hiking trip in the Tatras and Beskids, with accommodation in mountain refuges.

Bike Events (☎ 01225-480 130, ☎ 310 858), PO Box 75, Bath, Avon BA1 1BX, runs a two week bicycle trek from Kraków to Budapest via the Tatra Mountains and Slovakia, plus other Central Europe trips.

World Expeditions (☎ 01628-74174, fax 74312), 8 College Rise, Maidenhead, Berkshire SL6 6BP, organises two-week trekking and rafting tours in the Polish and Slovak Tatras, plus B&B in Kraków and Prague, for £730 from London.

Poland Tours (☎ 01784-247 286), 22 West View, Bedfont, Middlesex TW14 8PP, offers travellers cheap 10-day packages in the Polish mountain resorts, plus many other tours.

St Adalbert's Church in the southern corner of Rynek Główny dates back to the 10th century.

Archaelogical Museum, founded in 1850 and housed in a Carmelite Monastery later used as a jail.

Shopaholics absorb history and culture as they enjoy the shops and stalls at Cloth Hall.

Getting Around

The overwhelming majority of Kraków's tourist attractions are in or near to the Old Town, within easy walking distance from each other, so you won't have many rides on buses, trams or taxis unless you're staying well outside the centre.

Prices are given in US$.

TO/FROM THE AIRPORT

The airport in Balice, about 15km west of the city, is accessible by the frequent (every 20 minutes) and convenient bus No 152 from the bus stop on ul Lubicz just out of the main train station. There's also the infrequent and less convenient bus No 208 from Plac Nowy Kleparz, 1km north of the Old Town. A taxi between the airport and the city centre shouldn't cost more than $8.

PUBLIC TRANSPORT

Kraków's public transport is reasonably efficient, extensive, frequent and cheap. The two major means of transport, bus and tram, operate from around 5 am to 11 pm. There are also half-hourly night-time buses (6xx lines) on main routes. Timetables are posted at stops, but be a little bit flexible about their accuracy.

Information

Transport routes are included on most city maps, and there are also free tourist transport maps available (irregularly) from tourist offices. Easier to find is a small brochure published by the City Transport Company, MPK, which features information (in five languages, English included) about kinds of services, tickets and fares.

Tickets & Passes

Unlike in most Polish cities, fares on Kraków's public transport can be both flat-rate and time based. A flat-fare ticket ($0.40) allows for one trip, regardless of duration or distance, but if you change vehicle, you need another ticket. If you need to change, it can be better to buy a one hour ticket ($0.50) which allows as many changes as you wish, but you can't travel on one ticket longer than an hour. Night services cost $1 a fare. There are also daily/weekly passes valid for all buses and trams, for $1.60/4. There are no discounts for students with an ISIC card, nor are there any for senior citizens. Each piece of bulky luggage (legally anything measuring more than 60 x 40 x 20cm) is an additional flat-rate fare, but passengers with daily/weekly passes can carry their luggage free.

There are no conductors on board; you buy tickets beforehand and stamp them in the little machine near the door. Make sure you validate a ticket for every piece of your luggage. You can buy tickets from Ruch kiosks and other selected establishments recognisable by the MPK *bilety* (ticket) boards they display. Buy a bunch of them at once if you are going to use public transport regularly and buy enough tickets on Saturday morning to last you until Monday, as few kiosks are open on Sunday. Tickets can also be bought in the vehicle from the driver, but there's a surcharge (about 20%) and you need coins to pay the exact fare as they don't give change.

Your Ticket, Please ...

The plain-clothed ticket inspectors control tickets on city buses and trams more rigidly today than they did before, and foreign travellers are their favourite targets as they make easy prey. These inspectors tend to be officious, dogged and singularly unpleasant to deal with. If you are caught without a validated ticket for you or your luggage, it's best to pay the fine straight away. It's US$20 for you and US$10 for each piece of your luggage. Make sure to ask for a receipt. Never hand your passport over to inspectors, even if they threaten you with police intervention if you don't.

CAR & MOTORCYCLE

You won't enjoy having a vehicle in Kraków for two reasons – driving is not much fun in the city and you don't actually need to drive. The focus of attention is the Old Town, most of which is closed to traffic and where it's almost impossible to park. Around the Old Town, traffic is heavily congested and faces parking restrictions. Farther out, there's not that much to see, and you can easily get around by public transport or taxi. The city is fairly compact and travelling times are reasonable – this is not spread out like Los Angeles or Sydney.

Parking

There are two guarded car parks within the Old Town – on Plac Szczepański and Plac Św Ducha – and they are the most convenient places to leave your vehicle ($1 per hour) if you are lucky enough to find space there. If not, leave it in one of the guarded car parks in the surrounding area. Parking on the streets in the belt around the Old Town requires special tickets (*karta postojowa*) which you buy in a Ruch kiosk, mark with the correct month, day and time, and then display on your windscreen.

Car Rental

Avis, Budget, Hertz and other international agencies are well established in Poland these days, and there are also plenty of local operators in town. Most rental vehicles are European makes, such as Peugeot, Renault, Opel, Fiat, VW, BMW, Audi, Mercedes and Volvo.

Most companies offer one-way rentals within Poland (usually for some additional fee), but most will insist on keeping the car within Poland. None of them are likely to let you take their car beyond the eastern border.

Rental agencies will require you to produce your passport, a driver's licence held for at least one year, and a credit card. You need to be at least 21 or 23 years old to rent a car, and you may need to be older to rent a luxury model or 4WD.

Car rental is not cheap in Poland – the prices are comparable to, or even higher than, full-price rental in Western Europe –

and there are seldom any promotional discounts. As a rough guide only, economy models offered by reputable companies begin at around $60 a day plus $0.35 a kilometre, or $100 daily with unlimited mileage. Add $10 to $30 (depending on the model) a day for compulsory insurance. All companies have discount rates if you are going to use the car for a longer time, a week being the usual minimum period. The local operators are cheaper, but their cars and rental conditions may leave something to be desired.

It's usually cheaper to prebook your car from abroad rather than front up to an agency in Poland. This will also ensure that you have the car you need when you arrive; otherwise you may wait for a few days or, sometimes, a few weeks.

Major car rental companies operating in Kraków include:

Avis
  (☎ 421 10 66 or toll-free ☎ 0 8001 200 10)
  ul Basztowa 15 (in the LOT office)
Budget
  (☎ 637 00 89) ul Radzikowskiego 99/101
  (in Motel Krak)
Hertz
  (☎ 637 11 20 or toll-free ☎ 0 8001 HERTZ)
  Al Focha 1 (in Hotel Cracovia)
Europcar
  (☎ 633 77 73) ul Szlak 2.

TAXI

Taxis are easily available and not too expensive by western standards. As a rough guide, a 5km taxi trip will cost around $3, and a 10km ride shouldn't cost more than $5. Taxi fares are 50% higher at night (10 pm to 6 am) and on Sunday, and still more expensive outside the city limits. The number of passengers (usually up to four), or the amount of luggage, doesn't normally affect the fare.

There are plenty of taxi companies; their taxis are recognisable by the company's name and its phone number, marked either on a roof board or side doors. There are also pirate taxis (called by Poles the 'mafia'), which usually have just a small 'taxi' sign and may also have a name but no phone number. Mafia taxis are a plague in Warsaw and are recently spreading to Kraków. They occupy the main touristy taxi stands and tend to overcharge up to several times the normal fare. They should be avoided at all cost.

In Kraków, the mafia has so far only conquered the taxi stand in front of the main train station and the one at the back (the so-called Dworzec Wschodni), but be careful because it may spread farther. You'll easily recognise these taxis by the lack of phone numbers. You'll also notice the lack of official company taxis at these two stands – the mafia simply doesn't let them stay there.

Taxis can be waved down on the street, but it's much easier to go to a taxi stand *(postój taksówek)* where you'll almost always find a line of them. There are plenty of such stands and everybody will tell you where the nearest one is. Taxis can also be ordered by phone, usually for no extra charge, and should arrive within 10 minutes unless you request one at a specified time later on.

When you get into a taxi, make sure the driver turns on the meter. Also check whether the meter has been switched to the proper rate, which is identified by the number: '1' is the daytime rate, whereas '2' is the night rate.

Remember to carry small bills, so you'll be able to pay the right fare. If you don't, it's virtually impossible to get change back from a driver who's intent on charging you more. It's a good idea to find out beforehand how much the right fare should be by asking the hotel staff or an attendant at the airport.

Some of Kraków's better known companies include Radio Taxi (☎ 919), Tele Taxi (☎ 96 26), Wawel Taxi (☎ 96 66), Royal Taxi (☎ 96 23), Euro Taxi (☎ 96 64) and Express Taxi (☎ 96 29).

BOAT

From May to September, an excursion boat operated by the Anex company (☎ 422 08 55) chugs up the Vistula from the quay at the foot of Wawel. Excursions include one-hour return tours on weekdays ($2.50) and 1½-hour return trips to Bielany on week-ends ($3.50). The boat (which has a capacity for 200 passengers) doesn't depart if fewer than 35 people turn up for the trip.

BICYCLE

Kraków is not a good place for bikers. Traffic is heavy and road behaviour aggressive, and pollution can be appalling. There are virtually no bicycle lanes but many lunatic drivers. Potholes are deep and numerous, and the cobblestones in many streets can loosen your teeth. Tram tracks are treacherous, especially when wet.

Judging the pros and cons, it's probably better to leave your bike somewhere safe in your hotel and do the city sights on foot or by public transport, but if you decide otherwise, you'll need a good lock for wheels and frame.

Kraków has some bike shops (and sports/travel shops with bike sections), stocked with imported bikes and spare parts. There are very few places that rent out bikes. One is Jordan (☎ 421 21 25), ul Długa 9. A popular bike costs $1.50 per hour, $8 per day (24 hours), and you need to leave a deposit of $50.

WALKING

The best way to get around central Kraków is on foot, with occasional trips to the suburbs by public transport or taxi.

ORGANISED TOURS

Three travel agencies – Orbis (☎ 422 46 32) at Rynek Główny 41; Jan-Pol (☎ 421 42 06) in the Dom Turysty PTTK at ul Westerplatte 15/16; and Intercrac (☎ 422 58 40) in the Dom Polonii at Rynek Główny 14 – jointly operate tours in and outside Kraków. They include city sightseeing by coach ($25); the traces of Jewish culture ($24); the Wieliczka salt mine ($28); and the Auschwitz-Birkenau death camps ($27). Students get a 25% discount on the Wieliczka and Auschwitz tours. Contact any of the three operators for their free 'Cracow Tours' brochure with a full list and description of the tours.

A roughly similar program of tours (costing much the same) is offered by the Point travel agency operating from its two offices: in the Hotel Continental (☎ 423 78 94) at Al Armii Krajowej 11; and in the Hotel Ibis (☎ 421 84 33) at ul Przy Rondzie 2. Its tours can also be booked and paid for in several central hotels, including the Royal, Saski and Logos.

The Jarden Jewish Bookshop (☎ 421 71 66) at ul Szeroka 2, in Kazimierz's Jewish quarter, is the best known agency offering tours to discover Jewish heritage, including its showpiece – the Schindler's List tour. This two-hour tour, which includes the film's locations and other sites related to local Jewry, is conducted daily in summer (at other times on request) in a car or minibus and costs $15 per person.

All the above-listed tours are conducted in English; selected tours are programmed with German-speaking guides, and you may be able to have a French-speaking guide if you request one.

Note that even the cheapest tour won't be really cheap. Unless you specifically want some comfort and a foreign-language guide, it will cost you at most a third of the price to do any of these independently, plus you can take your time.

Some hotels, including Grand Hotel (☎ 421 72 55) and Hotel Polonia (☎ 422 12 33) arrange taxi trips on demand to Auschwitz ($75 per taxi for up to four people) and to other destinations.

Wędrowiec (Map 6; ☎ 421 89 08), in the kiosk at the car park on ul Powiśle at the foot of the Wawel, has guides in major western languages, who can show you around the city ($50 per group for any time up to five hours).

Almatur student agency (Map 4; ☎ 422 46 68) at ul Grodzka 2 offers hiking, kayaking, horse-riding, sailing etc holidays in summer. It also issues ISIC student cards.

Eko-Tourist travel agency (Map 4; ☎ 422 88 63, fax 423 16 97, email eko-tour@interkom.pl), ul Radziwiłłowska 21, is Kraków's first and still one of the few operators to deal with ecological tourism. It organises tours to national parks and also has a choice of tours for people with particular interests (bird-watching, rock-climbing, cycling, canoeing). Contact the agency in advance for its English-language catalogue. If you write to it, add the '31-026' postcode before 'Kraków'.

Quite the opposite to ecology, you can go on a tour to the Nowa Huta steelworks, organised through the local PTTK office (Map 2; ☎ 643 79 05). It needs at least two weeks advance notice and can provide English-speaking guides ($25) and a minibus ($40) to move around this huge place. You can also do the tour using your own transport, or in a taxi. The tour takes two to three hours, and no photos are allowed inside the steelworks.

Things to See & Do

Kraków's prime attraction is its historic centre consisting of the Old Town and Wawel. Together, they form pretty much a living museum of some eight centuries of art and architecture, where you'll find you want to spend most of your Kraków time. Perhaps the most enjoyable way of visiting the place is by aimlessly strolling about the streets, discovering this savoury palette of architecture, art, people, food, drink and, of course, entertainment.

The attractions in the following sections of this chapter have normally been listed in sequential order so you can conveniently connect them into a walking tour.

Prices are given in US$.

Highlights

- Wawel Castle and Cathedral – possibly the most important historic sights in Poland
- Kraków's magnificent Main Market Square
- The chancel of St Mary's Church with its stained-glass windows, wall paintings and an extraordinary Veit Stoss' Gothic altarpiece
- The Czartoryski Museum with its extensive and varied art collection including Leonardo da Vinci's enigmatic *Lady with Ermine*
- Charming Collegium Maius collection
- The world-class Museum of Pharmacy
- An evening of live *klezmer* music in one of the cafés on ul Szeroka
- Labyrinthine 700-year-old salt mine in Wieliczka
- Nights exploring fabulous cellar-vaulted pubs
- Beautiful salads at Chimera Salad Bar
- A dinner at Chłopskie Jadło

OLD TOWN

The Old Town (Stare Miasto) developed gradually throughout the centuries. Its plan was drawn up in 1257 after the Tatar invasions, and has survived more or less in its original form. The construction of the fortifications began in the 13th century, and it took almost two centuries to envelop the town with a powerful 3km chain of double defensive walls complete with 47 towers and eight main entrance gates, plus a wide moat.

With the development of military technology, the system lost its defensive capability and, apart from a small section to the north, was demolished at the beginning of the 19th century. The moat was filled and a ring-shaped park, the Planty, laid out on the site, surrounding the Old Town with parkland.

The Old Town has plenty of historical monuments, enough to keep you at least several days exploring. There are a dozen museums and nearly 20 churches here, not to mention scores of other important sights.

Noble, harmonious and oh so elegant, Kraków's Old Town has a unique atmosphere, felt as much in its busy street life during the daytime, as in its majestic silence late at night. Except for some enclaves, the quarter is car free or car limited-access area, so you can stroll largely undisturbed. It is best explored casually without a particular plan, savouring architectural details and the old-time air, while dropping into art galleries, trendy boutiques and cosy cafés and bars on the way.

The following places are shown on Map 4.

Main Market Square

Measuring 200m x 200m, Kraków's Main Market Square (Rynek Główny) is the largest medieval town square in Poland and reputedly in all of Europe. It's considered to be one of the finest urban designs of its kind. Its layout from 1257 has been retained to this day, though the buildings have changed over the centuries. Today most of them look neoclassical, but don't let the façades confuse you – the structures are older, sometimes considerably so, as can be seen in their doorways, architectural details and interiors. Their cellars date from medieval times. Walk around the square looking up at the houses' façades in detail from the street level up to the top – what a wealth of decorative detail it is!

In the past, the square was the marketplace and was crammed with vendors' stalls and houses. All that went in the 19th century, leaving behind three important freestanding buildings: the Cloth Hall, the Town Hall Tower and St Adalbert's Church. All that was left of the outdoor trade is a collection of flower stalls just opposite St Mary's Church, which have reputedly been trading on this site from time immemorial. This area is also the 'pasture' for Kraków's population of pigeons, thought to be the second largest in Europe after that of Venice.

Cloth Hall & Gallery of 19th Century Polish Painting The largest building on the square, the centrally positioned Cloth Hall (Sukiennice) was erected as a centre for the cloth trade in the 14th century, but was gutted by fire in 1555 and rebuilt in Renaissance style. In the late 19th century, arcades were added, giving the hall a more decorative appearance. The ground floor continues to be a trading centre, today for crafts and souvenirs, while the upper floor has been taken over by the Gallery of 19th Century Polish Painting, which is a branch of Kraków's National Museum (see the boxed text).

The gallery displays works by important painters of the period from Romanticism to the Young Poland movement, including Piotr Michałowski, Józef Chełmoński, Jacek Malczewski, Aleksander Gierymski and the leader of monumental historic painting, Jan Matejko. Matejko's two giant canvases, *Kościuszko pod Racławicami* (Kościuszko at the Battle of Racławice) and *Hołd Pruski* (Prussian Homage), attract perhaps the largest crowds. One of the most controversial is *Szał* (Ecstasy) by Władysław Podkowiński (see the boxed text).

Kraków's National Museum

The treasure trove of art, Kraków's National Museum (Muzeum Narodowe w Krakowie) began in 1879 with the painting of *Pochodnie Nerona* (Nero's Torches) by Henryk Siemiradzki (donated by the painter), and 20 years later its collection numbered 10,000 items. The museum's first exhibition room was in the refurbished Cloth Hall. Today the museum has eight outlets in the city, and only a small part of its 700,000-piece collection can be put on display. The branches (described separately in this chapter) include:

- Main Building (20th Century Polish Painting, Decorative Art, Arms and Uniforms)
- Cloth Hall (19th Century Polish Painting)
- Czartoryski Museum (Ancient Art, Decorative Art, West European Painting, Historical Objects up to 18th Century)
- Wyspiański Museum (Biographical Collection)
- Matejko House (Biographical Collection)
- Mehoffer House (Biographical Collection)
- Szołajski House (Polish Painting and Sculpture up to 1764)
- Centre of Japanese Art and Technology 'Manggha' (Old Japanese Art)

Each outlet displays a board featuring opening hours of all branches – take note that they don't differ from when this book was written. Also take note of the free-entry day (most likely to be Sunday), which will save you a couple of dollars on each admission. If you plan on visiting three or more branches and don't want to rush through them on the free-entry day, consider buying a special ticket ($5/3.50 for adult/student) which gives admission to all the permanent exhibitions of all the branches at any time. The ticket can be bought at any of the museum outlets.

The gallery is open Tuesday to Sunday from 10 am to 3.30 pm (Thursday till 6 pm).

Town Hall Tower The solitary 70m-high Town Hall Tower (Wieża Ratuszowa), next to the Cloth Hall, is all that is left of the 14th century town hall, pulled down in the 1820s because of its dilapidated state. The tower has miraculously survived, even though it too was in bad shape and leaning (the main reason for the leaning was reputedly a great hurricane in 1703). It has been extensively renovated over the past years (but it still leans 55cm off the vertical) and is open to visitors in summer.

You enter through a flight of stairs guarded by two lions (added in the 19th century) and climb a narrow staircase to the upper hall, from where you can look around through three windows (though the view is perhaps not as exciting as you would expect it to be). The tower is open from May to October, Wednesday to Friday from 10 am to 5 pm, Saturday and Sunday from 10 am to 4 pm. The spacious vaulted cellars under the tower, once the city jail, are now a café and theatre.

St Adalbert's Church The small domed St Adalbert's Church (Kościół Św Wojciecha), in the southern corner of the square, is one of the oldest churches in town – its beginnings dating back to the 10th century – but it has been rebuilt and altered on several occasions since. The cosy interior boasts modest baroque furnishings.

The church's original foundations can be seen in the basement (open in summer only), accessible by the external door from the south, adorned with a fine Romanesque doorway. This was once the main door to the church – note that the Rynek's level has risen over the centuries. A small exhibition in the basement features archaeological finds excavated from the square. These include the medieval wooden sewage pipes and a 12th century tomb with a preserved skeleton.

Monument to Adam Mickiewicz A few steps north of St Adalbert's Church, the monument of this great Romantic poet was unveiled in 1898, on the centenary of his birth. His statue is surrounded by four allegorical figures: the Motherland, Learning, Poetry and Valour (discover which is which). The monument's design, by Teodor Rygier, was chosen in a competition (in which Matejko also took part), and immediately sparked a wave of controversy, so that the artist had to alter some details.

The monument was pulled down by the Nazis in 1940 and found dismantled on a scrapheap near Hamburg after the war. It

The Painting that Scandalised the Public

The large-sized *Ecstasy* by Władysław Podkowiński (1866-95) is one of Poland's best known paintings and also one of the most controversial ones. The canvas depicts a naked woman with a sensual face and body, snuggled up to a huge wild black horse about to dash into a yawning chasm.

Painted by the artist in 1894 and shown the same year at an exhibition in Warsaw's Zachęta salon, it completely shocked the public, unused to such images. The scandal drew 12,000 people into the gallery in a month, a record-breaking figure for its time and a remarkable attendance even by today's standards.

Affected by the reception and a storm of critics, Podkowiński slit the canvas with a knife after the exhibition ended, in a desperate attempt to destroy it. He died just nine months later in a fit of madness, severely ill with tuberculosis, before reaching the age of 30.

Ecstasy is Podkowiński's last finished canvas. It's considered the finest and boldest achievement of his restless and unsatisfied artistic career. It has been reconstructed, yet the scars of the cutting are visible.

was reconstructed in 1955, it's an extremely popular rendezvous spot, always full of locals and visitors sitting all around. The Szopki competition is held here on the first Thursday of December (see Special Events in the Facts for the Visitor chapter).

Historical Museum of Kraków This museum (Muzeum Historyczne Krakowa) is accommodated in the large Krzysztofory Palace, in the northern corner of the square. It features a bit of everything related to the town's history, including old clocks, armour, medals, drawings, maps, plus a vast collection of paintings depicting Kraków's buildings, streets, squares and cityscapes. There's also a fine model of medieval Kraków as it looked in the late 15th century.

An exhibition related to Kraków's traditions and customs (including the Szopki and the Lajkonik) is to be opened on the 2nd floor – check when you come. The museum is open Wednesday, Friday, Saturday and Sunday from 9 am to 3.30 pm, and Thursday from 11 am to 6 pm. Saturday is free-entry day.

St Mary's Church Kraków's most important temple after the Wawel Cathedral, St Mary's Church (Kościół Mariacki), overlooks the main square from the east. The first church on this site was built in the 1220s and, typically for the period, was 'oriented' – that is, its presbytery pointed east. Following its destruction during the Tatar raids the construction of a mighty basilica started, using the foundations of the previous church. That's why the church stands at an angle to the square.

St Mary's is a great artistic achievement, where various styles from Gothic to Art Nouveau successively have left their imprint and harmoniously coexist, making an extraordinary final result. The church has been undergoing a thorough renovation over the past years, both on the outside and inside, and looks impressive. Its chancel is easily among the most amazing you can ever see in any church anywhere.

The church's main entrance, through a baroque porch added to the façade in the 1750s, is used by the faithful only; tourists enter through the side, southern door (where a small admission fee is charged), which gives access to the chancel. The chancel is illuminated by the original stained-glass windows dating from the late 14th century, considered some of Poland's oldest and most beautiful specimens. On the opposite side of the church, above the organ loft, is a fine Art Nouveau stained-glass window by Stanisław Wyspiański and Józef Mehoffer.

The colourful wall paintings designed by Matejko harmonise beautifully with the medieval architecture and make an appropriate background for the grand high altar, which is unanimously acclaimed as the greatest

Two Towers of St Mary's Church

St Mary's façade is dominated by two unequal towers. Why unequal? The story is that two brothers were commissioned for the construction, each for one tower. A bitter rivalry developed, in which each attempted to built his tower higher and grander. The younger brother, who ended up second, couldn't get over his defeat and killed his elder brother with a knife. Overcome by remorse, he then sunk the same knife into his own heart. The knife has been preserved as a record of the event and hangs at the eastern entrance to the Cloth Hall, opposite Mickiewicz's statue.

On a more factual note, the lower, 69m-high tower, topped with a Renaissance dome, serves as a bell tower and shelters five bells. The taller one, 81m high, has traditionally been the city's property and functioned as a watchtower. It's topped with a spire surrounded by turrets – a good example of medieval craftsmanship – and in 1666 it was given a 350kg gilded crown, 2.40m in diameter. The gilded ball higher up contains Kraków's written history.

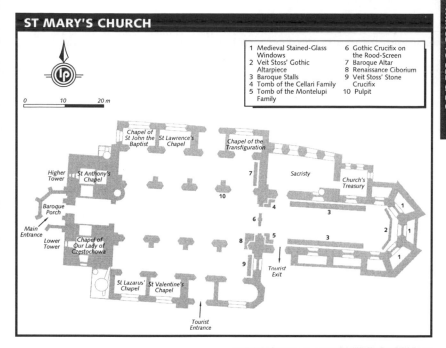

ST MARY'S CHURCH

1	Medieval Stained-Glass Windows	6	Gothic Crucifix on the Rood-Screen
2	Veit Stoss' Gothic Altarpiece	7	Baroque Altar
3	Baroque Stalls	8	Renaissance Ciborium
4	Tomb of the Cellari Family	9	Veit Stoss' Stone Crucifix
5	Tomb of the Montelupi Family	10	Pulpit

masterpiece of Gothic art in Poland. It is opened daily at 11.50 am and closed after the evening mass, except for Saturday when it's left open for the Sunday morning mass. Visits are from 11.30 am to 6 pm (from 2 pm on Sunday).

The altarpiece is certainly the main showpiece, but don't miss other precious works of art around, including the expressive stone crucifix on the baroque altar at the head of the right-hand aisle, another work by Veit Stoss, and the still larger crucifix placed on the rood-screen, attributed to pupils of the master. Also worth attention are the Renaissance ciborium (the place where the Host is kept), the ornate baroque stalls in the chancel, and the white-marble mannerist tombs of the Montelupi and Cellari families. There are more fine altarpieces and tombstones in the side chapels.

St Barbara's Church Just to the south of St Mary's Church is the small, charming St

High Altar of St Mary's Church

St Mary's famous altarpiece is a pentaptych (like a triptych, but consisting of a central panel and two pairs of side wings), intricately carved in limewood, painted and gilded. The main scene represents the Dormition of the Virgin while the wings portray scenes from the life of Christ and the Virgin. The altarpiece is topped with the Coronation of the Virgin and, on both sides, the statues of the patron saints of Poland, St Stanislaus and St Adalbert.

Measuring about 13m high and 11m wide, the pentaptych is the largest piece of medieval art of its kind. It took over 12 years for its maker, the Nuremberg sculptor Veit Stoss (known to Poles as Wit Stwosz), to complete this monumental work before it was solemnly consecrated and revealed in 1489.

Hejnał

Every hour the *hejnał* (bugle call) is played on a trumpet from the higher tower of St Mary's Church to the four quarters of the world in turn. Today a musical symbol of the city, this simple melody, based on five notes only, was played in medieval times as a warning call. Intriguingly, it breaks off abruptly in mid-bar. Legend links it to the Tatar invasions; when the watchman on duty spotted the enemy and sounded the alarm, a Tatar arrow pierced his throat in mid-phrase. The tune has stayed this way thereafter. Since 1927, the hejnał has been broadcast on Polish Radio every day at noon.

MARTIN HARRIS

Mary's Square (Plac Mariacki) which until the early 19th century was a parish cemetery. The 14th century St Barbara's Church (Kościół Św Barbary) bordering the square on the east was the cemetery chapel. Next to its entrance, there's an outer chapel featuring a stone sculptural composition of Christ and three apostles, attributed to the Veit Stoss school. There are some amazing tombstones in the church's external walls. The baroque interior boasts a fine high altar from 1692 and wall paintings from 1765. Look for an impressive early 15th century stone Pietà in a niche in the left-hand wall.

A passage which adjoins the church will take you onto the Little Market Square (Mały Rynek) which was once the second largest marketplace in town, trading mainly in meat.

North of the Market Square

The area to the north of Rynek Główny is noted for its regular chessboard layout. Its main commercial street, ul Floriańska, is part of the traditional Royal Way which leads from St Florian's Church to Wawel. There are important museums and churches in the area as well as other attractions you'll find while strolling about the streets.

Museum of Pharmacy Ulica Floriańska is the liveliest street of the Old Town and in it, at No 25, you'll find the little known Museum of Pharmacy (Muzeum Farmacji). Accommodated in a beautiful historic house (which has preserved its fine Gothic and Renaissance stone doorways and has an original ceiling covered with unique 17th century decorative paper), this is one of Europe's largest museums of its kind, and one of the best.

The 22,000-piece collection it houses, spread over the building's four levels and the cellars, features interiors of historic pharmacies, old laboratory equipment (including an unusual wooden microscope from about 1800), rare pharmaceutical instruments, heaps of glassware, stoneware, mortars, jars, barrels, medical books, documents, prescriptions etc. The oldest exhibits include an apothecary pottery vessel from Lebanon from around 1000 BC and Roman glass bottles.

This is a fascinating museum, worth visiting not only by specialists in the subject, and there are detailed descriptions of the contents in four languages. It is open on Tuesday from 3 to 7 pm and Wednesday to Sunday from 11 am to 2 pm.

Matejko House Just a few paces north from the Museum of Pharmacy, at ul Floriańska 41, is the Matejko House (Dom Matejki). An uncontested leader of national historical painting, and renowned for his powerful canvases documenting Polish history, Jan Matejko lived and worked here for the twenty most creative years of his life (1873-93).

Today Matejko House is a branch of the National Museum, open Tuesday to Sunday

The Słowacki Theatre has a 900 seat auditorium and has been the stage for major national dramas. The stage curtain is a gigantic painting by Henryk Siemiradzki.

from 10 am to 3.30 pm (Friday till 6 pm), which displays memorabilia of the artist and some of his paintings and drawings (his larger paintings are in the Cloth Hall gallery). The house itself is a 16th century structure, but was remodelled according to a design by Matejko himself.

Museum of Kraków's Theatre Theatre buffs might be interested in visiting the small Museum of Kraków's Theatre (Dzieje Teatru Krakowskiego), established in a 1474 Gothic building at ul Szpitalna 21, which traces the history of the city's theatre traditions. You'll find here a collection of theatrical items, costumes, stage projects, puppets, old photos, posters etc. It's open on Wednesday from 11 am to 6 pm, and Thursday to Sunday from 9 am to 3.30 pm.

Church of the Holy Cross Unprepossessing outside, the small 15th century Church of the Holy Cross (Kościół Św Krzyża) deserves a visit for its Gothic vaulting, one of the most beautiful in the city. An unusual design with the palm-like vault supported on a single central column, it was constructed in 1528 and recently thoroughly renovated. The set of baroque altars and stalls feels comfortable in the Gothic structure. Note the fragments of original Gothic and Renaissance frescoes on the walls, and the bronze baptismal font from 1423 on the right side at the entrance to the chancel.

Słowacki Theatre The large and opulent Słowacki Theatre (originally called the City Theatre) opened in 1893, and it reflects Kraków's high artistic aspirations of the day. The building was patterned on the Paris Opera, but various local motifs and decorative elements have been incorporated (eg the parapet which is reminiscent of that of the Cloth Hall). The theatre was the stage for premieres of major national dramas by Poland's greatest artists, including Adam Mickiewicz, Juliusz Słowacki and Stanisław Wyspiański.

Inside, the monumental staircase leads to the great 900 seat auditorium lined with four balconies. The highlight is the curtain which is actually a gigantic painting by Henryk Siemiradzki, full of allegoric figures representing Comedy, Tragedy, Dance, Music, Song etc.

Florian Gate The Florian Gate (Brama Floriańska) is the only one of the original eight city gates which was not pulled down during the 19th century 'modernisation'. It was built around 1300, although the top is a later addition. There's a fine statue of St Florian in the niche up on the gate's southern wall (from ul Floriańska), and a small shrine in the passageway. The adjoining walls together with two towers have also been left and today host an outdoor art gallery, where you are able to see and buy some amazing kitsch paintings.

Barbican The finest remnant of the medieval fortifications, the Barbican (Barbakan) is a powerful circular brick bastion adorned with seven turrets. There are 130 loopholes distributed on four levels in its massive walls (sometimes 3m thick). This remarkable piece of military architecture was built around 1498 as extra protection to the Florian Gate and was once connected to it by a narrow passage running over a moat. It's one of the very few surviving structures of its kind in Europe, the largest and arguably the most beautiful.

It's open for visitors Wednesday to Sunday from 9 am to 4 pm, and you can walk through the gallery which runs within the walls on the upper level around the whole structure.

Piarist Church The baroque Piarist Church (Kościół Pijarów) was built in 1718-28 at the end of ul Św Jana, and its location provides an attractive visual closing of the street. The beautiful late-baroque interior has been adorned with trompe l'oeil painting on the vault, which looks three dimensional and makes the nave seem loftier. There's also an unusual illusionistic high altar, in which the columns and saints have been painted, not carved. The whole, illuminated with artificial light, gives a rare impression of smoke or fog in the chancel.

Underneath the church is a spacious crypt, which is used as the site for art exhibitions, occasional theatre performances, and renowned Holy Sepulchres during Easter week.

Czartoryski Museum The Czartoryski Museum (Muzeum Czartoryskich), ul Św Jana 19, is one of the best and most frequently visited in town. Part of Kraków's National Museum, it was established in 1800 in Puławy by Princess Izabela Czartoryska as the first historical museum in Poland. It was secretly moved to Paris following the November Insurrection of 1830 (in which the family was implicated) and in the 1870s brought to Kraków.

The collection experienced another 'excursion' during WWII when the Nazis seized it and took it off to Germany, and not all the exhibits have been recovered. Even so, there's a lot to see, including Greek, Roman, Egyptian and Etruscan ancient art, Oriental armour, artistic handicrafts from Europe and Asia, and old European paintings, mainly Italian, Dutch and Flemish. The star pieces of the collection are Leonardo da Vinci's *Lady with the Ermine* (about 1485) and Rembrandt's *Landscape with the Good Samaritan*, also known as *Landscape before a Storm* (1638).

The museum is open Tuesday to Sunday from 10 am to 3.30 pm (till 6 pm on Friday). From mid-June to mid-September, the weekday opening hours are extended, from 9 am to 5 pm. Sunday is free-entry day.

St Mark's Church The late 13th century St Mark's Church (Kościół Św Marka) has been rebuilt several times since, yet its red-brick exterior still reflects much of its austere early-Gothic style. The interior has changed more and now shelters mostly 17th century baroque furnishings. The focal point is no doubt a beautiful high altar from 1613, covered with richly gilded mannerist ornamentation. The crucifix in the middle comes from the original, medieval church. Also of note is an unusual heart-shaped pulpit topped with a cross, with a cherub desperately hanging underneath.

Church of the Reformed Franciscans The rather unprepossessing 17th century Church of the Reformed Franciscans (Kościół Reformatów) is renowned for its crypt which holds coffins, each one containing a mummified body. The striking thing is that no particular embalming procedure has been applied; the bodies were just laid to rest here. The crypt has a unique microclimate which allowed the bodies to mummify naturally. It is closed to the public to maintain its atmospheric conditions, and is likely to remain so in the future.

West of the Market Square

Part of this sector was inhabited by Jews, who were moved out when the Kraków Academy was founded here in 1364. Since then it has traditionally been the university quarter, which still has its own peculiar atmosphere during the academic year.

Szołajski House This large building (Kamienica Szołajskich), at Plac Szczepański 9, was home to a branch of the National Museum which featured the painting and sculpture from the 14th to 16th centuries, before it closed down for renovation. Most of the collection are meanwhile stored, but some of the best pieces are temporarily presented in Wawel as an exhibition titled the Art More Precious Than Gold (see the Wawel section). The full collection will some day come back here or go to the House of Erazm Ciołek at ul Kanonicza 17.

Assembled from churches in the region, this is Poland's largest and best collection of late-Gothic and early-Renaissance altarpieces and Madonnas. The showpieces include the carved and painted *Virgin and Child of Krużlowa* from around 1410, arguably the finest of this sort in Poland, and the life-size *Christ on a Donkey* from around 1470, reputedly the best preserved sculpture of its kind in Europe.

Leonardo da Vinci's Enigmatic *Lady with Ermine*

Lady with Ermine by Leonardo da Vinci (1452-1519) is arguably Poland's most famous foreign painting. It's an oil portrait of a young woman handling an ermine, painted around 1485 on a walnut wooden panel measuring 55cm x 40cm. The painting is one of the finest of da Vinci's several woman portraits, in the same league as the *Mona Lisa* (or *La Gioconda*) and the *Virgin of the Rocks*. The model for the portrait was probably Cecilia Gallerani from the Milan court, painted when she was around 16 years old.

The early history of the painting is an enigma – the earliest written record which mentions it only dates from the end of the 18th century. The portrait was bought by Prince Adam Jerzy Czartoryski in 1800 in Italy, for the collection of his mother Izabela in Puławy, but there are no documents or details of the transaction. The painting was supposedly sold as an original work, but it was long considered a product of one of da Vinci's pupils or a copy, and was underestimated.

The painting was taken to Paris in 1831 then brought to Kraków for the new Czartoryski museum (which opened in 1876), but it wasn't put on display in either city, which only added to the mystery. It wasn't until the early decades of the 20th century that art historians really began to investigate the work's provenance. Following various comparative analyses and technical examinations of the painting in Poland and abroad, da Vinci's authorship has been determined almost without doubt, though some details are attributed to his pupils. The black background was added at some later stage and covered the original layer depicting some architectural motifs.

Shortly after the outbreak of WWII, the Nazis seized the Czartoryski collection and took it to Germany. The portrait was for a while on display in Berlin, before Kraków's notorious Nazi governor Hans Frank brought it in 1940 to Wawel castle, his temporary home. In 1944, when the Soviet front approached, he sent the painting to his villa in Bavaria, but it was found after the war and returned to Kraków.

Old Theatre Erected in 1798, the Old Theatre (Teatr Stary) is Poland's oldest theatre building operating uninterruptedly to this day. It was thoroughly refurbished in 1903-06, and large Art Nouveau stucco friezes have been added to the walls. There's a small Museum of the Old Theatre inside the building (open Tuesday to Saturday from 11 am to 1 pm, and one hour before performances) and the stylish Café Maska in the basement. The Old Theatre has long been one of Poland's most prestigious theatre companies (see the Entertainment chapter).

Palace of Art The Palace of Art (Pałac Sztuki) was built in 1901 for the Society of the Friends of Fine Arts. The project, in which some of the best local artists of the day had their hand, resulted in an interesting multistyle expression of the Young Poland movement – walk around it to see it all. The low-relief frieze running around the building was created by Jacek Malczewski. You'll find Matejko's bust on the eastern side (facing Plac Szczepański) and Wyspiański's bust on the opposite side. Don't miss an elaborate sculptural composition topping the southern façade. The door below leads to the spacious interior where temporary exhibitions of modern art are held – it's worth checking what's on.

Bunker of Art Another place to look for modern art is the Bunker of Art (Bunkier Sztuki), as the locals appropriately call this communist concrete production, reputedly the ugliest building within the Planty. Despite this, do go inside as interesting exhibitions can often be found here.

Collegium Maius Built as part of the Kraków Academy, the Collegium Maius is Poland's oldest surviving university building and one of the best examples of 15th century Gothic architecture in the city. It has a magnificent arcaded red-brick courtyard, with a well from 1517 in the middle, but what is still more interesting is the university collection kept inside the building.

You will be shown around the historic interiors where you'll find rare 16th century astronomic instruments, supposedly used by Nicolaus Copernicus, a bizarre alchemy room, old rectors' sceptres and, the highlight of the show, the oldest existing globe (from about 1510) that has the American continent marked on it. You will also visit an impressive Aula, a hall with an original Renaissance ceiling, crammed with portraits of kings, benefactors and professors of the university. It was here that Pope John Paul II and Czesław Miłosz received honorary doctorates.

The museum is open Monday to Friday from 11 am to 2.30 pm, and Saturday from 11 am to 1.30 pm. Saturday is entry-free day. All visits are in guided groups; tours begin every half-hour and there's usually one tour daily in English. Tours in French and German can be arranged on request. In summer it's advisable to reserve in advance, either personally in the museum office (2nd floor) or by phone (☎ 422 05 49). The courtyard is open from 7 am till dusk and can be entered free of charge.

St Anne's Church Built in 1689-1703 as a university church, just a few steps from the Collegium Maius, the baroque St Anne's Church (Kościół Św Anny) was designed by one of the best architects working in Poland in that period, Tylman van Gameren. It was long the site of inaugurations of the academic year, doctoral promotions, and a resting place for many eminent university professors. Today, it's still a popular venue for various university-related celebrations and for student weddings.

A spacious, bright interior fitted out with fine furnishings, gravestones and epitaphs, and embellished with superb stucco work by Baldassare Fontana and frescoes by Karol Dankwart and the Monti brothers – all stylistically homogeneous – puts the church among the best classical baroque buildings in Poland. There are many objects worth a closer look, including the high altar, pulpit, organ, stalls and the frescoes in the central dome.

The church is the place of the cult of St Jan Kanty (also known as Jan z Kęt), a clergyman, preacher, chronicler and longtime professor of theology at the Kraków Academy. When he died in 1473 he was already surrounded with an aura of holiness. He was canonised in 1767 and became a patron saint of the university. The chapel dedicated to the saint, in the right arm of the transept, features a marble coffin with his remains, supported by personifications of four university departments (Theology, Philosophy, Law and Medicine), and surrounded by four high columns topped with the saints.

Nowodworski Collegium Just opposite St Anne's Church, the Nowodworski Collegium (Kolegium Nowodworskiego) is the place where Poland's first grammar school was founded, in 1588. Today the rectorate and administration of the Collegium Medicum are here. The building has a beautiful arcaded baroque courtyard.

Collegium Novum Erected in 1883-87, the neo-Gothic Collegium Novum is one of the most recent additions to the collection of the Jagiellonian University's buildings within the Planty. Today it houses university authorities and administration.

Vaguely modelled on the Collegium Maius, the building shelters a large formal assembly hall (on the 1st floor) with coffered ceiling, decorated with historic paintings (among them the famous painting by Matejko depicting Copernicus at work), used for official inaugurations, doctoral promotions and some special occasions, plus music concerts and other cultural events.

South of the Market Square

The southern part of the Old Town is an elongated area, steadily narrowing south towards Wawel. This was once the settlement called Okół, which existed since around the 9th century at the foot of Wawel, long before the market square and a chessboard array of streets around it were laid out. As it developed spontaneously, Okół had no regular street layout and has none today. The main artery of this sector is ul Grodzka, dotted with several churches, while the parallel ul Kanonicza is perhaps the most picturesque of Kraków's streets.

Franciscan Church The mighty Kościół Franciszkanów was erected in the second half of the 13th century but repeatedly rebuilt and refurnished after at least four fires, the last and the most destructive being in 1850 when almost all the interior was burnt out. Of the present-day decorations, the most extraordinary are the Art Nouveau stained-glass windows in the chancel and above the organ loft, the latter being regarded among the greatest in Poland. All were designed by Stanisław Wyspiański, who also executed most of the frescoes in the presbytery and the transept.

The church is a single-naved construction but has a large chapel to each side of the nave. The one on the right-hand side shelters in its altar the much venerated 15th century painting of Our Lady of Sorrows (Matka Boska Bolesna). To the right is a fine mannerist tomb.

Adjoining the church from the south is the monastery, which has preserved its original Gothic cloister complete with fragments of 15th century frescoes. There's a valuable collection of portraits of Kraków's bishops on the cloister walls. The entrance to the cloister is from the transept of the church or from the outside through the eastern door next to the chancel.

Dominican Church The equally powerful Kościół Dominikanów, at the opposite end of the square, was also built in the 13th century and badly damaged in the 1850 fire, though its side chapels, dating mainly from the 16th and 17th centuries, have been preserved in reasonably good shape. The huge gable adorned with pinnacles, which tops the façade, is a post-fire product.

The entrance is through a neo-Gothic porch stuck to the façade, and on through a beautifully ornamented original 14th century doorway which leads into the church proper.

The first thing that strikes you inside is a collection of singularly monumental neo-Gothic furnishings, including confessionals, stalls and altarpieces. They were all made after the 1850 fire had consumed the previous furnishings.

Of the chapels, possibly the most important is St Hyacinthus' Chapel (Kaplica Św Jacka), accessible by a stairway along the left wall. Its sumptuous gilded altar boasts a marble coffin which contains the remains of the first Polish Dominican who died in 1257. At the head of the right aisle is the large Chapel of Our Lady of the Rosary (Kaplica Matki Boskiej Różańcowej), with the miraculous painting of the Virgin in its high altar.

The monastery, just behind the northern wall of the church, is accessible from the church through the side door underneath the staircase, or directly from the street. The cloister there has retained its Gothic shape pretty well and boasts a number of beautiful epitaphs, tombs and paintings.

Every day at 6.30 pm (except for the holiday period from July to mid-September and the 13th of each month), a few dozen Dominican monks, clad in their cream gowns, gather in the church's chancel for the vespers and sing their beautiful liturgic chants (in Latin), as they reputedly did for over 750 years. They usually conclude their half-hour worship with a procession to either St Hyacinthus' Chapel or the Chapel of Our Lady of the Rosary.

Archaeological Museum The Muzeum Archeologiczne (Poland's first archaeological museum, founded in 1850), ul Poselska 3, presents Małopolska's history from the Palaeolithic period till the early Middle Ages. One of the highlights of the collection is the 9th century tall stone statue of a Slav pagan god, Światowid. There's also a small exhibition featuring the art of Ancient Egypt, plus temporary displays.

The museum occupies a massive building of what was once a Carmelite monastery and later served as a prison for 153 years, until 1950. There's a beautiful garden beside it with a view of Wawel. The museum is open Monday to Wednesday from 10 am to 2 pm, Thursday from 1 to 4 pm, and Sunday from 11 am to 2 pm (closed Friday and Saturday).

Geological Museum Occupying part of the same complex of buildings as the Ar-

chaeological Museum (but the entrance is from ul Senacka 1/3), the Muzeum Geologiczne features minerals, fossils and Poland's largest collection of meteors. It's open on Tuesday from 10 am to 5.30 pm, Wednesday to Friday from 10 am to 3 pm and Saturday and Sunday from 10 am to 2 pm.

Cricoteka Cricoteka, in a fine Gothic house at ul Kanonicza 5, is a centre documenting the work of Tadeusz Kantor, principally his famous Cricot 2 avant-garde theatre. There's an exhibition hall in the basement where displays related to the theatre are held on a temporary basis. The ticket office stocks publications on Kantor's work. Serious theatre buffs and critics may be interested in contacting the centre's staff for specific information and to see the performances of Cricot 2 on video.

Wyspiański Museum Dedicated to one of Kraków's most beloved sons and the key figure of the Młoda Polska (Young Poland) movement, the Muzeum Wyspiańskiego reveals how many diverse branches of art Stanisław Wyspiański explored. A painter, poet and playwright, he was also a designer, particularly renowned for his stained-glass designs, some of which are on display.

His most unusual proposal was the 'Acropolis', a project to reconstruct Wawel as Poland's political, religious and cultural centre. There's a model made according to his design – an amazing mix of epochs and styles, a Greek amphitheatre and a Roman circus included. Wyspiański's vision has never been realised. Later calculations proved that the hill wouldn't support so many buildings squeezed onto its top. The museum was closed in 1998 for refurbishing – check whether it has reopened, and if the hours are still Tuesday to Sunday from 10 am to 3.30 pm (Thursday to 4.30 pm).

Church of SS Peter & Paul The first baroque building in Kraków, the Church of SS Peter and Paul (Kościół Św Piotra i Pawła) was erected by the Jesuits who had been brought to the city in 1583 to fight the Reformation. Designed on the Latin cross

Traditional music from all over Europe adds to the atmosphere of Kraków's streets and squares.

Church of Our Lady Queen of Poland, Nowa Huta, was designed by Bronisław Chromy.

Fine stained-glass windows in the richly decorated Tempel Reformed Synagogue in Kazimierz.

Austere Romanesque façade of St Andrew's.

The first Baroque Church of SS Peter and Paul.

Wyspiański's Stained-Glass Windows

While Stanisław Wyspiański was a master in many artistic fields, it's probably his stained-glass windows that most impress visitors. They all radiate with amazing Art Nouveau floral curving lines, usually arranged around a central theme, motif or figure, depending on the project's commissioner.

To see some of this work, the Wyspiański Museum may be a good point to start. It displays some of his designs, as does the Gallery of 20th Century Polish Painting in the National Museum's Main Building (where you can see the famous project of the stained-glass windows for the Wawel Cathedral, never realised). The most extraordinary project carried into effect is a set of windows in the Franciscan Church. There's also a fine large window, co-designed with Józef Mehoffer, in St Mary's Church. Other buildings which boast Wyspiański's designs include the House of Medical Association and the Hotel Pollera.

KRZYSZTOF DYDYŃSKI

---

layout and topped with a large dome, the church was built in 1596-1619 to become one of Poland's finest early-baroque churches. It has a refreshingly sober interior (compared to later baroque productions crammed with over-the-top ornate furnishings), except perhaps for the developed late-baroque high altar and the organ loft topped with the sculpture of an archangel.

The fine stucco decoration on the vault is work by Giovanni Battista Falconi, who was also the author of the statues of four Evangelists placed in the niches inside the dome. Just to the left of the high altar is the monumental tomb of Bishop Andrzej Trzebicki, made in black and white marble in 1679. The crypt in front of the high altar shelters the ashes of Piotr Skarga (1536-1612), a Jesuit priest, preacher and chronicler. The late-baroque figures of the Twelve Apostles standing on columns in front of the church are copies of the statues from 1723.

Collegium Iuridicum & Zoological Museum

Opposite the church, the Collegium Iuridicum was built in the early 15th century as part of the Kraków Academy, but

remodelled on various occasions later. It has a cosy arcaded courtyard and a marvellous doorway from 1680. There's a small Zoological Museum in the basement featuring collections of sea shells and butterflies from all over the world.

St Andrew's Church

Built towards the end of the 11th century, St Andrew's Church (Kościół Św Andrzeja) is one of Kraków's oldest and its austere Romanesque stone façade is preserved beautifully. As soon as you enter, though, you'll find yourself in a totally different world; the minute interior was subject to a radical late-baroque overhaul in the 18th century. Note the high altar and an unusual pulpit in the shape of a boat complete with the mast.

St Vladimir's Foundation

Accommodated in a restored historic house at ul Kanonicza 15, the foundation (Fundacja Św Włodzimierza), named after Vladimir the Great of Kiev who accepted the Byzantine Orthodox faith in 988, has a small gallery of icons dating from the 17th to 19th centuries. You can also visit a modern Orthodox chapel, adorned with paintings by the contemporary Kraków painter Jerzy Nowosielski. Taking inspiration from traditional Byzantine iconography, Nowosielski has applied modern techniques and forms and created an original and attractive style of painting expression. He is also the author of some of the painting work in the Orthodox Church (Cerkiew Prawosławna), at ul Szpitalna 24 in the Old Town, and in the Catholic Church of St Francis of Assisi (Kościół Franciszka z Asyżu), in the suburb of Azory, 3km north-west of the centre.

Archdiocesan Museum Opened in 1994, the Muzeum Archidiecezjalne, located in the 14th century house at ul Kanonicza 19, presents a collection of religious sculpture and painting, dating mostly from the 14th to 16th centuries, including five amazing Madonnas and Poland's oldest surviving painting on wooden board (dating from the 13th century).

Also on exhibition is the room where Karol Wojtyła (today's Pope John Paul II) lived in 1951-58, complete with the furniture and belongings, including his skis. He later lived (until 1967) in a spacious apartment in the adjacent house, which is also part of the museum, yet it has no original furnishing – it's just a display space for the religious art collection. The museum is open Tuesday to Saturday from 10 am to 3 pm.

St Giles' Church One of the oldest and smallest in town, St Giles' Church (Kościół Św Idziego; Map 5) was reputedly founded in 1086, but the Gothic building now existing dates from around 1320. Inside, there's a beautiful late-Renaissance high altar and unique marble stalls, assembled in 1626 from the elements of St Hyacinthus' tomb dismantled and removed from the Dominican Church. The church is only open for the Sunday mass (in English) at 10.30 am.

WAWEL

The very symbol of Poland, Wawel is saturated with Polish history as no other place in the country. It was the seat of the kings for over 500 years from the early days of the Polish state, and even after the centre of power moved to Warsaw, it retained much of its symbolic, almost magical power. Today a silent guardian of a millennium of national history, Wawel is about the most visited sight in Poland.

The following sites are on Map 5, Map 6 or the Wawel Cathedral map.

The way up the Wawel hill begins at the end of ul Kanonicza from where a lane leads uphill. Past the equestrian statue of Tadeusz Kościuszko, it turns to the left leading to a vast open central square surrounded by several buildings, of which the cathedral and the castle are the major attractions, and both can be visited.

Reserve at least three hours if you want anything more than just a general glance over the place. Note the different opening hours of the cathedral and the castle exhibitions (see below). In summer, it's best to come early as later there may be long queues for tickets. Avoid weekends, when Wawel is besieged by visitors. Bicycles are not allowed on the Wawel hill and there's nowhere to store them at the entrance.

Guide Services

Guides in Polish, English, German and French are available upon request at Wawel's Tourist Assistance Office (Biuro Obsługi Turystów; ☎ 422 16 97) in the entrance hall to the Royal Chambers exhibition in the castle. There's another guide service (☎ 422 09 04) at the entrance to the Wawel hill, opposite the statue of Kościuszko. A foreign-language guide will cost about $30 per group of up to nine people for a tour around the cathedral and all the exhibitions in the castle (admission fees are extra). It takes about three hours altogether. You can also take a guide for the cathedral-only tour, for a particular castle's exhibition or for any combination of your choice.

Wawel Cathedral

The national temple, the Wawel cathedral, has witnessed most of the royal coronations and funerals and is the last resting place for most of the Polish monarchs. Many outstanding artists had a hand in the gradual

Wawel Coronations

The Wawel Cathedral saw most of the coronations of Polish monarchs – of 19 kings and one queen, to be precise. The first Wawel coronation, of Władysław Łokietek, took place in 1320, and the last, of August III, in 1734. Before 1320, coronations were held in Gniezno's cathedral, where five Polish monarchs were crowned, including Poland's first king, Bolesław Chrobry, in 1024. Only two Polish kings were crowned outside Gniezno and Kraków: Stanisław Leszczyński (1704) and Stanisław August Poniatowski (1764), both in Warsaw's cathedral.

The Wawel coronations, which took place on Sunday, evolved into strictly scripted ceremonies, conducted over several days. They usually started with a funeral of the previous monarch, on the Saturday before the coronation day. After a solemn mass in the cathedral, the body was put to rest in the crypt.

The second part of the ceremony, also held on Saturday, was a penitential procession of the new monarch to the Skałka church, to pay homage to St Stanislaus. This was observed very strictly, perhaps to avoid the curse (see the boxed text on St Stanislaus later), and even Stanisław August Poniatowski, who was crowned in Warsaw, was obliged to do it. He actually had to do it twice: once in Warsaw before his coronation and then in Kraków during an official visit.

The coronation itself took place at the high altar of the cathedral and was an elaborate ceremony attended by the whole of the Church top hierarchy. The next day (Monday), a colourful pageant, headed by the king and the court, departed from Wawel for the (today nonexistent) town hall at the Main Market Square, to receive homage from the city council and to dub the knights. The ceremony was completed with a great outdoor popular party on the square, with music and tournaments for the knights, and free food and drink provided by the king.

After the capital was transferred to Warsaw, and the kings and court resided there (but continued to be crowned and buried in Kraków), the coronation ceremony became still more elaborate. It began with a funeral departing from St Florian's Church and proceeding along the Royal Way to Wawel, after the king's body had been brought from Warsaw. Similarly, the newly elected kings who arrived from Warsaw, began their coronation celebration with a festive pageant from St Florian's Church to Wawel.

creation of the cathedral, and have left behind a wealth of magnificent works of art and craft. It is an extraordinary artistic achievement and Poland's spiritual sanctuary.

The building you see is the third church on this site, erected in 1320-64. The original cathedral (known as St Gereon's Church) was founded around 1020 by the first Polish king, Bolesław Chrobry, and was replaced with a considerably larger Romanesque construction some 100 years later. It was completely burnt down in 1305 and only a crypt, known as St Leonard's Crypt, has survived. The present-day cathedral is essentially a Gothic structure but chapels in different styles were later built all around it.

The cathedral can be visited from 9 am to 3 pm, but on Sundays and holidays mass is held in the morning and visits are only from noon to 3 pm. From May to September, the opening hours are extended up till 5.30 pm. You can visit the cathedral's interior free of charge, but if you want to go up to the Sigismund Tower and down to the crypts you do need a ticket ($1.50, $0.75 for students). The box office is diagonally opposite the cathedral entrance in the Vicar's House.

Cathedral's Interior Before you enter, note the massive iron door and, hanging on a chain to the left, the prehistoric animal bones. They are believed to have magical

St Stanislaus – The Patron Saint of Poland

St Stanislaus, the first saint of Poland, was in his real life Kraków's bishop Stanisław Szczepanowski. In 1079 he was condemned to death by King Bolesław Śmiały (Boleslaus the Bold) for joining the opposition against the king and excommunicating him. According to the legend, the king himself carried out the sentence by beheading the bishop. The execution reputedly took place on the bank of the Vistula, south of Wawel.

The murder not only got the bishop canonised as patron saint of Poland, but it also cast a curse on the whole royal line. The first victim was the executioner himself, who was forced into exile. Successive kings built a commemorative church on the site of the crime (known as Skałka Church) and made penitential pilgrimages to it, but it didn't seem to help. In another desperate effort, a sumptuous mausoleum to the saint was erected in the very centre of the Wawel Cathedral, yet the curse continued to hang over the throne. It was believed, for example, that no king named Stanisław could be crowned and buried at Wawel, and indeed, two Polish monarchs bearing this name, Stanisław Leszczyński and Stanisław August Poniatowski, were crowned and buried elsewhere.

The curse went even further: no clergyman named Stanisław could become Kraków's bishop. The only one of that name in the town's history, Stanisław Dąbski, was elected in 1699, but fell ill and died just a few months later.

powers; as long as they are here, the cathedral will remain too. The bones were excavated in the grounds at the beginning of the 20th century.

Once inside, you'll immediately get lost amid a maze of sarcophagi, tombstones and altarpieces scattered throughout the nave, chancel and ambulatory. Among a score of chapels, the showpiece is the **Sigismund Chapel** (Kaplica Zygmuntowska) on the southern wall, referred to as 'the most beautiful Renaissance chapel to be seen north of the Alps'. From the outside, it's easily recognised by its gilded dome. Another highlight is the **Holy Cross Chapel** (Kaplica Świętokrzyska) in the south-western corner of the church, distinguished by the unique 1470 Byzantine frescoes and a marble sarcophagus from 1492 by Veit Stoss.

Right in the middle of the church is the laboriously decorated baroque **Shrine of St Stanislaus** (Mauzoleum Św Stanisława), dedicated to the bishop of Kraków who was canonised in 1253 to become the patron saint of Poland (see the boxed text above). The silver coffin, adorned with 12 relief scenes from the saint's life, was made in Gdańsk around 1670; the ornamented baldachin over it is about 50 years older.

Sigismund Tower The Sigismund Tower, which is accessible through the sacristy, shelters the Sigismund Bell, popularly called 'Zygmunt'. Cast in 1520, the bell is 2m high and 2.5m in diameter, and it weighs 11 tonnes, making it the largest bell in Poland. Its clapper weighs 350kg, and eight strong people are needed to ring the bell, which happens only on the most important church holidays and for significant state events.

Crypts Back down in the church, go downstairs (from the left-hand aisle) to the **Poets' Crypt** where two great Romantic poets, Adam Mickiewicz and Juliusz Słowacki, are buried.

Farther towards the back of the church in the same aisle you will find the entrance to **St Leonard's Crypt**, the only remnant of the 12th century Romanesque cathedral.

Follow through and you will get to the **Royal Crypts** (Krypty Królewskie) where, apart from kings, several national heroes including Kościuszko and Józef Piłsudski (see the two boxed texts later) are buried. Visit the Royal Crypts at the end of your cathedral tour, because the exit is outside the cathedral.

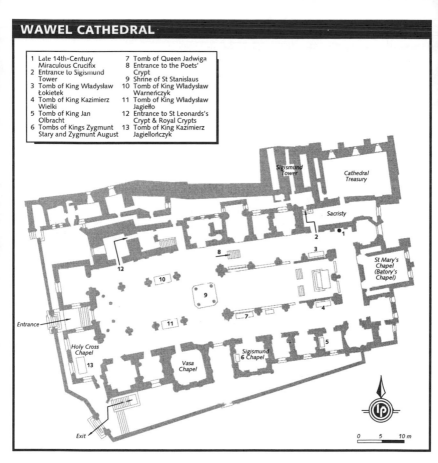

WAWEL CATHEDRAL

1 Late 14th-Century Miraculous Crucifix
2 Entrance to Sigismund Tower
3 Tomb of King Władysław Łokietek
4 Tomb of King Kazimierz Wielki
5 Tomb of King Jan Olbracht
6 Tombs of Kings Zygmunt Stary and Zygmunt August
7 Tomb of Queen Jadwiga
8 Entrance to the Poets' Crypt
9 Shrine of St Stanislaus
10 Tomb of King Władysław Warneńczyk
11 Tomb of King Władysław Jagiełło
12 Entrance to St Leonards's Crypt & Royal Crypts
13 Tomb of King Kazimierz Jagiellończyk

Cathedral Museum The Cathedral Museum (Muzeum Katedralne), diagonally opposite the cathedral, holds historical and religious objects from the cathedral. There are plenty of exhibits, including some amazing chasubles – note an extraordinary specimen from 1504 which depicts the life and death of St Stanislaus – but not a single original crown. They were all stolen from the treasury by the Prussians in 1795 and reputedly melted down. Each crown could easily contain 1kg of pure gold, not to mention their artistic value. The museum is open from 10 am to 3 pm (closed Monday).

Wawel Castle

The political and cultural centre of Poland until the early 17th century, the Wawel royal castle is, like the cathedral, the very symbol of Poland's national identity.

The castle is now a museum containing five separate sections in different parts of the building. The ticket office is in the passage leading to the castle's inner courtyard. You buy tickets here to all the castle's exhibitions, except the Lost Wawel.

Free-entry day to all the castle exhibitions (but not the cathedral) is Wednesday (June to September) and Sunday (remaining

Wawel Chakra

Once upon a time Lord Shiva threw seven magic stones towards seven parts of the world, and one of these landed in Kraków. As a gift to humanity, the places which had been hit radiated the god's energy. That's what legend says, but according to Hindu esoteric thinkers, these seven sites are indeed centres of supernatural energy which is reputed to give exceptional spiritual strengths. The centres, known as chakras (also spelled chakrams), are related to seven celestial bodies and include Delhi (Moon), Delphi (Venus), Jerusalem (Sun), Kraków (Jupiter), Mecca (Mercury), Rome (Mars) and Velehrad (Saturn). The seven earth chakras have their seven equivalent spiritual centres of power in the human body.

Kraków's chakra is nestled at Wawel, in the north-western corner of the royal castle's courtyard. It's believed to be centred in the chancel of St Gereon's Church, considered Wawel's first cathedral, founded around 1020. Only the foundations and crypt of this church have survived, but are off-limits to tourists. The holy stone which, as the legend has it, lies here is said not only to produce energy that revives life-giving forces, but also protects the city from misfortunes (as it did by saving it from destruction in WWII).

The history of the Wawel chakra is as esoteric as the chakra itself. It's not known whether the kings had any idea about what they were living on – at least there are no historic records about it. In the 19th century Wawel was becoming a legendary place, comparable to the Acropolis and Zion, but this was more due to its significance as a spiritual symbol of Poland in the time when the country formally no longer existed, rather than as a source of a supernatural energy.

The Pandora's box of controversy was probably opened by a Hindu traveller who visited Kraków in the early 1920s and, for some reason, expressed particular interest in St Gereon's Church. The following years witnessed a number of other Hindu visitors. All came specifically to the ruined church where they meditated for hours in deep silence, to the increasing astonishment of the Wawel management. The management was perhaps in for an even bigger shock when an Indian government delegation led by Prime Minister Nehru kindly asked if they could include the ruin in their official Wawel tour and be left alone inside.

The chakra has drawn in all sorts of dowsers who come with divining rods and wands. According to their measurements, Wawel radiates stronger energy than any other known site in Poland (the far second strongest is Częstochowa). They also confirmed that the main source of radiation lies underneath the chancel of St Gereon's Church. The studies published by them after a complex research of Wawel are full of diagrams, figures and comments, all of which seem to confirm the uniqueness of the place and its supernatural properties.

Predictably, the Wawel chakra draws people in. They flock to this particular corner of the courtyard and stand immobile for minutes or hours, attracting the curiosity of unaware passers-by and ironic smiles from those who don't believe in such things. No matter which side you take, Wawel has yet another attraction, even though the Wawel management plays down the existence of any chakra.

MARTIN HARRIS

months). The number of visitors per day is limited, so you should be early for your free tickets, especially in the summer season.

Castle's History The original small residence was built in the early 11th century by King Bolesław Chrobry, beside the chapel dedicated to the Virgin Mary (known as the Rotunda of SS Felix and Adauctus). King Kazimierz Wielki turned it into a formidable Gothic castle. It was burnt down in 1499, and King Zygmunt Stary commissioned a new residence. Within 30 years a splendid Renaissance palace, designed by Italian architects, had been built. Despite further extensions and alterations, the Renaissance structure, complete with a spacious arcaded courtyard, has been preserved to this day.

Repeatedly sacked and devastated by Swedes and Prussians, the castle was occupied after the third partition by the Austrians, who intended to make Wawel a citadel. A fancy plan to rebuild the royal seat included turning the castle into barracks, and the cathedral into a garrison church, moving the royal tombs elsewhere.

The Austrians succeeded in realising some of their projects. They turned the royal kitchen and the coach house into a military hospital, and razed two churches standing in the outer courtyard to make room for a parade ground. During the work, they stumbled upon the perfectly preserved pre-Romanesque Rotunda of SS Felix and Adauctus and pulled down a good part of it. They also enveloped the whole hill with a new ring of massive brick walls, largely ruining the original Gothic fortifications.

Only in 1918 was the castle recovered by Poles and restoration work begun. It was continued after WWII and succeeded in recovering a good deal of the castle's earlier external form and its interior decoration.

Royal Chambers The Royal Chambers (Komnaty Królewskie) are the largest and most impressive exhibition and you should head there first; the entrance is in the south-eastern corner of the courtyard. Proceeding through the apparently never-ending chain of rooms on the two upper floors of the castle, all restored to their original Renaissance and early-baroque style and crammed with period furnishings and works of art, you'll get an insight into how the royalty once lived.

While strolling around, note the amazing tiled stoves, coffered ceilings and doorways carved in stone. You'll also see heaps of magnificent old tapestries hanging on the walls all over the place – this collection is actually Wawel's most precious possession. Largely assembled by King Zygmunt August, it once numbered 356 pieces but only 136 survive. Even so, this is probably the largest collection of its kind in Europe.

The two biggest (and probably most impressive) interiors you'll pass on your way are the Senators' Hall, originally used for the senate sessions, court ceremonies, balls and theatre performances, and the Audience Hall, also known as the Throne Hall. Look at the coffered ceiling of the latter, with 30 surviving carved heads (known as Wawel heads) of a total of 194 that once adorned this place.

The Royal Chambers are open Tuesday to Saturday from 9.30 am to 3 pm (on Friday until 4 pm), and Sunday from 10 am to 3 pm. From May to September, the exhibition is open half an hour longer from Tuesday to Friday. Entry costs $3 ($1.50 for students).

Oriental Art The exhibition of Oriental Art (Sztuka Wschodu) features a collection of 17th century Turkish banners, weapons and an embroidered tent, all captured after the Battle of Vienna, displayed along with a variety of old Persian carpets, Chinese ceramics and other Oriental objects. The opening hours are the same as those of the Royal Chambers and the entrance is from the north-western corner of the courtyard. Tickets are $1.50 ($0.75 for students).

Crown Treasury & Armoury The Crown Treasury (Skarbiec Koronny), housed in vaulted Gothic rooms surviving from the 14th century castle, is in the north-eastern part of the castle. The most famous object here is the 13th century Szczerbiec or

Jagged Sword which was used at all Polish coronations from 1320 onwards. This apart, you'll find here a varied and interesting collection that include chalices, monstrances, maces, house altars, clocks and an amazing golden pendant with mountain crystal dating from the 11th century.

The adjacent Armoury (Zbrojownia) has a collection of old weapons from various epochs (mainly from the 15th to 17th centuries) as well as replicas of the banners of the Teutonic Knights captured at the battle of Grunwald in 1410. The Treasury and Armoury are open on the same days and hours as the Royal Chambers, and the joint admission ticket costs $3 ($1.50 for students).

Lost Wawel The Lost Wawel (Wawel Zaginiony) exhibition is installed in the old royal kitchen. Apart from the remnants of the late 10th century Rotunda of SS Felix and Adauctus, reputedly the first church in Poland, you can see various archaeological finds (including amazing old ceramic tiles from the castle's stoves) as well as models of the previous Wawel churches. The entrance is from the outer side of the castle. The exhibition is open daily except Tuesday, from 9.30 am to 3 pm; entry is $1.50 ($0.75).

Art More Precious Than Gold This enigmatically named exhibition (Sztuka Cenniejsza niż Złoto) is not listed on Wawel's information boards, yet it's well worth a visit. Its core is the 40-piece selection of Gothic painting and sculpture, the highlights of the extensive collection from the Szołajski House, currently in restoration. Added to the exhibition are some castle interiors, including the Hen's Foot Tower (Kurza Stopka).

Wawel Dragon

Kraków's Dragon, from a woodcut by Sebastian Münster, in *Cosmographia*, 1550.

According to legend, once upon a time there lived a powerful prince, Krak or Krakus, who built a castle on a hill named Wawel on the bank of the Vistula and founded a town named after himself. It would have been paradise if not for a dragon living in a den underneath the castle. This fearsome and ever-hungry huge lizard decimated cattle and sheep, and was not averse to human beings, especially pretty maidens.

The wise prince ordered a sheep's hide to be filled with sulphur, which was set alight, and the whole thing was hurled into the den. The voracious beast devoured the bait in one gulp, only then feeling the sulphur burning in its stomach. The dragon rushed to the river, and drank and drank and finally exploded, giving the citizens a spectacular fireworks display. The town was saved. The dragon has become the symbol of the city immortalised in countless images, and a sculpture has been cast and placed where the beast once lived.

The entrance to the exhibition is from the inner courtyard through the same gate as to the Royal Chambers – inquire at the Tourist Assistance Office (Biuro Obsługi Turystów) which sells the tickets. All visits are by guided tour with a maximum of 10 people. Tours start on the hour, Tuesday to Sunday, from 10 am to 3 pm. The Gothic art on display will return to its legitimate owner, the National Museum, as soon as the museum is able to present it.

Dragon's Den

You can complete your Wawel trip with a visit to the Dragon's Den (Smocza Jama), the home of the legendary Wawel Dragon (Smok Wawelski). The entrance to the den is next to the Thieves' Tower (Baszta Złodziejska) sited at the western edge of the Wawel hill.

You'll get a good panorama over the Vistula and the suburbs farther to the west, including the Centre of Japanese Art and Technology on the far bank of the river, and Kościuszko's Mound far away on the horizon.

You descend 135 steps to the den, then walk another 70m through its interior and emerge onto the bank of the Vistula next to the fire-spitting bronze dragon, the work of the renowned contemporary sculptor, Bronisław Chromy. The den can be visited May to September, daily from 10 am to 5 pm.

SOUTHERN SUBURBS
Stradom

Stradom, immediately south-east of Wawel, is a small district sandwiched between the Old Town and Kazimierz. It's not a prime tourist destination, but it is close enough for anyone to visit its various attractions (see Map 5).

Bernardine Church Sitting just at the foot of the Wawel hill, the impressive Bernardine Church (Kościół Bernardynów) was built in 1659-80 on the site previously occupied by a more modest construction that was ruined by the Swedes. Its spacious three-naved interior is crammed with overwhelming baroque furnishings, including

the mid-18th century sumptuous altars supported on heavy twisted columns.

St Anne's Chapel at the head of the left aisle shelters the late-Gothic wooden statue of St Anne, sculptured in the workshop of Veit Stoss in the early 16th century, which somehow survived the destruction of the former church. On the side wall of the same chapel hangs an unusual painting of the Danse Macabre.

Missionaries' Church Another elaborate baroque affair, the nearby Missionaries' Church (Kościół Misjonarzy), was erected in 1719-28, taking inspiration from Italian examples in Rome. Behind the monumental façade, the single-naved interior is lined on both sides with chapels illuminated by the light reflected from the mirrors hanging high in the nave – quite an unusual and ingenious concept – and topped with a vault adorned with fine wall paintings.

Natural History Museum This small museum (Muzeum Przyrodnicze) features some stuffed animals typical of Poland, however the highlight is the prehistoric woolly rhinoceros found at the foothills of the Carpathians in present-day Ukraine. The reconstructed rhinoceros, its skeleton and a plaster cast, show the position in which it was found (see the boxed text Woolly Rhinoceros). The museum is open Tuesday to Friday from 9 am to 2 pm.

Kazimierz

Today one of Kraków's inner suburbs located within walking distance south-east of Wawel, Kazimierz used to be an independent town with its own municipal charter and laws. Its colourful history was determined by its mixed Jewish/Polish population, and though the ethnic structure is now wholly different, the architecture gives a good picture of its past, with clearly distinguishable sectors of what were Christian and Jewish quarters. The suburb boasts some important tourist sights, including good churches, synagogues and museums.

Woolly Rhinoceros

While Kraków is well known for its cultural attractions, few people know that it also shelters some precious natural relics, including the world's only complete specimen of the woolly rhinoceros (Coelodonta antiquitatis), the animal which inhabited the region about 30,000 years ago. It was found in 1929 in an ozocerite (earth wax) mine in Starun, south of Lviv, then taken to Kraków and reconstructed. Examination of the creature has revealed that it was a young female which could have weighed up to three tonnes.

The animal was preserved in a remarkably good state thanks to the site's favourable conditions – a combination of ozocerite and salty groundwater. The animal's skin – almost 1cm thick – has lost the hair, though some of it has been found nearby. The skin was put onto a hypothetical model of the animal and completed with re-created eyes, hoofs and horns which hadn't survived. The skeleton has been reconstructed separately, using the original bones, most of which survived although some were found broken.

MARTIN HARRIS

Christian Quarter The western part of Kazimierz was traditionally Catholic since the town's early days, when several churches were built. Although Jews also settled here, particularly from the early 19th century until WWII, the quarter largely preserved its original character and its churches, which are now the major tourist sights. You can easily get there from the Old Town and Wawel on foot, either along the Vistula bank, or by Stradomska and Krakowska streets.

Pauline Church The Pauline Church (Kościół Paulinów) is commonly known as the Skałka (the Rock) due to its location, for it was built on a rocky promontory that is no longer pronounced. Today's mid-18th century baroque church is the third building on the site, previously occupied by a Romanesque rotunda and later a Gothic church. The place is associated with Bishop Stanisław (Stanislaus), canonised in 1253 and made patron saint of Poland. His shrine is in the Wawel Cathedral – read the boxed text about the saint in the Wawel section.

The memory of the saint still lives on in the church's late-baroque dim interior. You can even see the tree trunk (on the altar in the left-hand chapel closest to the high altar), believed to be the one on which the king performed the crime of beheading the bishop. The body is supposed to have been dumped into the pond in front of the church.

The pond was later transformed into a stylish pool. It is lined with a balustrade and fronted with a baroque gate, with a sculpture of St Stanislaus placed in the middle. The water is said to have miraculous powers.

The cult of the saint has turned the place into a national pantheon; the crypt underneath the church shelters the tombs of 12 eminent Poles including medieval historian Jan Długosz, composer Karol Szymanowski, and painters Jacek Malczewski and Stanisław Wyspiański.

On the Sunday following 8 May (the saint's feast day) a well attended procession, with almost all the episcopate present, leaves Wawel for the Skałka church.

St Catherine's Church One of Kraków's most monumental churches which has retained its original Gothic shape, St Catherine's Church (Kościół Św Katarzyny) was founded in 1363 by King Kazimierz Wielki and completed some 35 years later, though the towers have never been built. A large, richly decorated stone Gothic porch on the southern wall was added in the 1420s. The church was once on the corner of Kazimierz's market square but the area was built up in the 19th century.

The showpiece of the lofty and spacious whitewashed interior is the singularly im-

Kazimierz's Chequered Jewish-Polish History

Kazimierz was founded in 1335 by King Kazimierz Wielki (hence its name) just on the southern outskirts of Kraków. Thanks to numerous privileges granted by the king, it developed swiftly and soon had its own town hall and a market square almost as vast as that of Kraków, and two large churches. The town was encircled with defensive walls and by the end of the 14th century came to be the most important and wealthiest city of Małopolska after Kraków.

The first Jews came to settle in Kazimierz soon after its foundation, but it wasn't until the end of the 15th century that their numbers began to grow quickly, following their expulsion from Kraków in 1494 by King Jan Olbracht (John Albert). They settled in a relatively small prescribed area of Kazimierz, north-east of the Christian quarter, and the two sectors were separated by a wall.

The subsequent history of Kazimierz was punctuated by fires, floods and plagues, with both communities living side by side, confined to their own sectors. The Jewish quarter became home to Jews fleeing persecution from all corners of Europe, and it grew particularly quickly, gradually determining the character of the whole town.

At the end of the 18th century Kazimierz was administratively incorporated into Kraków and in the 1820s the walls were pulled down. At the outbreak of WWII Kazimierz was a predominantly Jewish quarter, with a distinctive culture, colour and atmosphere. However, the Jews were exterminated by the Nazis in the concentration camps; of about 70,000 Kraków Jews (most of whom lived in Kazimierz) in 1939, only some 6000 survived the war. The current Jewish population in the city is estimated at between 100 and 150.

During the communist rule, Kazimierz was largely a forgotten place on Kraków's map, partly because the government didn't want to touch the sensitive Jewish question. In the early 1990s, the suburb slowly made its way onto the pages of tourist publications, yet its grubby appearance, along with the rather limited interest of Poles in the Jewish legacy, didn't help much to promote it. Then came Steven Spielberg to shoot his *Schindler's List* and all changed overnight.

Actually Kazimierz was not the setting of the movie's plot – most of the events portrayed in the film took place in the Płaszów death camp, the Podgórze ghetto and Schindler's factory, all of which were farther to the south-east, beyond the Vistula. Yet the film turned the world's attention to Kraków's Jewry as a whole, and since Kazimierz is the only substantial visual relic of Jewish heritage, it has benefited the most. 'Schindler's Tourism' now draws in crowds of visitors – Poles and foreigners alike – to the place which hardly saw any tourists a decade ago. Isn't it a bitter irony that a couple of hours on screen can mean more than half a millennium of history?

As a result of the state's long neglect, the quarter still looks dilapidated except for some of its small enclaves which have been restored and revitalised by private entrepreneurs. A more comprehensive development program is hindered by limited funds and, particularly, unsettled titles of real estate once belonging to the Jews.

posing richly gilded early-baroque timber high altar from 1634. Also worth noticing are the large mannerist funeral monument from 1618, the wooden statue of St Rita from the late 15th century, and the painting of the Danse Macabre. All three are near each other in the right-hand aisle. Adjoining the church is the monastery cloister (accessible from the church) which features some well preserved Gothic wall paintings.

Corpus Christi Church Founded in 1340, the Corpus Christi Church (Kościół Bożego Ciała) was the first church in Kazimierz and for a long time the parish church. Its exterior reflects its original Gothic style, but the interior has been almost totally fitted out with baroque furnishings, including the huge high altar, impressive massive stalls in the chancel (among the most beautiful in Kraków) and a boat-shaped pulpit. Note the only surviving early 15th century stained-glass window in the presbytery.

Town Hall & Ethnographic Museum

Kazimierz's town hall was built in the late 14th century in the middle of a vast market square (Plac Wolnica is all that's left of it) and was significantly extended in the 16th century, at which time it acquired its Renaissance appearance. It no longer serves its original purpose; now it shelters the Ethnographic Museum (Muzeum Etnograficzne) which has one of the largest collections in Poland (about 60,000 exhibits), though only a small part of it is on display.

The permanent exhibitions feature the interiors of traditional peasant houses that have been faithfully reconstructed (ground floor), folk costumes from all over Poland and many traditional customs, including some extraordinary Nativity scenes (1st floor), and folk painting and woodcarving – mostly religious (2nd floor). The museum is open on Monday from 10 am to 6 pm, Wednesday to Friday from 10 am to 3 pm, and Saturday and Sunday from 10 am to 2 pm (free entry on Sunday).

Bonifrater Church

Characterised by its decorative three-tier façade, the Bonifrater Church (Kościół Bonifratów) is a late-baroque structure, erected in 1739-58. Its single-naved interior has an illusionistic wall painting on the vault and the miraculous statue of Jesus of Nazareth in its high altar.

Jewish Quarter

Kazimierz's Jewish quarter occupied an area of not more than 300m x 300m, yet in the course of centuries it came to be a centre of Jewish culture as nowhere else in the country.

In WWII, the Jews were slaughtered by the Nazis and with them disappeared all the folklore, life and atmosphere of the quarter. Today only the architecture reveals that this was once a Jewish town.

Miraculously, all seven synagogues survived the war in better or worse shape, but only one of them continues to function as a place of worship, and two more have been turned into museums.

Ul Szeroka (literally, Wide Street) was traditionally the central street of the Jewish quarter. Appropriately named, it's wide and short, and looks more like an elongated square than a street, now packed with tourist cars. Ul Józefa was historically the main entry to the Jewish town from the Christian sector in the west.

Old Synagogue & Museum of History and Culture of Kraków Jewry

The Old Synagogue (Stara Synagoga) sits at the southern end of ul Szeroka. The name is not accidental, for this is the oldest Jewish religious building in Poland, dating back to the end of the 15th century. Damaged by fire in 1557, it was reconstructed in Renaissance style by the Italian architect Matteo Gucci. It was plundered and partly destroyed by the Nazis, but later restored to its previous form and today houses the Museum of History and Culture of Kraków Jewry.

The prayer hall with a reconstructed bimah (raised platform at the centre of the synagogue where the Torah is read) in the middle and the original aron kodesh (the niche where Torah scrolls are kept) in the eastern wall, houses an exhibition of liturgical objects related to Jewish culture. The adjacent rooms are dedicated to Jewish traditions and paintings, and on the upper floor you can see old photographs depicting Jewish martyrdom during WWII.

The museum is open on Wednesday, Thursday, Saturday and Sunday from 9 am to 3.30 pm and Friday from 11 am to 6 pm. It's closed on the first Saturday and Sunday of each month, in which case it opens on the following Monday and Tuesday from 9 am to 3 pm. Saturday is a free-entry day.

Isaac's Synagogue

Built in 1640-44, this is Kraków's largest synagogue. Damaged during WWII, it was restored in the mid-1990s and is today open as a museum. You can see the remains of the original stucco and wall painting decoration, and watch two short historic documentaries about Kraków's Jewry. More documentary films may be available as well as some temporary exhibitions. The place is open from 9 am to 7 pm daily except on Saturday and Jewish holidays.

Poper's Synagogue This small baroque synagogue with thick walls and buttresses was founded in 1620 by the wealthy merchant Wolf Poper. It was damaged during the Nazi occupation and its interior decoration hasn't survived. Today it's an artistic centre for children, and the synagogue's main room serves as the exhibition hall.

Remuh Synagogue This is the smallest synagogue in Kazimierz and the only one regularly used for religious services. Established in 1553 by a rich merchant, Israel Isserles, but associated with his son Rabbi Moses Isserles, a philosopher and scholar, the synagogue is open to visitors Monday to Friday from 9 am to 4 pm.

Remuh Cemetery The cemetery is just behind Remuh Synagogue. It was founded at the same time as the synagogue itself, but it was closed for burials in the early 19th century, when a new, larger cemetery was established.

During WWII, Nazis razed the tombstones to the ground. However, during postwar conservation work, Polish workers discovered old tombstones under a layer of earth. Further systematic work led to the discovery of about 700 gravestones, some of them outstanding Renaissance examples four centuries old. It seems that the Jews themselves buried the stones to avoid their desecration by the foreign armies which repeatedly invaded Kraków in the 18th century. The tombstones have all been meticulously restored, making up one of the best preserved Renaissance Jewish cemeteries anywhere in Europe. The tombstone of Rabbi Moses, dating from 1572, is right behind the synagogue. You can recognise it by the stones placed on top in an expression of respect.

Tempel Reformed Synagogue Kazimierz's newest synagogue, which dates from 1862, is a good-size neo-Romanesque building which has a large prayer hall with a balcony running all around. Walls and ceiling are richly decorated with colourful floral and geometric patterns, and there are fine stained-glass windows. The interior was being thoroughly renovated in 1999, but is likely to be completed by now.

New Jewish Cemetery Much larger than the old Remuh graveyard, the new Jewish cemetery is behind the railway track (the entry is at ul Miodowa 55, just past the railway bridge). It was established around 1800 and is the only current burial place for Jews in Kraków. Its size gives an idea of how large the Jewish population must have been. There are still about 9000 surviving tombstones – the oldest dating from the 1840s – some of which are of great beauty. In contrast to the manicured Remuh cemetery, the newer one is completely unkempt, which makes it an eerie sight. The entrance to the cemetery is through the funeral building you'll see to your right or through the gate in the fence – whichever you find open.

Podgórze

Podgórze is a vast suburb south of Kazimierz, beyond the Vistula. While Kazimierz was the place where the Jews lived for centuries, Podgórze marks the tragic end of their history. It was here that the Jews were herded into the ghetto established during WWII, and later exterminated in Płaszów concentration camp (see the boxed text later), just to the south, or sent to Auschwitz and Bełżec and gassed there.

The suburb features various places of interest, both related and unrelated to the Jewish issues. An easy way to explore places linked to Jewish history is by taking the 'Schindler's List' tour, which is run by the Jarden Jewish Bookshop at ul Szeroka 2. You can also put together your own tour using the following descriptions.

Museum of National Remembrance Accommodated in the former Pharmacy under the Eagle (Apteka pod Orłem) of Tadeusz Pankiewicz, at Plac Bohaterów Getta 18, the museum (Muzeum Pamięci Narodowej) features old photos from the Jewish ghetto in Podgórze and the concentration camp in Płaszów. It's a small but chilling collection. There's also a small display of pharmaceutical equipment. The museum is open weekdays from 10 am to 4 pm and Saturday from 10 am to 2 pm.

The museum's location in Pankiewicz's pharmacy is not incidental. He was the only Pole of non-Jewish descent who stayed in the ghetto after it was established. He lived and worked within the walls until the ghetto's liquidation, eye-witnessing all the horrors of the arrests, round-ups, purges, deportations and killing of the Jews. His pharmacy was open 24 hours a day and served as a meeting place and point of contact with the outer world. Pankiewicz survived the war and in 1947 published his memoirs from that tragic period (later translated into several languages, including English and Hebrew). He died in 1993 and is buried at the Rakowicki Cemetery.

Schindler's Factory Oscar Schindler's Rekord enamelware factory was at ul Lipowa 4. In 1948 the premises were taken over by the Telpod state electronic company, but the main gate hasn't changed much except for the Telpod board placed above it. Enter through the left door of the gate (open weekdays till about 6 pm) and you'll get to the staircase which features prominently in the film as the staircase leading to Schindler's office.

The previous Schindler's office and the main factory hall are off-limits. The 50m-high chimney, which also features in the film, no longer exists; it was pulled down in 1998 because it was in danger of collapsing. The commemorative plaque placed after the film was shot was reputedly taken away by some passionate visitors. The factory's administration charges $1.50 to visit the place, so it's possible that somebody will approach you at the staircase and request payment (which should be done in the factory's reception desk at a different entrance).

Jewish Ghetto

Soon after the Nazis occupied Poland, an intensive persecution of Polish Jews began. In all Polish cities with a significant Jewish population, Jews were forcibly displaced and moved to enclosed areas called ghettos. In Kraków, the ghetto was established in March 1941 in the Podgórze suburb. It was surrounded by a 3m-high wall designed in the shape of Jewish gravestones, and was accessible by four guarded gates. About 12,000 Jews were initially squeezed into the 320 buildings existing within the walls.

After the Nazis agreed on their infamous 'final solution' in January 1942, the Jews were gradually displaced from the ghettos to the concentration camps. In Kraków, about 11,500 Jews were sent from the Podgórze ghetto to the concentration camp in Bełżec in two great displacement actions of June and October 1942 (Płaszów camp was not finished at that time), and the ghetto area was reduced.

In the final displacement actions in March 1943, 6000 Jews were sent to the Płaszów camp and another 1000 to Auschwitz, while some 3000 people were shot dead in the ghetto itself. The ghetto was eventually liquidated on 13 March 1943 and the walls pulled down. Only two small fragments of the walls remain – at ul Lwowska 27 and behind the primary school No 28 at ul Limanowskiego 62.

Podgórze changed considerably after the war, so much so that Steven Spielberg decided to shoot ghetto scenes for his film in Kazimierz, which was less altered. One of the ghetto gates was re-created off ul Szeroka.

Zucher's Synagogue Podgórze had its own synagogue, at ul Węgierska 5. It was a fair-sized brick building erected in 1879-81, but only the façade survived WWII. It has been restored and a modern structure built behind, and it now houses Starmach Gallery, one of the most prestigious private art galleries in town.

St Joseph's Church Overlooking the spacious Rynek Podgórski, the large neo-Gothic St Joseph's Church (Kościół Św Józefa) is neither very old (it dates from 1909) nor probably very important as an historic monument, but it has an amazing ornate fairy-tale façade. Its central spire was clearly modelled upon that of St Mary's Church. The spacious interior with a wide transept features neo-Gothic furnishings, including the altars, organ and confessionals.

St Benedict's Church The origins of the small St Benedict's Church (Kościół Św Benedykta) are shrouded in the mists of obscurity. It was probably built as early as the 11th century, but was reshaped on various occasions. It sits on a hilltop, reputedly on the site of a pagan ritual centre. The church is locked save for two masses a year (on 21 March on St Benedict's day, and on the Tuesday after Easter Sunday), but its surroundings provide wide views over Podgórze. It was here that Spielberg filmed the scene of Schindler on horseback looking at the ghetto.

The red-brick construction you see near the church is the fort built by the Austrians in 1852 as part of Kraków's vast fortification system.

Krakus' Mound Believed to be the grave of Krakus, the legendary founder of Kraków, Krakus' Mound (Kopiec Krakusa) is a 16m-high structure of earth and sand built atop a natural hill (Map 2). Archaeological excavat-ions placed it at around the 7th century but didn't shed much light on the purpose of its building and the functions it played.

Płaszów Concentration Camp

The building of the camp began in November 1942 on the grounds of two neighbouring Jewish cemeteries in the Płaszów suburb, just 1km south of the Podgórze ghetto. The camp expanded quickly throughout 1943, particularly after Amon Goeth was appointed its commanding officer in February 1943. It was initially a coercive labour camp, but it was turned into a concentration camp in January 1944.

The changed situation on the eastern front forced the Nazis to cut short plans to expand the camp, and to cancel building projects for gas chambers and a crematorium. The camp's liquidation began in July 1944 and it took half a year to demolish the camp completely in an attempt to hide the crimes. Even the ashes of the burned victims were taken away and spread over the fields. The last liquidation squads left the place three days before the arrival of the Soviet troops on 15 January 1945. By then virtually nothing was left of the camp. Today it's a large rugged bush area increasingly circled by villa suburbs. Two monuments have been placed on the site to pay homage to the victims.

KRZYSZTOF DYDYŃSKI

Monument to victims killed at Płaszów

About 35,000 prisoners, mostly Jews but also Poles, Hungarians and Gypsies, went through Płaszów during its two years in operation. Of these, about 8000 people were murdered in Płaszów itself, while most others were transported to other camps to meet their death. There were no gas chambers, so the main method of extermination was mass execution. Amon Goeth was notorious in passing arbitrary sentences and personally shooting prisoners. He was tried in Kraków in 1946 and sentenced to death by hanging

Kraków's Mounds

Kraków is exceptional among Polish cities in having mounds. These are cone-shaped hills of earth erected by human hands, of which the two oldest, Krakus' Mound in Podgórze and Wanda's Mound in Nowa Huta, are both approximately 16m high and date back to about the 7th century. Little is known about what they were raised for.

A third mound was erected in Zwierzyniec in the early 1820s, and here the purpose was absolutely clear: to pay tribute to Tadeusz Kościuszko, a widely venerated national hero who fought for independence first in America then in Poland. No wonder then that the mound was raised with the enthusiastic participation of thousands of volunteers, and eventually reached a height of 34m.

Continuing the tradition, a fourth mound went up in the woodland park of Las Wolski in the mid 1930s, to honour Marshal Józef Piłsudski, the man who brought about Poland's independence after WWI.

It can't come as a surprise that Cracovians have already raised another mound, dedicated to one more eminent city citizen, Pope John Paul II, even though he is still alive. Built in 1997 in the garden of the Resurrectionist Seminary on ul Pawlickiego, this is Kraków's smallest mound. It's topped – you guessed it – with a large cross.

MARTIN HARRIS

Whatever the answers might be, the mound provides sweeping views all around, including Wawel and Nowa Huta. Nearby, to the west, you can see an old quarry with high cliffs all around it. The Płaszów concentration camp was re-created here for Spielberg's film.

WESTERN SUBURBS
Piasek & Nowy Świat

These two suburbs (Map 4), immediately to the west of the Old Town, were for centuries just collections of loosely scattered houses, repeatedly ravaged by foreign assaults. Solid progress didn't come until the

Most of the citizens of Kraków are practising Roman Catholics. Pope John Paul II, the first Polish Pope, has inspired greater involvement and expression of the faith.

Golgotha in the Carmelite Church where you'll find a miraculous painting of Our Lady of the Sand.

High Altar, Cistercian Abbey, Nowa Huta.

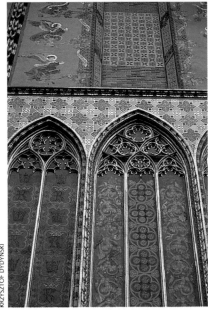

Exquisite chancel, St Mary's, Rynek Główny.

late 19th century, when many wealthy citizens settled here, favouring this quiet area over the overcrowded and busy Old Town. Accordingly, a good part of the architectural fabric dates from the turn of the 19th century and includes some fine Young Poland examples.

Carmelite Church The Carmelite Church (Kościół Karmelitów) was founded in 1395 by Queen Jadwiga and King Władysław Jagiełło, but it was wrecked almost completely during the Swedish invasion of 1655-56 and reconstructed two decades later in baroque style. Its interior boasts a massive high altar, ornate stalls and an organ, but the church's most precious possession is the miraculous painting of Our Lady of the Sand (Matka Boska Piaskowa), in the large chapel to the right of the nave.

The image was painted in the late 15th century directly onto the southern external wall of the church, and it didn't take long before miracles occurred in increasing numbers. A chapel was built to protect the painting and accommodate the faithful. King Jan Sobieski prayed here to the Virgin before heading for the Battle of Vienna, which he eventually won. In 1883 the image was crowned – the crowns of the Virgin and the Child were designed by Matejko.

Mehoffer House In this house, at ul Krupnicza 26, Wyspiański was born in 1869. Long after his death, Józef Mehoffer bought the house in 1930 for his studio and family residence. Since 1995 it has been Mehoffer's biographical museum featuring the artist's paintings, drawings and stained-glass designs, all displayed in the house's authentic interior, full of period furniture and family mementos. The museum is open Tuesday to Sunday from 10 am to 3.30 pm (on Wednesday till 6 pm).

Capucine Church The small Capucine Church (Kościół Kapucynów) was built in the late 17th century, and its interior decoration is modest. The main attraction is the mechanised *szopka* (Nativity scene), displayed here during the Christmas period.

Adjoining the church is the early 18th century Loreto House (Domek Loretański), modelled, like many others across Europe, on the famous Casa Santa in Loreto, Italy. Inside the house is a small chapel which features the statue of Our Lady of Loreto and a fine tabernacle in its altar, and Art Nouveau wall paintings by Jan Bukowski all around. The entrance to Loreto House is from the right aisle of the church, through the Chapel of the Crucified Christ (note the crucifix in the altar).

House under the Singing Frog This fanciful building (Dom pod Śpiewającą Żabą), on the corner of ul Retoryka and ul Piłsudskiego, was designed by Teodor Talowski and built in 1890. Watch out for the singing frog. You'll find some other unusual creations by the same architect a few steps south along ul Retoryka.

National Museum's Main Building The massive edifice called the Main Building (Gmach Główny), on the corner of Al Mickiewicza and Al 3 Maja, is the National Museum's largest exhibition space. It houses three permanent sections: Gallery of 20th Century Polish Painting; Decorative Art; and Polish Arms and Uniforms – plus various temporary exhibitions.

The largest of the three sections, the painting gallery, features an extensive collection of Polish painting (and some sculpture) covering the period from 1890 until the present day. There are several stained-glass designs (including the ones for Wawel Cathedral) by Wyspiański, and a good selection of Witkacy's paintings. Jacek Malczewski and Olga Boznańska are both well represented. Of the more recent artists, note the works by Kantor and Nowosielski, Kraków's best known post-war painters.

The museum is open Tuesday to Sunday from 10 am to 3.30 pm (on Wednesday till 6 pm). Sunday is a free-entry day for all the permanent galleries (but not for temporary exhibitions). Next to the entrance to the museum building is a large monument dedicated to Wyspiański.

Zwierzyniec

Once the hunting grounds for the kings, Zwierzyniec is today predominantly a villa suburb with large stretches of green areas. Its main attraction is arguably Kościuszko's Mound, but you can visit other sights en route if you decide to stroll around the area (all on Map 3).

Błonia Just west of the National Museum's Main Building, the 43 hectare Błonia is the largest green area near the city centre. Once a marsh, it was drained and is today a vast meadow, the venue for a variety of activities and events from parachute competitions to the masses celebrated by Pope John Paul II during his visits to his motherland. On his last visit, in June 1999, a crowd of 1.5 million people gathered here.

You may find a circus or a fair, or sometimes just grazing cows, the beneficiaries of a 14th century privilege granted by King Kazimierz Wielki to the local peasants, and honoured to this day.

Zwierzyniec's Churches Zwierzyniec has three historic churches, all a stone's throw away from each other, close to the Vistula. The most important, the **Church & Convent of the Premonstratensian Nuns** (Kościół i Klasztor Norbertanek) is a large fortified complex right on the river bank. It dates from the 12th century but its present-day appearance is the result of numerous changes and extensions which continued well into the 17th century. The interior shelters the unusual neoclassical colonnade from 1777 in the chancel, the oratorium at the back of the church separated by a screen, and the 1876 wall paintings on the vault.

Up the hill are the charming octagonal timber **St Margaret's Chapel** (Kaplica Św Małgorzaty) from 1690 and the Romanesque stone **Holy Saviour's Church** (Kościół Św Salwatora), both locked except for Sunday mass. The latter is one of Kraków's oldest churches; excavations have shown that the first building was erected here in the 10th century, and some fragments of the original structure can be seen.

Kościuszko's Mound The mound (Kopiec Kościuszki) was constructed in 1820-23, soon after Kościuszko's death, to pay tribute to the man who had embodied the dreams of independent Poland in times of foreign occupation. It measures 34m and due to its position, sitting on a natural hill, it commands a spectacular view over the city and is one of the area's popular tourist attractions.

The entrance to the walk up the mound is through a small neo-Gothic chapel. It's open May to September, daily from 9 am to 7 pm; and from 10 am to 5 pm the rest of the year.

The large brick construction around the mound is a fort built by the Austrians in the 1840s. Part of it is now a hotel and another part accommodates the small Kościuszko Museum (Muzeum Kościuszkowskie) which displays memorabilia related to the hero. It's open daily except Monday from 10 am to 4 pm.

Bus No 100 will take you (every hour or so) directly to the mound from Plac Matejki opposite the Barbican (Map 4). Otherwise you can walk all the way via Błonia or take tram No 1, 6 or 32 to the end of the line in Zwierzyniec and then continue on foot along the tree-shaded, car-free Al Waszyngtona (a 25 minute walk).

NORTHERN SUBURBS
Kleparz

Kleparz, just north of the Old Town, was once an independent town, founded by King Kazimierz Wielki in 1366. Strategically set on the Warsaw and Wrocław roads, the town was known far and wide for its numerous inns and taverns, to accommodate visitors who arrived late and found Kraków's gates closed.

In 1792 Kleparz was incorporated into Kraków, but it wasn't until the second half of the 19th century that it really developed, fuelled by the proximity of the train station (built in 1844-47). It was then that the vast square of Plac Matejki (part of what previously was Kleparz's main market square), was laid out and lined with monumental buildings.

Tadeusz Kościuszko – Polish-American Hero of Independence

Born in 1746 to a noble family in Poland's far eastern province (now part of Belarus), Kościuszko completed military school in Warsaw and then went to Paris to continue his military studies. On returning to Poland he fell in love with the daughter of a general, but was unable to win his permission for the marriage and, following an unsuccessful attempt to elope with her, he was forced to flee Warsaw. He went to France then, in 1776, to America, where he joined the local forces fighting for independence from Britain.

During the following five years, he was involved in most major engagements of the American independence campaign, including the Battle of Saratoga, the Battle of Ninety-Six and the blockade of Charleston. In recognition for his contribution, he was granted US citizenship and made a brigadier general in the US Army. Yet, in 1784 he decided to go back to Poland, which was in an increasingly difficult political situation.

The return was a disappointment. It wasn't until 1789 that he was offered a major military position. Meanwhile, he lived a humble life in the countryside and had another broken love affair with the daughter of another general who didn't give his consent to marriage.

Kościuszko was certainly more fortunate on the battlefield, which he had an opportunity to prove again following the invasion of Poland by the Russian army in 1792. The aggression was launched by Empress Catherine the Great to break the local reforms introduced in the aftermath of the fully liberal constitution which was passed in 1791. It was met with a strong defence by the Poles, culminating in the Battle of Dubienka in 1792, in which Kościuszko largely contributed to the victory of Polish troops. His fame reached international proportions, so much so that the new French government gave him honorary French citizenship. King Stanisław August Poniatowski raised him to the rank of general.

In March 1794 Kościuszko swore the oath of national uprising against the occupants, the ceremony watched by a thick crowd that flocked to Kraków's main square. A few months later he commanded the famous Battle of Racławice, when legions of Polish peasants equipped with just scythes won a smashing victory over the well armed Russian troops.

To attract more peasant volunteers for further formations, Kościuszko issued a manifesto suspending serfdom, but this was met with resistance by the aristocracy. This proved to be a turning point in the campaign's fortunes. Kościuszko was forced to retreat to Warsaw and led a heroic two month defence of the city against massive attacks of the combined Prussian-Russian armies, before it was captured. He tried to continue fighting in Wielkopolska, but was wounded and taken prisoner by the Russians at Maciejowice. Without its leader, the insurrection was soon over and it was just a matter of months before the three occupying powers divided among themselves the remaining chunk of Poland.

Jailed in St Petersburg, Kościuszko was freed in 1796 soon after the death of Catherine the Great. He went to the USA, where he became a close friend of Thomas Jefferson, but returned to France in 1798, hoping to gain Napoleon's aid in Poland's independence cause. Napoleon didn't want to commit himself, however.

Disillusioned and embittered, Kościuszko retired from public life, retreating to a country estate in France, then in Switzerland, where he died in 1817. A year later, his remains were brought to Kraków and buried among the Polish kings in the crypt of the Wawel Cathedral.

Grunwald Monument The huge Grunwald Monument (Pomnik Grunwaldzki), in the middle of Plac Matejki (Map 4), commemorates the Battle at Grunwald of 1410, when Polish-Lithuanian troops under King Władysław Jagiełło defeated the Teutonic Knights, killing their grand master, Ulrich von Jungingen, and marking the beginning

KRZYSZTOF DYDYŃSKI

Grunwald Monument

of the order's decline. Erected in 1910 in quincentenary of what was Poland's greatest and most decisive medieval battle, the monument was destroyed by the Nazis on their entering the city in 1939 and was re-created in 1975. It's a figurative composition topped with an equestrian statue of Jagiełło, noted by theatrical gestures of the figures, including the agonising von Jungingen.

St Florian's Church One of Kraków's five oldest churches, the Kościół Św Floriana was built in 1185-1212, yet because of its location outside the city walls it was repeatedly ravaged by enemies and rebuilt by the local clergy. The present-day form dates from the 17th century reconstruction, and the baroque façade has been adorned with the statue of St Florian.

The three-naved interior is also in baroque style throughout, including its high altar featuring the painting of St Florian of 1683. The chapel in the right aisle closest to the high altar shelters a fine late-Gothic triptych carved in wood.

House under the Globe Erected in 1904-06, the House under the Globe (Dom pod Globusem), ul Długa 1, is considered one of the best architectural achievements of the Young Poland movement. Its massive spire is topped with a globe and the façade is adorned with decorative details. The interior decoration is largely the work of Józef Mehoffer, but the house is now the office of a book publisher, and tourists are not allowed to visit it.

Perhaps the only way to see the representative hall on the 1st floor, with the wall paintings by Mehoffer, is to turn up at one of the book promotions which are held here from time to time.

Church of the Nuns of the Visitation Designed by Giovanni Solari and built in 1686-95, the Church of the Nuns of the Visitation (Kościół Wizytek) has avoided fires and destruction and is today one of the best examples of Kraków's baroque architecture, despite its rather small size and simple structure. It has a fine decorative façade, adorned with rich ornamental and sculptural detail, and a sumptuous single-naved interior with a large high altar and lots of good stucco work all over the place.

Rakowicki Cemetery

The large Rakowicki Cemetery (Cmentarz Rakowicki) was founded in 1803 and today is Kraków's most exclusive necropolis, after the Wawel Cathedral and Pauline Church.

The cemetery is the final resting place for many prominent citizens, including the painters Jan Matejko, Piotr Michałowski, Wojciech Kossak and Józef Mehoffer, plus plenty of renowned university professors, politicians, lawyers and doctors. In a way, the cemetery is a reflection of the last two centuries of Kraków's history.

St Florian – the Patron Saint of Firefighters

St Florian was a Roman soldier who died a martyr's death. In 1184, by the request of Polish Prince Kazimierz Sprawiedliwy (Casimir the Just), Pope Lucius III presented the saint's relics to the Wawel Cathedral. However, legend has it that the oxen pulling the cart with the holy relics stopped in Kleparz and wouldn't move any farther until the relics were unloaded. The event was interpreted as St Florian's will about his resting place, and Prince Kazimierz commissioned a church to be built at the place to shelter the saint's remains.

Kraków's defensive gate and the street leading to the main square were named after the saint. It's today the only surviving medieval gate and the city's busiest street.

When the capital was moved from Kraków to Warsaw, St Florian's Church was given an important role in the royal funeral ceremonies. It was the place where a king's body, just arrived from the capital, was deposited before its final journey, in which it was carried in a much celebrated procession to the Wawel Cathedral. St Florian's Church also became the starting point for the coronation processions, from where a newly elected king, arriving in Kraków, proceeded in a joyful pageant to the Wawel Cathedral for his coronation. In fact, St Florian's Church came to be commonly considered as the beginning of the Royal Way.

St Florian's supernatural powers made him a protector of natural disasters, particularly fires. He was reputedly seen in the skies during Kraków's huge fire of 1528, which he miraculously extinguished with a bucket of water from the heavens. He is now the patron saint of firefighters.

St Florian's day is 4 May. A solemn procession used to proceed from the Wawel Cathedral to St Florian's Church on that day every year until the early 20th century. The celebrations are now held locally with the participation of the city's firefighters.

Even if the names don't tell you much, it's worth coming here for the wealth of beautiful tombs, funeral monuments and chapels that make up some of Poland's largest and finest collections of funerary sculpture. It's also one of the most diverse assemblages, containing just about every style from Ancient Egypt to contemporary. Finally, it's a tranquil tree-shaded place, contemplative, surrounded by a nostalgic atmosphere.

The Rakowicki Cemetery is no longer in use. Some of the eminent city dwellers are now buried in the Military Cemetery, just to the north. Here you will find the tombs of Kantor, Piotr Skrzynecki and the parents of Pope John Paul II.

The cemeteries look most impressive on 1 and 2 November, when thousands of people come to pray for the souls of the dead, placing flowers, wreaths and lighting candles on the graves of their relatives. Don't miss coming if you are in town around that time – it's a unique experience.

EASTERN SUBURBS
Wesoła

The suburb of Wesoła, just east of the Old Town, developed along the old trail to Mogiła, today ul Kopernika. Most of the sights are along this tree-shaded street, within easy walking distance of each other.

St Nicholas' Church Dating from the 12th century, St Nicholas' Church (Kościół Św Mikołaja) was repeatedly destroyed and rebuilt over the centuries. Its current form is the result of the reconstruction of 1677-84, after the Swedes had burned it almost completely in their devastating invasion of 1655-56.

The church's interior, along with the high altar, organ and sumptuous stalls, is in baroque style, but note some older objects: the 16th century bronze baptismal font, just to the left of the high altar; and the fine 15th century Gothic pentaptych, at the head of the right aisle. The oldest relic, however, is the 14th century stone 'lantern of the dead', transferred here from St Valentine's leprosarium in Kleparz. It's Poland's only monument of its kind. It stands outside the church, next to the chancel, from the street side.

House of the Medical Association The interior of this house (Gmach Towarzystwa Lekarskiego) was built in 1904, and was designed by Wyspiański. Of particular note is the stained-glass titled *Apollo – Solar System* and the decorative balustrade of the staircase.

Jesuit Church Built in 1909-21, the monumental Jesuit Church (Kościół Jezuitów) is one of Poland's most original ecclesiastical buildings of the early 20th century. Largely overlooked by tourist guides (perhaps because it is considered 'not old enough' by Kraków standards), it's an interesting piece of architecture designed by Franciszek Mączyński. The architect took elements from various styles, but transformed it all creatively into an original work. Some of the best local artists contributed to the church's fittings and decoration.

The first thing you'll notice from a distance is a strikingly high bell tower (one of Kraków's tallest church spires), looking a bit like a lighthouse. The main doorway is topped with an amazing statue of Christ, a work by Xawery Dunikowski.

Once inside, you are enveloped by colourful Art Nouveau wall paintings by Jan Bukowski, an artist responsible for mural decorations in several other churches, including the Loreto Chapel of the Capucine Church. He also designed a collection of elaborate neo-baroque confessionals.

Both side altars are large dynamic figurative compositions carved in white marble by Karol Hukan, while the high altar is an unusual composition – a colonnade topped with a half-dome modelled on Renaissance patterns.

Botanical Garden Established in 1783, this is Poland's oldest botanical garden (Ogród Botaniczny; Map 3). Initially encompassing 2.5 hectares, it was extended in 1819 when an area with a pond was adjoined and transformed into an English-style landscaped park. Many trees planted then are today the core of the arboretum. The garden was further extended after WWII, and a new glasshouse was built. The garden now covers 9.8 hectares and shelters about 6000 plant species and strains.

The garden is open April to October daily from 9 am to 7 pm (shorter hours in autumn), but the glasshouses are only open from 10 am to 1 pm except on Friday. There's a small botanical museum (open on Sunday only, from 9 am to 4 pm) in the palace-like neoclassical building from 1788, at the entrance to the botanical garden. It was a Jesuit residence and later housed an astronomical observatory, which moved out in the 1970s.

Czyżyny
Polish Aviation Museum Established in 1964 on what was Poland's first airfield, the Muzeum Lotnictwa Polskiego is by far the country's biggest museum of its kind. It features about 150 aircraft, including aeroplanes, gliders and helicopters, dating from 1915 on. Displayed indoor and outdoor, exhibits include a rare Russian M-15 flying boat from 1917 (the world's only complete surviving specimen) and German warplanes from WWI. The museum also shelters one of the world's biggest collections of aviation engines, numbering about 200 pieces, the oldest of which dates from 1908.

The museum is off Al Jana Pawła II, halfway between the Old Town and Nowa Huta (Map 3). It's open May through November, Tuesday to Friday from 9 am to 4 pm, Saturday from 10 am to 3 pm and Sunday from 10 am to 4 pm.

OUTER SUBURBS & OUTSKIRTS
Tyniec
The small and distant suburb of Tyniec, about 10km south-west of the centre, is the site of the **Benedictine Abbey** (Klasztor Benedyktynów) perched on a cliff above the Vistula. The Benedictines were brought to Poland in the second half of the 11th century, and it was in Tyniec that they estab-

lished their first home. The original Romanesque church and the monastery were destroyed and rebuilt several times. Today, the church is essentially a baroque building though the stone foundations and the lower parts of the walls, partly uncovered, show its earlier origins.

You enter the complex through a pair of defensive gates, resembling the entrance to a castle, and find yourself in a large courtyard. At its far end is an octagonal wooden pavilion which protects a stone well dating from 1620.

The monastery cannot be visited but the church is open to all. Behind a sober façade, the dark interior is fitted out with a mix of baroque and rococo furnishings. The organ is plain but has a beautiful tone, and concerts are held here in summer. Check the current schedule and program with the Cultural Information Centre (see the Entertainment chapter) and try to make your trip coincide with a concert – a much more attractive bet than just visiting the building. To get to the abbey take bus No 112 from Rynek Dębnicki, near Rondo Grunwaldzkie.

Las Wolski

The 485 hectare Las Wolski (Wolski Forest), 6km west of the city centre, is by far the largest forested area within the city limits (reputedly one of the largest woodland city parks in Europe). It's a popular weekend destination among the city dwellers thanks to the beauty of the forest itself and the attractions it shelters.

Church & Hermitage of the Camaldolese Monks This church and hermitage (Kościół i Erem Kamedułów) overlook the Vistula from the top of the Srebrna Góra (Silver Mountain), on the southern edge of the Las Wolski. The Camaldolese order is known for its very strict monastic rules and ascetic way of life. It attracts curiosity – and a few ironic smiles – for its 'Memento Mori' motto ('remember you must die').

The order was brought to Poland from Italy in 1603 and in the course of time founded a dozen monasteries scattered throughout the country. However, today only two survive.

Apart from Poland and their native Italy where four hermitages still exist, the

So You Wanna Be a Camaldolese Monk ...

To start with, it's a decision of a lifetime. Once an aspirant takes the monastic vows, only the pope can release him, if the reasons are sufficiently important. It's a one-way life trip into loneliness, austerity and silence. It's a life spent in contemplation and prayer, without friends and enemies, in possibly ultimate intimacy with faith and truth, face to face with God.

The Camaldolese monks live in seclusion in hermitages and have contact with each other only during prayers, and some don't have any contact with the outer world at all. They are vegetarian and have solitary meals in their 'homes', with only five common meals a year. There's no TV or radio, and the conditions of life are austere. The hermits don't sleep in coffins as rumoured, but they do keep the skulls of their predecessors in the hermitages. Though they presumably think about death constantly, they seem in no hurry to meet it and many monks reach the age of 80 or 90.

The Camaldolese day doesn't vary much throughout the year. The monks get up at 3.30 am and spend their time in prayer in their hermitages and in matins in the church, before collecting their breakfast from the kitchen at 7 am. The period from 8 to 11.30 am is spent on labours related to the monastery maintenance, after which the monks can dedicate themselves to their midday prayer and collect their lunch. They have free time until 2 pm, when afternoon prayer is held for half an hour, and the monks return to the monastery maintenance tasks for another two hours. Supper comes at 5 pm and is followed by vespers until 8 pm, when the day ends.

Camaldolese can only be found at two places in Spain and one in South America.

Kraków was the first of the Camaldolese seats in Poland; a church and 20 hermitages were built between 1603 and 1642 and the whole complex was walled in. Not much has changed since. The place is spectacularly located and can be visited.

You approach it through a long walled alley that leads to the main gate. Once inside, you come face to face with the massive white limestone façade of the church, 50m high and 40m wide. The spacious, single-nave interior is covered by a barrel-shaped vault and lined on both sides with ornate baroque chapels. The simple tomb slab of the founder, Mikołaj Wolski, is placed just behind the entrance so that the faithful have to walk over it – a gesture of humility. His portrait hangs on the wall above the tomb.

Underneath the chancel of the church is a large chapel used for prayers and, to its right, the crypt of the hermits. Bodies are placed into niches without coffins and then sealed. Latin inscriptions state the age of the deceased and the period spent in the hermitage. The niches are opened after 80 years and the remains moved to a place of permanent rest. It's then that the hermits take the skulls to keep in their shelters.

In the garden behind the church are 14 surviving hermitages where several monks live (others live in the building next to the church), but the area is off-limits to tourists. You may occasionally see hermits in the church, wearing fine cream gowns.

Men are able to visit the church and the crypt any day from 8 to 11 am and 3 to 4 pm (till 5 pm in summer), but women are allowed inside only on major holidays. There are 12 such days during the year: 7 February, 25 March, Easter Sunday, Sunday and Monday of the Pentecost, Corpus Christi, 19 June, the Sunday after 19 June, 15 August, 8 September, 8 December and 25 December. These days apart, both men and women can enter the church to take part in two Sunday masses (at 7 and 10 am), though the visit is limited to attending church only.

The hermitage is 7km west of the city centre. Take tram No 1, 6 or 32 to the end of the line in Zwierzyniec and change for any westbound bus except No 100. The bus will let you off at the foot of Srebrna Góra, from where it's a 10 minute walk up the hill to the church.

Zoological Garden After visiting the church you can either come back the same way or walk north for 20 minutes through the forest to the zoo (Ogród Zoologiczny), open daily from 9 am till sunset. Founded in 1929, the 20 hectare zoo is home to about 2000 animals representing 300 species from around the world, including South American condors, Chinese leopards and rare Hawaiian geese. The zoo's attractive natural setting adds to its appeal. Bus No 134 from the zoo will bring you back to the city.

Piłsudski's Mound Piłsudski's Mound (Kopiec Piłsudskiego), 1km north of the zoo, is the largest of the city mounds, erected in honour of the marshal after his death in 1935. It was actually begun in 1934, when Piłsudski was still alive (which in itself tells something about the respect held for the marshal), and completed in 1937. After WWII the communist government felt uncomfortable about a monument dedicated to men who had defeated the Soviets, and pulled down the memorial stone using an army tank. A replica was placed on the summit in the early 1990s.

Nowa Huta

The youngest and largest of Kraków's suburbs, Nowa Huta (New Steelworks) is a result of the postwar rush to industrialise. In the early 1950s a gigantic steelworks and a new town to serve as a dormitory for the workforce, was built 10km east of the city centre. The steel mill accounted for nearly half of the national iron and steel output and the suburb has become a vast urban sprawl populated by over 200,000 people.

Because of an increasing awareness of environmental issues, the industry management was forced to cut production at the plant and reduce the workforce, but the

Marshal Józef Piłsudski – Father of the Second Republic

Marshal Józef Piłsudski is widely admired in Poland, for various reasons. It was he who realised the long-awaited dream of sovereign Poland after WWI, thus becoming the father of national independence. He was also the last great independent Polish leader, a man of authority who commanded respect and contrasted sharply with the subsequent communist puppets. Finally, the marshal was the last of Poland's rulers who defeated the Russians in battle.

Piłsudski was born in 1867 in the Vilnius region, then part of Poland under Russian occupation. As a teenager, he entered the underground anti-tsarist circles in Vilnius, but was arrested in 1887 and sent to a prison in Siberia for five years. Once freed, he returned to Poland and joined the newly founded Polish Socialist Party (PPS) in Warsaw. He was again arrested in 1900 and sent to a jail in St Petersburg, but escaped the following year and took refuge in Kraków (then under the less oppressive Austrian occupation), which became the base for his anti-tsarist activities until WWI.

In 1908 the PPS, under the leadership of Piłsudski, formed paramilitary squads, which in time developed into the Polish Legions, the military force of the still formally nonexistent Poland. During WWI, the legions fought under Piłsudski for the nation's independence. The opportune moment came in November 1918, after Germany's capitulation. The marshal came to Warsaw, took power on 11 November and proclaimed Poland a sovereign state.

In 1919 Piłsudski launched a massive offensive towards the east, capturing vast territories which had been Polish before the 18th century partitions. However, the Soviet counter-offensive pushed westward, and by mid-1920 the Red Army approached Warsaw In the battle for the city in August 1920 (known as the Miracle on the Vistula), the Polish Army under Piłsudski outmanoeuvred and defeated the Soviets. It may well be that this victory saved the weakened Western Europe, or at least Germany, from Bolshevik conquest.

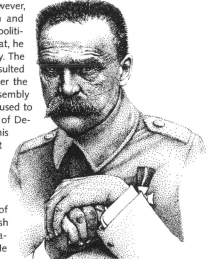

After independent Poland was safely back on the map, Piłsudski stepped down in 1922. However, disillusioned with the economic recession and governmental crisis, he reappeared on the political scene in May 1926. In a classic coup d'état, he marched on Warsaw at the head of the army. The three day street fighting which broke out resulted in 400 dead and over 1000 wounded. After the government resigned, the National Assembly elected Piłsudski president. However, he refused to take the post, opting instead for the office of Defence Minister, which he maintained until his death. There are no doubts, though, that it was Piłsudski who ran the country from behind the scenes for a decade, until he died in 1935 of cancer.

Despite his obvious faults and dictatorial-style rule, Piłsudski was buried in the crypt of Kraków's Wawel Cathedral among Polish kings, which in itself reflects the degree of national respect and admiration held for him. He continues to be widely admired today.

KATE NOLAN

mammoth plant is still kept working at high gear (and smoking badly), despite the fact that it's unprofitable.

If you want to see the steelworks in action from the inside, you can go on a tour (see the Organised Tours section in the Getting Around chapter).

Even if you are not interested in the steelworks, you might still visit the suburb. It is a shock after the medieval streets of the Old Town. Tram No 4 or 15 from the central train station (as well as minibuses from ul Wiślna just off Rynek Główny) will drop you at Plac Centralny, the suburb's central square. A huge fat Lenin statue stood here but has gone along with communism.

It actually doesn't matter where you start your sightseeing; the landscape varies little throughout the suburb, and you'll need a city map so as not to get lost. Some locals fantasise about transferring Warsaw's Palace of Culture and Science out here, making the place a perfect open-air museum of Stalinist architecture. It would also provide a landmark while you navigate this grey concrete desert.

On a more serious note, there are some real sights, including an interesting collection of old and new churches.

Cistercian Abbey The abbey (Opactwo Cystersów), on ul Klasztorna in the Mogiła suburb, on the south-eastern outskirts of Nowa Huta, is the most important historic monument in the area. The Cistercians came to Poland in 1140 and founded their first monastery in Jędrzejów, 80km north of Kraków. They later established several other abbeys throughout the country, including this one in Mogiła, in 1222.

The abbey has a church, a monastery, and a vast garden-park. The church, open most of the day, has a large three-naved interior with a balanced mix of Gothic, Renaissance and baroque furnishings and decoration. The prime destination for most of the faithful is the Chapel of the Crucified Christ, separated by a decorative wrought-iron screen, in the left-hand transept. The wooden statue of Christ dates from the 15th century and must certainly possess strong miraculous powers, as you can tell from the number of votive offerings and grooves in the floor formed over centuries by worshippers moving around the altar on their knees. Curiously, the Christ has 'real' hairs, and some pilgrims believe that they grow.

The high altar boasts an amazing Gothic polyptych carved in 1514, and behind it are beautiful stained-glass windows made in modern times according to medieval patterns. Parts of the walls are covered with Gothic frescoes, painted in the 16th century, and there's a fine Renaissance tombstone from 1596 in the right-hand transept.

Nowa Huta – A Communist Fantasy

The postwar communist regime deliberately built Nowa Huta steelworks in Kraków to give a 'healthy' working-class and industrial injection to the strong aristocratic, cultural and religious traditions of the city. Other, more rational reasons counted less. It was not of any importance, for example, that Kraków had neither ores nor coal deposits and that virtually all raw materials had to be transported from often distant locations. The project didn't take into account that the site boasted one of the most fertile soils in the region, nor that construction of the complex would destroy villages with histories going back to the early Middle Ages.

The communist dream hasn't materialised exactly as planned. Nowa Huta hasn't in fact threatened the deep traditional roots of the city. Worse, it actually became a threat to its creators, with strikes breaking out here as frequently as anywhere else, paving the way for the eventual fall of communism. The steelworks did, however, affect the city in another way: it brought catastrophic environmental pollution which threatens people's health, the natural environment and the city's historical monuments.

If you arrive at a reasonable time of day, inquire at the monastery's gate, and one of the monks will probably guide you around the Gothic-vaulted cloister where you'll see fragments of wall paintings and interesting tomb slabs in the walls. Note an extraordinary 13th century doorway which leads from the cloister to the church.

St Bartholomew's Church Just across the street from the abbey is the charming wooden St Bartholomew's Church (Kościół Św Bartłomieja), built here in 1466. Side chapels were added in the mid-18th century, but the main Gothic structure has remained unchanged, making it the only surviving three-naved medieval timber church in Poland. It's normally open only for the Sunday religious service, but inquire at the house at the back of the church, and a nun may open it for you. The interior's walls and ceiling are covered with beautiful figurative-ornamental decoration, all done in 1776.

Church of Our Lady Queen of Poland Commonly known as the Arka Pana (Lord's Ark), this was the first new church to be permitted by the regime in Nowa Huta after WWII, and was completed in 1977 (up to that year, Nowa Huta had only the two old churches described previously). It's in the north-western part of the suburb, on ul Obrońców Krzyża.

The Ark is an interesting though rather heavy, boat-shaped construction, with, inside, a large, expressive modern sculpture of Christ, designed by Bronisław Chromy. Even more impressive, however, is a collection of six amazing wooden pietàs by naïve sculptor Antoni Rząsa, placed at the entrance to the Chapel of Reconciliation (Kaplica Pojednania). The chapel (open from 6 to 8.30 am and 4.30 to 6.30 pm) is underneath the church; the entrance is from the street level.

Church of Our Lady of Częstochowa The most recent addition to Nowa Huta's churches is the huge, spacious and bright Kościół Matki Boskiej Częstochowskiej, on Al Solidarności. Built in 1984-95, it

looks from the outside a bit like an ultra-modern shopping centre.

Nowa Huta's Cultural Centre Nowa Huta has a large cultural centre, just off Plac Centralny. It has an auditorium and an art gallery, and many cultural activities – pop in to check what's on.

Wieliczka

Just outside the administrative boundaries of Kraków, 15km south-east of the city centre, Wieliczka is famous for its **salt mine** (kopalnia soli), which has been operating uninterrupted for at least 700 years, making it the oldest Polish industrial plant in continuous operation.

The mine is renowned for the preservative qualities of its microclimate, as well as for its health-giving properties. An underground sanatorium has been established at a depth of 211m, where chronic allergic diseases are treated.

The mine has a labyrinth of tunnels – about 300km of them, distributed over nine levels, the deepest being 327m underground. A section of the mine is open to the public, and it is a fascinating trip. The Wieliczka mine is on UNESCO's World Heritage list.

You visit three upper levels of the mine, from 64m to 135m below the ground, walking through an eerie world of pits and chambers, all hewn out by hand from solid salt. Some have been made into chapels, with altarpieces and figures included, others are adorned with statues and monuments – all carved of salt – and there are even underground lakes.

The highlight is the ornamented **Chapel of the Blessed Kinga** (Kaplica Błogosławionej Kingi), actually a fair-sized church 54m x 17m and 12m high. Every single element here, from chandeliers to altarpieces, is of salt. It took over 30 years (1895-1927) to complete this underground temple, and about 20,000 tonnes of rock salt had to be removed. Occasional masses and concerts are held here.

The mine is open from 16 April to 15 October daily from 7.30 am to 6.30 pm, and

THINGS TO SEE & DO

the rest of the year from 8 am to 4 pm. All visitors are guided in groups; the tour takes about two hours and costs $7 ($3.50 for students under 25 years of age). You walk about 2km through the mine – wear comfortable shoes.

The temperature in the mine is 14°C all year round. In the summer season, when the mine is often overrun by visitors, tours start every five minutes or so, but in winter tours depart every half-hour to an hour, when enough tourists have turned up.

Tours are in Polish, but from May to September there are English-language tours ($8, no student discounts) scheduled a few times a day. Last summer they started at 10 am, 12.30 and 3 pm, but there may be more – check with the tourist offices or call the mine (☎ 278 73 02, ☎ 278 73 66). Alternatively, you can hire an English-speaking guide ($40 per group plus $5 entry ticket per person) – call a day before to book on the above phone numbers. Brochures in English are available at the souvenir kiosk by the entrance to the mine.

There's a **museum** accommodated in 16 worked-out chambers on the 3rd level of the mine, where the tour ends. It features a collection of objects related to the mine (captions are in Polish only). You need a separate ticket ($3, $1.50 for students) if you want to visit it. From here a lift takes you back up to the outer world.

There's another **museum** in Wieliczka, in the local castle near the mine (open daily except Tuesday, from 9 am to 3 pm), which has exhibits on the archaeology and history of the region, and a collection of some 200 old saltcellars.

The easiest way to get to Wieliczka from Kraków's centre is by Lux-Bus minibus – they depart frequently all day long from near the bus terminal, and will let you off close to the mine ($0.50). There are also trains from the Kraków Główny station, but they run irregularly and will leave you farther away from the mine.

WHAT'S FREE

It's easy to spend a fortune on sightseeing, tours and entertainment, but some of the most enjoyable things cost nothing. In Kraków, you may consider some of the following free sights and activities (all detailed in this book):

- Enjoy the charming Main Market Square
- Visit the Wawel castle on Sunday (Wednesday in summer)
- Catch a glimpse of the trumpeter playing the hejnał on the hour, from the higher tower of St Mary's Church
- Stroll about the narrow cobbled streets of the Old Town
- Take advantage of a free-admission day (once a week) in all the sections of the National Museum and most other city museums
- Explore the city churches, all of which (except for the chancel of St Mary's Church) are free to visit
- Watch out for Kraków's colourful buskers, often to be found on the main square and the adjacent streets
- See the vast collection of amazing kitsch paintings at the open-air gallery on the walls adjoining the Florian Gate
- Have a laugh at Andrzej Mleczko's gallery of cartoons
- Catch a free concert, show or exhibition, going on around the centre (check the program with the cultural centre)
- Keep yourself up to date on Polish contemporary arts by visiting art galleries scattered around the centre
- Contemplate the nostalgic air of the peaceful Rakowicki Cemetery with its amazing old tombstones
- Go rock climbing on Zakrzówek Rocks, just a short distance from Wawel
- Pump yourself up with supernatural energy produced by the Wawel chakra

ACTIVITIES
Swimming
Outdoor Pools Kraków has several outdoor pools, normally open June to August, from about 10 am to 6 pm, if the weather is clement. Entry is $1.50 to $2 and you can stay as long as you want. The outdoor pools include:

Clepardia
(Map 3; ☎ 415 16 74) ul Mackiewicza 14
Krakowianka
(Map 2; ☎ 266 52 81) ul Żywiecka Boczna
Wisła
(Map 3; ☎ 610 15 62) ul Reymonta 22

Indoor Pools Several sports clubs have indoor pools, which can be used by anybody. The opening hours may be extensive (even 7 am to 10 pm), but people who are not associated with the clubs may be limited to specific times. The fee is $1.50 to $2 per hour. Most club pools close for July and August. These apart, two Kraków hotels have small pools which can be used by non-guests, and they don't close for the summer holidays. Places with pools include:

Hotel Forum
(Map 5; ☎ 261 92 12) ul Konopnickiej 28
Hotel Continental
(Map 3; ☎ 637 50 44) Al Armii Krajowej 11
Korona
(Map 5; ☎ 656 13 68) ul Kalwaryjska 9
Tomex
(Map 2; ☎ 644 28 95) ul Ptaszyckiego 4
Wisła
(Map 3; ☎ 610 15 62) ul Reymonta 22

Tennis

There's quite a number of tennis courts across the town, many belonging to sports clubs, but also some hotel courts and new private facilities. Most courts are open till dusk, though some are lit and open longer. The surface is not always in good shape but more inconvenient is that few courts have rackets and balls for rent. The court costs about $3 an hour, a bit more on weekends. Places where facilities can be found include:

Hotel Forum
(Map 5; ☎ 261 92 12) ul Konopnickiej 28
Hotel Piast
(Map 3; ☎ 636 46 68) ul Radzikowskiego 109
Centrum Tenisowe
(Map 3; ☎ 425 29 98) ul Na Błoniach 1
Nadwiślan
(Map 5; ☎ 422 21 22) ul Koletek 20
Olsza
(Map 5; ☎ 421 10 69) ul Siedleckiego 7

Fitness Centres

Kraków has an increasing number of gyms and fitness centres, including:

Fitness Club A & J
(☎ 421 95 34) ul Miodowa 21
Fitness Club M & M
(☎ 421 71 18) ul Stolarska 13
Fitness Club
ul Krakowska 21
Kontur
(☎ 429 12 13) ul Krakowska 5
Studio Rekreacji Relax
(☎ 411 03 60) ul Mogilska 70

Horse Riding

Most horse stables are outside Kraków. One of the few within the city limits is Stadnina Koni Decjusz (☎ 425 24 21), ul Kasztanowa 1. It welcomes both experienced riders and beginners and has instructors who speak English. An hour in the saddle will cost from $5 to $7.

Rock Climbing

Kraków is one of the few European cities with cliffs good for rock climbing right in the city. The rocks, up to 30m high, are in Zakrzówek, just 2km south-west of Wawel. They are popular with locals, who come to climb here mostly on weekends. A short walk south-west of the rocks is a picturesque reservoir surrounded by cliffs (a quarry used to be here) but swimming is forbidden.

LANGUAGE COURSES

The most reputable facility is the Instytut Polonijny Uniwersytetu Jagiellońskiego (Polonia Institute of the Jagiellonian University; Map 2; ☎ 429 76 32, fax 429 93 51), ul Jodłowa 13. The institute conducts a variety of lectures on Polish issues (history, culture, literature etc) throughout the year, and it has regular one and two-semester classes of Polish language costing $1700 per semester.

In July and August, the institute runs the Szkoła Letnia Kultury i Języka Polskiego (Summer School of Polish Language and Culture). The school offers a choice of three, four and six-week Polish language courses, conducted on eight levels, from 'survival' to 'native speaker', and provides accommodation and board. Courses cost $830/1110/1440, respectively, including bed and full board plus the tourist program. Contact the school well in advance for full details.

From September to June, the school has its office at ul Garbarska 7A, 31-131 Kraków (☎ 421 36 92, fax 422 77 01, email plschool@jetta.if.uj.edu.pl). In July and August, it opens at ul Piastowska 47, 30-067 Kraków (☎ 637 96 76, fax 637 96 63).

Even if you are not interested in the courses, you may want to visit the institute grounds at ul Jodłowa 13 in the suburb of Przegorzały, 5km west of the city centre. The showpiece here is a mock-Renaissance castle spectacularly set on the high cliff overlooking the Vistula. It was built by the Germans during WWII as a sanatorium for Nazi officers. It now houses a restaurant (Kurdish cuisine) and a café, the terraces of which provide a fabulous view over the Vistula meandering below.

On a clear day, you can occasionally spot the peaks of the Tatras 100km to the south. The student compound is in the woods beyond the castle.

Kraków has several other language schools, which are not as renowned but cheaper and can schedule their courses more flexibly, depending on the tourists' needs. If they don't have a course running when you come they can arrange teachers for individual classes ($14 to $18 an hour). The schools include:

Berlitz
  (☎ 632 90 75, fax 632 90 73)
  Al Słowackiego 64
Mały Rynek
  (☎/fax 422 78 57) Mały Rynek 3
Poliglota
  (☎ 421 81 28) Plac Szczepański 3
Prolog
  (☎/fax 422 72 28) ul Kościuszki 24

Places to Stay

In Kraków, as in other Polish cities, the choice of accommodation has grown and diversified considerably over recent years, but prices have risen. This trend is expected to continue in the near future: you'll have a wider choice but you'll pay more. On the whole, hotels in Kraków are cheaper than in Warsaw, but a bit more expensive than in other large Polish cities.

In Poland everyone, both locals and foreigners, pays the same price for accommodation (except for some youth hostels which may charge foreigners a little more than nationals). Prices listed in this chapter are for the high season (roughly from May to September). Most hotels reduce their rates by about 10% to 20% at other times.

Kraków is Poland's premier tourist destination, so finding a reasonable room in summer can sometimes be tricky and may involve a bit of legwork. Fortunately, several large student hostels open during that time, which normally meets the demand for budget lodging.

If possible, check the room before accepting, especially in budget and mid-range places. Don't be fooled by the hotel reception areas, which may look great in contrast to the rest of the establishment. If you ask to see a room, you can be pretty sure that they won't give you the worst one, which might happen otherwise.

All three tourist offices are likely to help you find somewhere to stay. If they can't find anything at a reasonable distance from the centre, they will send you to some workers' hostels in Nowa Huta or other outer suburbs which almost never fill up. In any case, they won't leave you on the street – at least that's what they claim.

If you want to be absolutely sure of not ending up in Nowa Huta, consider booking ahead. If you don't, try to arrive reasonably early in the day to allow some time for possible hotel hunting. And don't panic; if all else fails, there are almost always private rooms, available through either the Wawel-tour office (see Private Rooms later) or from the people hanging around it.

All room prices are given in US$.

PLACES TO STAY – BUDGET

Despite its touristy status, budget accommodation in Kraków is in good supply and fairly rated. The other side of the coin is that it's usually of pretty regular standard, and few of these places are within a reasonable distance from the centre; most are scattered all over the middle and outer suburbs, requiring some commuting.

Budget accommodation covers camping grounds, hostels and private rooms, plus some suburban hotels, which despite their 'Hotel' name, are hostels rather than hotels. You shouldn't normally pay more than around $30 per double in any of the places in this section.

Camping

Kraków has several camping grounds. None of them are close to the centre but all are linked to it by frequent public transport. Camping in your own tent costs around $3 to $4 per person plus another $3 to $4 for the tent. Consider the opening and closing dates as guidelines only – they may differ depending on the weather, tourist traffic etc.

Camping Smok *(Map 3; ☎ 429 72 66, ul Kamedulska 18)* is 4km west of the centre, 1km beyond Kościuszko's Mound. It's small, quiet and pleasantly located, and normally operates from June to September. From Kraków Główny train station, take tram No 2 to the end of the line in Zwierzyniec and change there for any westbound bus except No 100.

Camping Clepardia *(Map 3; ☎ 415 96 72, ul Pachońskiego 28A)*, 4km north of the centre, also operates from June to September. It has a tent space and several double cabins with bath ($30). Guests have free access to the outdoor swimming pools next to the camp site. Bus No 115 will bring you from the main train station in 15 minutes.

Camping Krakowianka (Map 2; ☎ *266 41 91, ul Żywiecka Boczna 4*), on the road to Zakopane, 6km south of the centre, is open from May to September. It's probably the lowest priced camping site in town and also has cheap cabins ($35 for a six-bed cabin). There's also the budget all-year *Hotel Krakowianka* on the grounds ($30 for a triple without bath). You can get there from the main train station by tram No 19 or bus No 119.

Camping Krak (Map 3; ☎ *637 21 22, ul Radzikowskiego 99*) is next to the *Motel Krak* on the Katowice road, about 5km north-west of the centre. It's the city's largest, best equipped and most expensive camping ground and is open from June to mid-September. The traffic noise may be considerable. Bus No 501 from the main train station goes there.

Camping Wieczysta (Map 3; ☎ *411 57 11, ☎ 422 57 11, ul Chałupnika 16*) is the most central, about 3km north-east of the Old Town, however it's only open in July and August. You can get there from the train station by bus No 124, or take tram No 4, 5, 10 or 15 and walk the remaining 1km.

Youth Hostels

Polish youth hostels *(schroniska młodzie-żowe)* are operated by Polskie Towarzystwo Schronisk Młodzieżowych (PTSM), a member of Hostelling International. Poland has currently about 130 all-year hostels and 440 seasonal ones, open in July and August only. Youth hostels are open to all, members and nonmembers alike, and there is no age limit. Curfew is usually 10 pm, sometimes 11 pm, but some hostel staff may be flexible about this. Most hostels are closed between 10 am and 5 pm. Checking-in time is usually up till 9 or 10 pm.

Hostels cost $3 to $6 per bed in a dorm for Poles, and about $1 more for foreigners. Singles and doubles, if there are any, cost about 20% to 50% more. The youth hostel card gives a 25% discount off these prices for nationals and, in some places, for foreigners. If you don't have your own bed sheet or a sleeping bag, the staff will provide a sheet for about $1.

Given the low prices, hostels are popular with both Poles and foreigners so can be often full. Particularly busy months are May and June when hostels are packed with Polish school groups, sometimes well beyond their capacity. In July and August it's usually much easier to find a bed.

Kraków has currently two official PTSM hostels. The main one is the all-year *youth hostel* (Map 4; ☎ *633 88 22, fax 633 89 20, ul Oleandry 4*), 2km west of the train station. To get there, take tram No 15 and get off just past the Hotel Cracovia. From the hostel, you have only a 10 minute walk to the Old Town. With its 380 beds, this is the largest youth hostel in the country but it nonetheless fills up at times. It has some doubles, triples and quads, but if anything is available it's more likely to be a bed in one of the large dorms sleeping 14 to 18 guests. Foreigners pay about $6 a bed in rooms up to quads and $5 in larger dorms. The curfew is 11 pm.

The other *youth hostel* (Map 3; ☎ 637 24 41, ul Szablowskiego 1C) is 4km north-west of the Old Town. Tram No 4 or 13 from the train station will let you off nearby. It's more spartan and less convenient than the Oleandry hostel but cheaper – just about $4 a bed. It has 40 all-year beds (difficult to find unoccupied) and an additional 200 seasonal beds in July and August (which are not as hard to come by). Check by phone for vacancies before you go.

There was another all-year youth hostel in Kraków, attractively set in part of a former convent overlooking the Vistula, at ul Kościuszki 88 in Zwierzyniec, but it closed down in 1999 and it's unknown when and where it's going to move. Check with a tourist office when you arrive.

Student Hostels

There are a number of student dorms operating as student hostels each summer (July to mid-September, approximately). Tourist offices tend to keep track of them, so ask about which ones are currently open.

They are most likely to include the four hostels of the Jagiellonian University: the closest one to the centre, *Hotel Studencki*

Wall-to-wall artworks for sale at the base of Florian Gate, through an archway off ul Pijarska.

Tram and bus are the main means of transport, but this historic tram only takes you back in time.

Bistro Bar Różowy Słoń (ie the Pink Elephant) is a fast food chain famous for its poster decorations.

Façade of Restauracja pod Aniołami, where you dine in fantastic vaulted cellars.

Alfresco cafés at Rynek Główny, the largest medieval town square in Poland.

Żaczek (Map 4; ☎ *633 54 77, Al 3 Maja 5)*, just round the corner from the Oleandry youth hostel; the *Hotel Studencki Nawojka* (Map 4; ☎ *633 52 05, ul Reymonta 11)*, 2km west of the centre; the *Hotel Studencki Bydgoska* (Map 3; ☎ *637 44 33, ul Bydgoska 19)*; and the *Hotel Studencki Piast* (Map 3; ☎ *637 49 33, ul Piastowska 47)* a little farther to the west. Any of these will cost no more than \$18/25 a double without/with bath, and all have heaps of rooms in summer which rarely fill completely. It's worth remembering that each has a limited number of rooms available year-round.

Another student facility, the *Letni Hotel AWF* (Map 3; ☎ *648 02 07, Al Jana Pawła II 82)*, is 4km east of the train station, midway to Nowa Huta, and is easily reached by the frequent trams Nos 4, 5, 10 and 15. This large 320 bed hostel has singles/doubles with bath for \$14/18 and its own cafeteria serving inexpensive meals. HI members get discounts on room prices.

Cheaper but not as good is *Hotel Letni Collegium Medicum* (Map 3; ☎ *636 14 09, ul Racławicka 9A)*, 2km north-west of the centre and accessible from the station by tram Nos 4 and 12. Beds in doubles or triples without bath go for about \$7.

Next to the latter is the 200 bed *Strawberry Hostel* (Map 3; ☎ *636 15 00, ul Racławicka 9)*, only open in July and August. It costs \$10 a bed in doubles, triples or quads with shared facilities. It can be reached by the same trams as above, or watch out for the guys from the hostel who often wait at the main train station (outside the stairs leading up from the platforms) to take tourists back by van.

Other Hostels & Hotels
There are a dozen other hostels scattered throughout the city.

The well run all-year *Schronisko Turystyczne Express* (Map 3; ☎ *633 88 62, ul Wrocławska 91)*, 2.5km north-west of the centre, is a cross between a private guesthouse and a youth hostel. Unlike youth hostels, it doesn't close during the day and has no curfew. It has 80 beds distributed in doubles (\$7 per person) and six-bed dorms

(\$6). Advance reservations are essential – there may be no vacancies for a month ahead. Bus No 130 from the main train station goes there; get off at the fifth stop.

The *Dom Wycieczkowy Chałupnik* (Map 4; ☎ *633 75 01*, ☎ *633 47 21, ul Kochanowskiego 12)* is about the most central budget all-year hostel. It's not a Sheraton but what would you expect for \$7 per head in doubles or quads with shared facilities, within a mere 10 minute walking distance from the Main Market Square.

There are a number of budget hostels and hotels further away from the centre, mostly in the eastern part of the city, including Nowa Huta. By and large they are not particularly inspiring (nor is the area), but they can offer shelter if nothing more central or attractive is available.

You can try, for example, the large 300 bed *Hotel Czyżyny* (Map 2; ☎ *644 67 00*, ☎ *643 08 98, ul Centralna 32)* which charges \$13/22/30 a single/double/triple, or the quiet 160 bed *Hotel Luna* (Map 2; ☎ *644 63 09, Osiedle Na Skarpie 18)* which charges \$16/25/30. The tourist offices know more places like these.

Private Rooms
Waweltur (Map 4; ☎ 422 19 21, ☎ 422 16 40), ul Pawia 8, next door to the KART tourist office, arranges accommodation in private rooms for \$18/26 a single/double. These are rooms in flats or houses rented out by owners. Most are a reasonable distance from the centre, but there are some scattered around the outer suburbs, so check the location carefully before deciding.

The office is open Monday to Friday from 8 am to 8 pm and Saturday from 8 am to 2 pm. The staff will show you what's available and point the location on the map; you then decide, pay and go to the address they give you. A minimum three day rental can apply for some rooms, but there are usually owners who will rent out their rooms even for one day.

It's always better to take the room for as short a time as possible then pay for additional days, rather than pay up front for several days for something which may look

How Much is a Double Room with Bath?

Room prices are usually displayed at the hotel reception desk. You are most likely to see details for a *pokój 1-osobowy* (single room) and a *pokój 2-osobowy* (double room), accompanied by some of the following descriptions:

bez łazienki – without bath
z łazienką – with bath (toilet, shower and basin)
z prysznicem or *z natryskiem* – with shower (but no toilet)
z umywalką – with basin (but nothing else)

There will usually be some other entries, including:

apartament – suite
opłata za dodatkowe łóżko – charge for an extra bed
opłata za telewizor – charge for a TV set

The prices normally include VAT, so you just pay what is written, unless indicated otherwise.

MARTIN HARRIS

attractive but turns out to be a disaster. You never know who your host will be and what kind of room you'll get.

You may also be offered a private room by someone on the street outside. The tourist offices don't recommend these services, but if you decide to use them (if, for example, the office has run out of rooms or is closed), ask to see the location on the map before agreeing to go, and pay only after you have seen the room and accepted it. And by the way, try to negotiate the price.

PLACES TO STAY – MID-RANGE

This section includes hotels where a double room will cost somewhere between $30 and $60. For this, you can stay in the very centre, even sometimes within a few blocks of the main square. Most of the hotels listed here offer a choice of rooms with or without bath, although the former will usually be outside this price bracket. Breakfast is not included in the price, unless specified.

In the Centre

There's quite a choice of mid-range accommodation within or near the Old Town. The places are not always good value, but will save you time on public transport and money on evening taxi returns to your cheap suburban shelter after a night out. They are all on Map 4, unless marked.

There are three affordable hotels near the main train station. **Hotel Warszawski** (☎ 422 06 22, ul Pawia 6) costs about $40/55/65 for singles/doubles/triples without bath, $55/75/85 for the much better, refurbished rooms with bath, all with breakfast.

The **Hotel Polonia** (☎ 422 12 33, ul Basztowa 25), just around the corner from the Warszawski, is marginally cheaper. **Hotel Europejski** (☎ 423 25 10, ul Lubicz 5) has been partly revamped and costs much the same as Warszawski.

All three are often full and fairly noisy because of heavy traffic.

Hotel Saski (☎ 421 42 22, fax 421 48 30, ul Sławkowska 3) is ideally located in a historic townhouse just off Rynek Główny. It costs $35/40/50 for singles/doubles/triples without bath, $55/75/85 with bath – good value so close to the main square. Note the century-old lift, still in working order.

Hotel Pokoje Gościnne SARPu (☎/fax 429 17 78, ul Floriańska 39) is also a good place to stay, if you are lucky enough to get a room there. This former architects' dormitory offers six rooms only, one single ($40), four doubles ($50) and one triple ($70). Two adjacent rooms share one bath, cooking stove and fridge. The place is on the top, 4th floor of a historic building.

The big, ugly and crowded *Dom Turysty PTTK (☎ 422 95 66, ul Westerplatte 15/16)*, just 500m south of the train station, costs $35/50 a single/double without bath, $60/75 with bath (all including breakfast). There are no longer eight-bed budget dorms. There's a cheap cafeteria on the premises (open from 7 am to 10 pm). The hotel also has a left-luggage room – a useful facility if you don't get a bed here and have to look for one elsewhere.

You may also try the *Hotel Wawel-Tourist (☎ 422 67 65, ul Poselska 22)*, which has doubles without/with bath and breakfast for $38/50. Better still, check the small *Pensjonat i Restauracja Rycerska (Map 5; ☎ 422 60 82, fax 422 33 99, Plac Na Groblach 22)*, at the foot of Wawel, which offers doubles without/with bath for $35/45, breakfast included. On the opposite, northern edge of the Old Town, is the reasonable *Pokoje Gościnne Jordan (☎ 421 21 25, fax 422 82 26, ul Długa 9)* which costs $34/50 a single/double with bath and breakfast.

In the Suburbs

If nothing can be found in the centre, you'll probably have to try somewhere farther afield. The closest option, the *Mini Hotel (Map 5; ☎ 656 24 67, fax 656 59 56, Plac Wolnica 7)*, is in Kazimierz within walking distance of the Old Town. Justifiably named, the hotel offers just one single ($36), one double ($55), one triple ($65) and one suite ($70). All rooms have private baths and all are on the top, 3rd floor of the building, providing views over the square or the church.

A short walk farther south, beyond the bridge, is the former sports *Hotel Korona (Map 5; ☎ 656 15 66, ul Kalwaryjska 9/15)*,

in Podgórze, which costs $30/40/50 for a single/double/triple with bath. From the main train station, take tram No 10.

Another sports accommodation, the *Hotel Wisła (Map 3; ☎/fax 633 49 22, ul Reymonta 22)*, 2km west of the Old Town, is good value for $35 a double or triple with bath, but it seldom has vacancies. Tram No 15 from the train station will let you off nearby.

One kilometre farther west, the *Hotel Nauczycielski Krakowiak (Map 3; ☎ 637 73 04, fax 637 73 25, Al Armii Krajowej 9)* is reasonable for $28/32 a single/double with private bath and it is easier to find a vacancy here.

PLACES TO STAY – TOP END

This section includes anything that costs more than $60 for a double room. All the hotels listed below have rooms with private baths, and breakfast is included in the price.

In the Centre

There are a dozen upmarket options in the Old Town, which is certainly Kraków's most atmospheric area. You don't need a fortune to stay in this historic centre, but rooms run out fast in the good-value places, so advance booking is recommended, if not essential. Note that few central hotels have their own car parks, so motorised guests need to park their cars on public parks. All hotels are on Map 4 unless marked.

The *Dom Gościnny UJ (Jagiellonian University Guest House; ☎/fax 421 12 25, ul Floriańska 49)* is a good (but often full) place. The hotel has 15 singles ($45) and eight doubles ($70). Rooms are spacious, quiet and clean, and have large beds, desk, telephone and private bath. Double rooms are excellent value.

The university operates another, slightly cheaper hotel, the *Bursa im St Pigonia (☎ 422 30 08, ul Garbarska 7A)*, just northwest of the Old Town. This absolutely quiet place, well off the street, costs about $40/65 a single/double. A bonus is a cheap car park in the grounds.

The *Hotel Polski (☎/fax 422 11 44, ☎/fax 422 14 26, ul Pijarska 17)* is a compromise between price and comfort, with singles/doubles for $65/95.

Another affordable option, the **Hotel Royal** (Map 5; ☎/fax 421 58 57, ul Św Gertrudy 26/29) near the Wawel castle, has a two star 'budget' section (☎ 421 46 61) rated at $45/70 a single/double, and a more comfortable three star section (☎ 421 49 79) for $60/110. Both sections offer spacious rooms and reasonable standards. Choose a room from the Planty side to avoid tram noise.

You may also check the **Hotel Pollera** (☎ 422 10 44, fax 422 13 89, ul Szpitalna 30) which has a good choice of singles/doubles/triples with bath for $65/75/90, and some cheaper rooms with shower only (the toilet is outside). The two stained-glass windows you'll see in the main staircase are designed by Stanisław Wyspiański.

You probably couldn't ask for a more central location than at the **Dom Polonii** (☎ 422 61 58, fax 422 43 55, Rynek Główny 14). It has just two doubles ($60 each) and one double suite ($100).

Nearby is the new **Hotel Rezydent** (☎ 429 50 18, fax 429 55 76, ul Grodzka 9), which has comfortable suites to sleep one/two guests for $100/145. Another new place, the **Hotel Wit Stwosz** (☎ 429 60 26, fax 429 61 39, ul Mikołajska 28), is also good value at $80/110 a double/triple.

There are a few reasonable places just west of the Old Town, including the modern, glass-fronted **Hotel Logos** (☎ 632 33 33, fax 632 42 10, ul Szujskiego 5) with singles/doubles for $70/80; and the **Hotel Fortuna** (☎/fax 411 08 06, ul Czapskich 5) which charges $50/70. The latter has recently opened a new, more comfortable outlet, the **Hotel Fortuna Bis** (☎/fax 430 10 25, ul Piłsudskiego 25), which costs $60/80 – good value.

You have a choice of posh hotels in the Old Town, including the **Hotel Francuski** (☎ 422 51 22, fax 422 52 70, ul Pijarska 13). Opened in 1912, it was fully refurbished in the early 1990s and the hotel combines elegant fin-de-siècle interiors with modern facilities. Singles/doubles are $120/160.

Another luxurious option, the **Grand Hotel** (☎ 421 72 55, fax 421 83 60, ul Sławkowska 5/7), is housed in a 19th-century building with partly preserved Art Nouveau decoration. Its old-fashioned singles/doubles cost $160/190, and there are also some more spacious and comfortable suites.

The **Hotel Elektor** (☎ 421 80 25, fax 421 86 89, ul Szpitalna 28) is another exclusive if pricey place. Set in a meticulously restored historic building, this classy small hotel offers singles/doubles for $230/260.

Not as posh as the Elektor but cheaper is the **Hotel Pod Różą** (☎ 422 12 44, fax 421 75 13, ul Floriańska 14), which costs $100/120 a single/double.

In the Suburbs

There are so many hotels in the heart of the city that few travellers stay far away from the centre. But you may consider staying in one of the inner suburbs, particularly in Kazimierz which has a choice of upmarket accommodation.

Possibly the most attractive option here is the **Hotel Alef** (Map 5; ☎ 421 38 70, ul Szeroka 17) which offers five large, somewhat rustic but charming suites. None has a TV but all provide a great view over the street. Each costs $70/80/100 for one/two/three people.

The nearby **Hotel Ester** (Map 5; ☎ 429 11 88, ul Szeroka 20) offers similar views, but is more elegant and comfortable and costs $115/135/160 a single/double/triple.

Other Kazimierz options include the **Hotel Regent** (Map 5; ☎ 422 54 56, fax 422 94 10, ul Bożego Ciała 19), and the **Hotel Pensjonat Kazimierz** (Map 5; ☎/fax 421 66 29, ul Miodowa 16). Both charge around $100 a double.

Directly opposite the latter is the small **Hotel Franciszek** (Map 5; ☎/fax 656 05 98, ul Miodowa 15), which costs $120/150 for a suite for two/three people.

The modern **Hotel Ibis** (Map 3; ☎ 421 81 88, fax 411 47 95, ul Przy Rondzie 2) is also quite close to the centre, 1km east of the main train station, and linked by frequent trams. Part of the French Ibis chain, the hotel offers satisfactory standards at fair prices: $80/100 a single/double.

Orbis runs two large Soviet-era hotels, a reasonable distance from the centre: the more central three star **Hotel Cracovia** (Map 4; ☎ 422 86 66, fax 421 95 86, Al Focha 1), rated at $100/150 a single/double, and four star **Hotel Forum** (Map 5; ☎ 261 92 12, fax 269 00 80, ul Konopnickiej 28), which at $160/200 is among the most expensive hotels in town. Set in large concrete blocks, neither is particularly romantic, but they offer a range of contemporary facilities and are therefore popular with the business community.

There are half a dozen upmarket hotels farther outside the city centre, including the **Hotel Demel** (Map 3; ☎ 636 16 00, fax 636 45 43, ul Głowackiego 22), the **Hotel Continental** (Map 3; ☎ 637 50 44; fax 637 59 38, Al Armii Krajowej 11), and the **Hotel Piast** (Map 3; ☎ 636 46 00, fax 636 47 74, ul Radzikowskiego 109).

All of these will suit visiting business people due to their facilities, even though not many tourists opt to stay so far from the centre.

Places to Eat

By Polish standards, Kraków is a food paradise. The Old Town is tightly packed with gastronomic venues – reputedly 350 of them – catering for every pocket from rock bottom to topnotch. Privatisation has eliminated most of the old proletarian eateries, whereas many excellent places have popped up in their place offering diners superior fare at affordable prices.

FOOD

Poland was for centuries a cosmopolitan country and its food has been influenced by various cuisines. The Jewish, Lithuanian, Belarusian, Ukrainian, Russian, Hungarian and German traditions have all made their mark. Polish food is hearty and filling, with thick soups and sauces, abundant in potatoes and dumplings, rich in meat but not in vegetables.

Polish Cuisine

Poland's most internationally known dishes are the *bigos* (sauerkraut with a variety of meats), *pierogi* (ravioli-like dumplings stuffed with cottage cheese or minced meat or cabbage and wild mushrooms) and *barszcz* (red beetroot soup, originating from Russian borsch). Favourite Polish ingredients and herbs include dill, marjoram, caraway seeds and wild mushrooms.

Typical starters include *tatar* (raw minced beef accompanied by chopped onion and raw egg yolk), *śledź w oleju* (herring in oil), *śledź w śmietanie* (herring in sour cream) and *nóżki w galarecie* (jellied pig's knuckles).

Poland is a land of hearty soups such as *żurek* (rye-flour soup thickened with sour cream), *botwinka* (beet greens soup), *kapuśniak* (sauerkraut soup), *krupnik* (barley soup), *flaki* (seasoned tripe cooked in bouillon with vegetables) and *chłodnik* (cold beetroot soup with sour cream and fresh vegetables).

Among the main courses, the most common dishes include *kotlet schabowy* (breaded pork cutlet), *golonka* (boiled pig's knuckle served with horseradish), *zraz* (stewed beef in cream sauce), *gołąbki* (cabbage leaves stuffed with minced beef and rice) and *schab pieczony* (roast loin of pork seasoned with prunes and herbs).

Wild mushrooms *(grzyby)* have always been great favourites in Poland, either boiled, pan-fried, stewed, sautéed, pickled or marinated. Cucumbers are served freshly sliced in sour cream *(mizeria)* or dill *(ogórek kiszony)*. *Ćwikła* is a boiled and grated beetroot with horseradish. Potatoes are made into dumplings, patties or pancakes *(placki ziemniaczane)*.

Kopytka are chunks of dough served with a semi-sweet sauce, while *knedle* are dumplings stuffed with plums or apples. A traditional Polish dessert is *mazurek* (shortcake). In early summer you can get fresh strawberries, raspberries or blueberries with cream.

Eating Habits

Poles start off their day with breakfast *(śniadanie)* which is roughly similar to its western counterpart and may include bread and butter *(chleb z masłem)*, cheese *(ser)*, ham *(szynka)*, eggs *(jajka)*, and tea *(herbata)* or coffee *(kawa)*.

The most important and substantial meal of the day, the *obiad*, is normally eaten somewhere between 1 and 5 pm. Obiad has no direct equivalent in English: judging by its contents, it is closer to western dinner, but timing is closer to lunch. Put simply, it's a dinner at lunch time. The third meal is supper *(kolacja)*, which is often similar to breakfast.

Etiquette and table manners are more or less the same as in the west. When beginning a meal, whether it's in a restaurant or at home, it is good manners to wish your fellow diners *smacznego*, or 'bon appetit'. When drinking a toast, the Polish equivalent of 'cheers' is *na zdrowie* (literally 'to the health').

Eateries

With the move towards capitalism, there has been a dramatic development on the gastronomic scene. A constellation of western-style eating outlets – almost nonexistent in communist Poland – such as bistros, snack bars, pizza houses, salad bars and fast-food joints sprang up to serve things which were previously uncommon or unobtainable. Most of the famous international fast-food chains, including McDonald's, Burger King, KFC and Pizza Hut, have already conquered Polish cities, including Kraków, and stacks of Polish imitations have settled in.

The prices have obviously gone up in the process, but you now have a decent choice, can eat and drink till late, and it's all still cheaper than in the west. Following are the major types of eateries, from bottom to top. All prices are in US$.

Milk Bar The cheapest place to eat is a milk bar (bar mleczny), a sort of no-frills self-service cafeteria which serves mostly vegetarian dishes. You can fill up completely for about $2. The 'milk' part of the name is to suggest that the menu is based on

dairy products, though this is changing as the bars increasingly venture into the carnivorous territory.

Milk bars open around 7 to 8 am and close at 6 to 8 pm (earlier on Saturday); only a handful are open on Sunday. The menu is posted on the wall. You choose, then pay the cashier who gives you a receipt which you hand to the person dispensing the food. Once you've finished your meal, carry your dirty dishes to a designated place, as you'll see others doing. Milk bars are popular and there are usually lines to the counter, but they move quickly. Smoking is not permitted and no alcoholic beverages are served.

Milk bars were created to provide cheap food for the less affluent, and were subsidised by the state. The free-market economy forced many to close, but a number have survived and some do a good job. Kraków still has plenty of them.

Jadłodajnia This is also a budget eatery, roughly similar to a milk bar (self-service, no alcohol, similar opening hours), but it often has a family atmosphere and the food usually tastes home-cooked. There are quite

Some Tips About Restaurant Menus

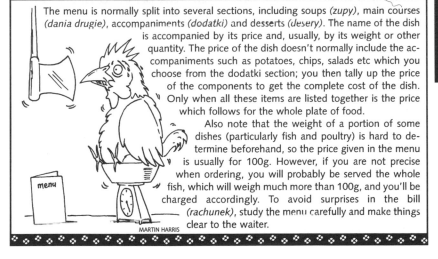

The menu is normally split into several sections, including soups (zupy), main courses (dania drugie), accompaniments (dodatki) and desserts (desery). The name of the dish is accompanied by its price and, usually, by its weight or other quantity. The price of the dish doesn't normally include the accompaniments such as potatoes, chips, salads etc which you choose from the dodatki section; you then tally up the price of the components to get the complete cost of the dish. Only when all these items are listed together is the price which follows for the whole plate of food.

Also note that the weight of a portion of some dishes (particularly fish and poultry) is hard to determine beforehand, so the price given in the menu is usually for 100g. However, if you are not precise when ordering, you will probably be served the whole fish, which will weigh much more than 100g, and you'll be charged accordingly. To avoid surprises in the bill (rachunek), study the menu carefully and make things clear to the waiter.

MARTIN HARRIS

a number of jadłodajnias in Kraków and some are excellent value.

Café A café *(kawiarnia)* in communist Poland was essentially a meeting place rather than an eating place. Many cafés have now introduced meals, which can be more attractive and cheaper than those of some restaurants.

Cafés tend to open around 10 am and close at any time between 9 pm and midnight. Almost all cafés are smokers' territory, and given Polish smoking habits, the atmosphere can be really dense.

Restaurant Restaurants *(restauracja)* are the main places for meals with table service. They range from unpretentious cheap eateries where you can have a filling meal for less than $5 all the way up to luxurious establishments that may leave a sizeable hole in your wallet. Many restaurants serve Polish food, but there has been a considerable expansion of ethnic outlets in Kraków.

Restaurants generally open either around 9 to 10 am (and then they usually have a breakfast menu) or about noon. Closing time varies greatly from place to place, but many places stay open until 11 pm or midnight. Most of the top-class restaurants have their menus in Polish and English and/or German, but don't expect foreign-language listings in cheap eateries, nor waiters speaking anything but Polish.

DRINKS
Nonalcoholic Drinks
Tea & Coffee Poles are passionate tea drinkers, consuming it with each meal and still more in between. Tea *(herbata)* is served in a glass, rarely in a cup, and is almost never drunk with milk. Instead, a slice of lemon is a fairly popular addition, plus a lot of sugar.

Coffee *(kawa)* is another popular drink, and you can find it in just about every café and restaurant. For a long time the most common serving manner was the so-called *kawa parzona*, a concoction made by putting a couple of teaspoons of ground coffee directly into a glass and topping it with

boiling water. It's still common in the countryside but in the cities you can finally have your espressos and cappuccinos.

Soft Drinks Coke, Pepsi and other soft drinks, either bottled or canned, are readily available everywhere. Mineral water *(woda mineralna)* comes from springs from different parts of the country, and is both good and cheap.

Alcoholic Drinks
Beer Polish beer *(piwo)* comes in a number of local brands, the best of which include Żywiec, Okocim and EB. Beer is readily available in shops, cafés, bars, pubs and restaurants – virtually everywhere. Depending on the class of the establishment, a half-litre bottle of Polish beer will cost anything from $1 to around $2.50. Not all cheap establishments may serve it cold, so ask for *zimne piwo* (cold beer) when ordering.

Wine Wines have traditionally come from the ex-Eastern bloc, mostly from Hungary and Bulgaria, and if you're not too fussy they are acceptable and cheap. Western wines, particularly French, German and Spanish, are increasingly available in shops and restaurants, though some of them are expensive. Pay attention to the price on the menu, which may be for a glass, not a bottle.

Spirits Vodka *(wódka)* is the national drink, which the Poles claim was invented here. In Poland, vodka is drunk neat, not diluted or mixed, and it comes in a number of colours and flavours, including *myśliwska* (vodka flavoured with juniper berries), *wiśniówka* (flavoured with cherries), *żubrówka* (flavoured with grass from the Białowieża forest) and *jarzębiak* (flavoured with rowanberry). The best known, however, is clear vodka, which comes in a myriad brand names, which seasoned drinkers easily distinguish.

A half-litre bottle of vodka costs $5 to $7 in a shop, but in restaurants it can double or even triple in price. Clear vodka should be served well chilled though this does not always happen in lower-class establishments.

Coloured vodkas don't need much cooling and some are best drunk at room temperature.

PLACES TO EAT – BUDGET

Kraków has a great number and variety of budget eateries, including the jadłodajnias. These small places offer you hearty Polish meals tasting as if they were cooked at home. They serve both vegetarian and non-vegetarian fare, including some typical Polish specialities such as barszcz, pierogi and kotlets.

All the places are shown on Map 4, except a few that are marked. They all open somewhere between 9 am and noon, and close early, usually around 6 to 7 pm, and even earlier on Saturday. Only a few open on Sunday.

One of the oldest and best known of these is the legendary *Jadłodajnia u Stasi (ul Mikołajska 16)* just off Mały Rynek, deservedly popular among the locals for its food. The place is open Monday to Friday from 12.45 pm until 'the meals run out', which usually happens at around 4 pm though the most attractive dishes run out much earlier. The jadłodajnia is off the street. Enter the gate, head for the backyard and join the queue – which may give some indication of the popularity of the place.

If the queue is too long for you, try next door at *Jadłodajnia u Górala (ul Mikołajska 14)* which is also besieged at lunch time. Other similar places include the *Jadłodajnia Anna Kwaśniewska (ul Sienna 11)*; *Kuchnia Staropolska u Babci Maliny (ul Sławkowska 17)* in the basement of the building of the Polska Akademia Umiejętności; *Jadłodajnia Kuchcik (ul Jagiellońska 12)*; *Bar Grodzki (ul Grodzka 47)*; *Jadłodajnia Bistro Stop (ul Św Tomasza 24)*; *Jadłodajnia Sąsiedzi (ul Szpitalna 40)*; and *Jadłodajnia Jak u Mamy (ul Św Tomasza 2)*.

You also have *Jadłodajnia Oleandry (ul Oleandry 1)* in the building of the Rotunda Student Club (useful if you are staying in the Oleandry youth hostel), and the tiny five-table jadłodajnia-like place named *Restauracja Pod Wieżyczką (ul Radziwiłłowska 35)* near the train station. Also similar in

style and budget is *Restauracyjka Pigoniówka (ul Garbarska 7A)* and *Gospoda na Zwierzyńcu (ul Zwierzyniecka 7)*.

In Kazimierz, one of the best eateries of this kind is *Bistro Pod 13-ką (Map 5; ul Miodowa 13)*.

In Podgórze, try the *Jadłodajnia Amicus (Map 5; Rynek Podgórski 9)*.

Any of the above places can leave you perfectly full for $3 to $5 but if this is too much, look for a bar mleczny where you can cut that in half and still have a filling two-course meal. Understandably, these are not particularly atmospheric places and the clientele (which can include some seasoned drinkers trying to save for vodka by cutting their food expenses) may be a bit weird, but you won't find many other establishments around this part of the world that serve soups for $0.25 each. Milk bars are particularly useful for very cheap early breakfasts, when most eateries, including jadłodajnias, are still closed.

Central milk bars include the *Bar Mleczny Pod Temidą (ul Grodzka 43)*, *Bar Mleczny Dworzanin (ul Floriańska 19)*, *Bar Mleczny Barcelona (ul Piłsudskiego 1)*, *Bar Mleczny Warszawianka (ul Dunajewskiego 4)* and *Bar Mleczny Górnik (ul Czysta 1)*. In Kazimierz, you have *Bar Mleczny Pod Filarkami (ul Dietla 87)* and *Bar Mleczny Syrena (Map 5; ul Starowiślna 93A)*.

Vegetarians will probably welcome the cheap and pleasant *Bar Wegetariański Vega (ul Św Gertrudy 7)*, one of the few exclusively vegie places in town, which serves tasty pierogi, crêpes, tofu, salads etc. The same people have recently opened another *Bar Wegetariański Vega (ul Krupnicza 22)*, which is equally agreeable and recommended.

Another good place which is turning into a chain, *Bar Bistro Różowy Słoń (Pink Elephant; ul Straszewskiego 24)*, soon gained popularity thanks to a varied menu (which includes salads, spaghetti, pierogi, barszcz and 20-odd flavours of crêpes) served at low prices in cheerful pop-art surroundings. It now has two other central outlets: at ul Sienna 1 and ul Szpitalna 38.

Salad lovers shouldn't miss *Salad Bar Chimera (ul Św Anny 3)* in attractive vaulted cellars. In summer, an umbrella-shaded open-air section opens in the backyard of the building. It offers an amazing array of fresh, good, cheap salads. Encouraged by the success, *Chimera II (ul Gołębia 2)* has opened, and serves budget Georgian food in similarly amazing vaults, and has live jazz and ethnic music on some evenings.

The folksy *Kawiarnia u Zalipianek (ul Szewska 24)* provides a choice of popular dishes. *Bistro Piccolo Chicken Grill (ul Jagiellońska 2)* serves a variety of chicken dishes. Fish eaters may try the inexpensive *Bar Rybny (ul Karmelicka 16)* which offers a choice of fish.

If crêpes are all you're after, check the budget crêperie *Naleśniqi (ul Szewska 27* and *Plac Mariacki 2)*. Both locations have a range of sweet and savoury crêpes. *King Pie (ul Sławkowska 20* and *ul Karmelicka 8)* serves delicious fresh pies for less than US$1 each.

Taco Mexicano (ul Poselska 20) brings a Mexican breeze to town. Opened in 1993, the place has quickly gained popularity among locals and visitors for its pretty authentic food at low prices. You, too, can have your enchiladas, burritos and tacos and wash them down with café carajillo or tequila. There's another less crowded outlet of *Taco Mexicano (ul Starowiślna 15A)*. Alternatively, try *El Paso Tex Mex Saloon (ul Św Krzyża 13)*, which does much the same for marginally more.

Over recent years, there has been a rash of Vietnamese eateries opening across the city centre and its environs, including *Bar Azjatycki Asia (ul Św Tomasza 6)*; *Bar Orientalny Lychee (ul Floriańska 27)*; and *Bar Dam (ul Basztowa 15)*. You also have *Bar Hoang Hai (Map 5; ul Stradomska 13)* in Stradom, and *Restauracja Orientalna Thien Long (Map 5; Plac Wolnica 7)* in Kazimierz. None of them will charge more than $3 for the copious main-course plate, or $1 for a bowl of soup.

Also located in Kazimierz is *Restauracja Ganges (Map 5; ul Krakowska 7)*. It is

---

Bagels

Roughly similar to American bagels, Kraków's *obwarzanki (obwarzanek* in singular) are hard ring-shaped bread rolls. Their tradition goes back to the town's early days and has Jewish roots. Baked according to centuries-old recipes, these savoury biscuits are made from a roll of dough which is twisted like a screw and shaped into a ring of about 10cm in diameter. They are then fried in oil with honey and seasoning.

The obwarzanki are produced by various bakeries and sold almost exclusively in the streets from small carts. Many come powdered with poppy seeds, but there are also varieties sprinkled with salt crystals or sesame seeds. An obwarzanek costs US$0.20. Buy them in the morning; by the afternoon they can become rock hard.

❖ ❖ ❖ ❖ ❖ ❖ ❖ ❖ ❖ ❖ ❖ ❖ ❖ ❖

Kraków's first Indian kitchen, and it too is very moderately priced.

Several Mediterranean and Middle Eastern short-order restaurants have popped up over recent years, including the *Akropolis Grill (ul Grodzka 9)*; *Grill Aladyn (ul Św Jana 3)*; and *Marhaba Grill (ul Grodzka 45)*. A hearty, copious plate in any of these won't cost more than around $7.

Given the abundance and diversity of cheap places to eat, *McDonald's (ul Floriańska 55)* wouldn't seemingly deserve a mention, but it does. It occupies a spacious two storey premises with the lower level in medieval cellars. Locals joke that this is probably the most original Big Mac – the ultimate icon of modern junk culture served in 600-year-old brick vaults.

The same applies to *Pizza Hut (Plac Św Marii Magdaleny)*. The ground level is pleasant, but go downstairs to the cellars – they're amazing. The company has opened a small *take-away outlet (ul Grodzka 57)*, round the corner, where it sells pizzas by the portion – convenient if you just want a small snack while tramping around.

Among other pizza houses, arguably the best places include the *Pizzeria Cyklop (ul*

Mikołajska 16) – the only one that has a wood-burning brick oven and *Pizzeria Grace (ul Św Anny 7, ul Sienna 17* and *ul Św Jana 1).*

Don't miss trying the *obwarzanki*, ring-shaped pretzels powdered with poppy seeds, a local speciality sold by pushcart vendors.

PLACES TO EAT – MID-RANGE

Included in this section are restaurants where an average main course will cost about $6 to $9. Of course, the final bill will depend on other components of your meal, such as a starter, soup and dessert, and alcoholic drinks, but you can roughly assume that a dinner for two will cost around $30. All the restaurants listed here are on Map 4 unless marked.

Restauracja Chłopskie Jadło (Map 5; ☎ 421 85 20, *ul Św Agnieszki 1),* in Stradom, a short walk south of Wawel, looks like a rustic country inn somewhere at the crossroads in medieval Poland, and serves traditional Polish 'peasant grub', as its name says. Live folk music on some evenings adds to the atmosphere. It's one of Kraków's most unusual culinary adventures, and at very reasonable prices; don't miss this opportunity.

Restauracja Korsykańska Paese (☎ 421 62 73, ul Poselska 24) offers Corsican and some mainland French cuisine, including fine seafood. The food is good, prices acceptable and the interior bright and cheerful. Not without reason the place is often packed solid. Another French-inspired establishment, the *Restauracja Guliwer (☎ 430 24 66, ul Bracka 6)* comes with some samples of Provençal cuisine in pleasant Mediterranean surroundings.

Next door to the Guliwer, the *Gospoda CK Dezerter (☎ 422 79 31, ul Bracka 6)* offers regional food with elements of traditional Austro-Hungarian cuisine.

The appropriately named *Surrestaurant Szuflada (☎ 423 13 34, ul Wiślna 5)* is perhaps the most eccentric place in town in which Salvador Dali would have probably felt entirely at home, even though the food served here hasn't yet reached the class of the décor.

Meats, Meats & More Meats

A Pole usually doesn't consider a dish a serious meal if it comes without a chunk of meat *(mięso).* The most commonly consumed meat is pork *(wieprzowina),* followed by beef *(wołowina)* and veal *(cielęcina).* They are the staple of every restaurant, from rock bottom to the very top. Among the commonest dishes are the following:

befsztyk – beef steak
bryzol – grilled beef steak
golonka – boiled pig's knuckle served with horseradish, a favourite for many Poles
gołąbki – cabbage leaves stuffed with minced beef and rice, and occasionally with mushrooms
gulasz – goulash; originally Hungarian
kotlet schabowy – a fried pork cutlet coated in breadcrumbs, flour and egg, found on every menu
pieczeń wołowa/wieprzowa – roast beef/pork
polędwica pieczona – roast fillet of beef
rumsztyk – rump steak
schab pieczony – roast loin of pork seasoned with prunes and herbs
stek – steak; in obscure restaurants you may find that it's minced meat
sztuka mięsa – boiled beef served with horseradish
zraz zawijany – stewed beef rolls stuffed with mushrooms and/or bacon and served in sour cream sauce

Italian culinary matters have recently been enlivened, putting several new eateries on the city map. Of these, *Ristorante Avanti (☎ 430 07 70, ul Karmelicka 7)* has become a local favourite, thanks to good food and prices, not to mention its décor. For a more striking décor, however, go to *Restauracja Cherubino (☎ 429 40 07, ul Św Tomasza 15)* which serves Italian and Polish dishes for a little more than the Avanti.

Other reasonable Italian restaurants include *Ristorante Corleone (☎ 429 51 26,*

Vegetarians, Don't Worry

Kraków is quite vegie-friendly. Polish cuisine includes some vegetarian specialities, which appear on the menus of the jadłodajnias, milk bars and some upmarket restaurants. Typical Polish vegetarian cuisine includes:

botwinka – soup made from the stems and leaves of baby beetroots; often includes a hard-boiled egg; served in summer only
chłodnik – another summer soup, but this one is cold; made from beetroot with sour cream and fresh vegetables; originally Lithuanian but widespread in Poland
knedle – dumplings stuffed with plums or apples
kopytka – Polish gnocchi; noodles made from flour and boiled potatoes
leniwe pierogi – boiled noodles with cottage cheese
naleśniki – crêpes; fried pancakes, most commonly filled with cottage cheese *(z serem)* or jam *(z dżemem)*; served with sour cream and sugar
pierogi – dumplings made from noodle dough, stuffed and boiled; the most popular are those filled with cottage cheese *(z serem)*, with blueberries *(z jagodami)* or with cabbage and wild mushrooms *(z kapustą i grzybami)*
placki ziemniaczane – fried pancakes made from grated raw potatoes bound with egg and flour; served with sour cream *(ze śmietaną)* or sugar *(z cukrem)*
zupa jarzynowa – mixed vegetable soup
zupa szczawiowa – sorrel soup, most likely garnished with hard-boiled egg

ul Poselska 19); and **Ristorante Caruso** *(☎ 422 60 61, ul Grodzka 39)*. And you still have **Ristorante da Pietro** *(☎ 422 32 79, Rynek Główny 17)*, one of the first real Italian eateries in town, which continues to serve good food in its attractive spacious cellar setting.

For Jewish food, go to **Café Alef** *(Map 5; ☎ 421 38 70, ul Szeroka 17)*; or **Café Ariel** *(Map 5; ☎ 421 79 20, ul Szeroka 18)*, next

to one another in Kazimierz. Both serve traditional Jewish dishes, cakes and desserts, and a hearty kosher beer. Their interiors are furnished in a manner reminiscent of the 19th century, and have a cosy intimacy. In the evening, both cafés have live performances of *klezmer* music.

In Podgórze, south across the Vistula from Kazimierz, is **Restauracja A Dong** *(Map 5; ☎ 656 48 72, ul Brodzińskiego 3)*, reputedly the best Chinese eatery in town (also serving Vietnamese fare).

PLACES TO EAT – TOP END

All the following restaurants are shown on Map 4.

Restauracja pod Aniołami *(☎ 421 39 99, ul Grodzka 35)* offers excellent typical Polish food in some of the most amazing surroundings. It's in fantastic vaulted cellars, beautifully decorated with traditional household implements and old crafts. It's easily one of the best options for that special dinner in the city.

Another marvellous place, **Restauracja Cyrano de Bergerac** *(☎ 411 72 88, ul Sławkowska 26)* serves fine authentic French food in one of the city's loveliest cellars. It's not exactly a budget eatery, and the portions are not overly copious, but it's certainly less than you'd pay in Paris.

Cheaper is **Restauracja u Szkota** *(☎ 422 15 70, ul Mikołajska 4)* which also enjoys a lovely cellar location. It occupies three intimate cosy vaults while a fourth has been made into a captivating bar. Despite its name (Scottish Restaurant), the cuisine is largely Polish, except for good Irish cider and a long list of whisky varieties.

Leaving medieval cellars for a while, **Restauracja Chimera** *(☎ 423 21 78, ul Św Anny 3)* is a ground level, well appointed place that does beautiful traditional Polish cooking at reasonable prices.

A famous Kraków eatery, **Restauracja Wentzl** *(☎ 429 57 12, Rynek Główny 19)*, has re-opened after decades out of business. Set in fabulous Gothic cellars, the place has been decorated in a striking modern style and even has a rotating dance floor. It does fine European cuisine at high prices.

Another local icon, **Restauracja Tetma-jerowska** (☎ *422 06 31, Rynek Główny 34*), is one of the city's most formal and expensive eateries. Accumulating its fame over a century, it serves international and Polish dishes in an elegant 1st floor historic interior topped with a beamed wooden ceiling and a fine mural running around the walls. The food is consistently good.

CAFÉS

Kraków has traditionally had a wealth of cafés, a good number of them located in historic buildings and their medieval cellars. Until recently they focused on coffee and sweets and were predominantly meeting places rather than eating places. Now most have introduced food menus, and some have even changed the sign, replacing 'Café' with 'Restaurant'. And they've all extended their once limited drink repertoire. In effect, the distinction between café, restaurant and bar is becoming blurred. All the following places are on Map 4.

Kraków's most famous café is the legendary **Jama Michalika** (*ul Floriańska 45*). Established in 1895, it was traditionally a hang-out for painters, writers and all sorts of artists. Decorated with works of art of the time, the place gives the impression of a small fin-de-siècle museum. It's nonsmoking – one of the few such cafés in the city.

For the best choice of coffee in town, go to **Sklep z Kawą Pożegnanie z Afryką** (*Coffee Shop Farewell to Africa; ul Św Tomasza 21*). It is a shop-cum-café which sells about 70 kinds of coffee, half of which can be drunk inside at the tables. Coffee is prepared in sophisticated coffee makers and spring water is used, not tap water which is pretty bad in Kraków. This is also a nonsmoking venue.

Smokers can try **Café Larousse** (*ul Św Tomasza 22*) just a block away. Papered in leaves from a Larousse dictionary (hence its name), this tiny place of only four tables (predictably often full) serves a choice of exotic coffees. Alternatively, go to the charming, bohemian **Café Camelot** (*ul Św Tomasza 17*), decorated with amazing pieces of folk art.

Café Botanica (*ul Bracka 9*) feels like a greenhouse or garden, filled with plants, with even the chairs and tables designed to match the whole. You enter a completely different world in **Kawiarnia Wiśniowy Sad** (*ul Grodzka 33*) which has a nostalgic air of Chekhov's days. Around the corner, the quiet **Caffeteria pod Błękitnym Kotem** (*ul Poselska 9*) has a choice of salads and other simple dishes.

Kawiarnia Esplanada (*ul Św Tomasza 30*) is Kraków's only reading café, with shelves full of books (in Polish only) and good coffee. **Kawiarnia Filmowa Graffiti** (*ul Św Gertrudy 5*) is a film café, decorated with film paraphernalia and equipped with a big screen, where old classics are screened on some evenings. **Kawiarnia Buschmann** (*ul Szpitalna 34*) is a quiet old-style two level café with period furnishing to match the whole.

If coffee is more important than the surroundings, go to the new, modern **Tribeca Coffee** (*ul Karmelicka 8*).

For a cup of good tea, there's probably nothing better than the famous Viennese **Demmers Teehaus** (*ul Kanonicza 21*) which sells heaps of tea varieties, many of which you can try in an intimate tearoom in the cellar.

Some of the best bread, croissants etc in town are sold in **La Croissanterine Fleury Michon** (*ul Floriańska 40*).

Entertainment

Kraków has a lively cultural life, particularly in the theatre, music and visual arts, and there are numerous annual festivals. The Centrum Informacji Kulturalnej (Cultural Information Centre; ☎ 421 77 87, fax 421 77 31) at ul Św Jana 2 just off the main square will provide detailed information on what's on. It publishes a comprehensive Polish/English monthly magazine, *Karnet*, listing cultural events, and sells tickets for some of them. The office is open Monday to Friday from 10 am to 7 pm, Saturday from 11 am to 7 pm.

Another local what's on monthly paper, *Miesiąc w Krakowie* (This Month in Kraków), is also comprehensive and detailed but is mostly in Polish. The two leading local papers, *Gazeta Krakowska* and *Gazeta Wyborcza*, list programs of cinemas, theatres, concerts etc. The Friday edition of the latter has a more comprehensive what's-on section that includes museums, art galleries and outdoor activities. Posters are an important source of information as well, so keep your eyes open when strolling about the streets.

You will find all the places in this chapter on Map 4, unless otherwise stated.

PUBS & BARS

There are perhaps 100 pubs and/or bars in Kraków's Old Town alone. Many are in vaulted cellars, often very attractive. Most pubs are open till at least midnight, and some don't close until the wee hours of the morning.

To name a few, just to help you start your exploration, there is: *Klub Kulturalny (ul Szewska 25)*; *Music Bar 9 (ul Szewska 9)*; *Pub Pod Papugami (ul Św Jana 18)*; *Black Gallery (ul Mikołajska 24)*; *Pub Uwaga (Mały Rynek 3)*; and *Nowy Kuzyn (Mały Rynek 4)*.

Then there is: *Free Pub (ul Sławkowska 4)*; *Pub u Kacpra (ul Sławkowska 2)*; the *Fischer Pub (ul Grodzka 42)*; and *Old Pub (ul Poselska 18)*.

Welcome to the Polish Pub

The fashion for all things western has brought pubs to Poland. They first appeared in 1990 in Warsaw and spread like wildfire to other cities and farther on down to the province. Warsaw has already a hundred or two of them and Kraków probably even more.

Some pubs tend to mimic their English/Irish/Scottish siblings, including the brands of beer on offer. A draught Guinness or a bottled Heineken will be served to you for roughly the same price as at home. Other pubs follow local style, and offer mostly Polish beer. Today, the name 'pub' is used indiscriminately to label just about any place which has a few tables and chairs and serves beer.

Until not long ago, most Polish pubs were strictly drinking venues, with occasional packets of chips the only food on offer. In recent years, some pubs have introduced a food menu, which may be an interesting proposition, if you don't mind thick clouds of fumes. Virtually all pubs are smoking venues, and in some places those sensitive to cigarette smoke might find an oxygen mask essential.

MENU
SMOKED CHICKEN
SMOKED SALMON
SMOKED TROUT
SMOKED CHEESE
SMOKED CHIP
SMOKED SAUS
SMOKED OYSTERS
SMOKED HAM

MARTIN HARRIS

After that, try out the *@tmosfera (Plac Szczepański 7)*; *Piwnica Pod Kominkiem (ul Bracka 13)*; and *Pub Pod Jemiołą (ul Floriańska 20)*.

Also include in your pub crawl *CK Browar (ul Podwale 7)*, in the basement of the Elefant department store, which serves beer straight from its own in-house brewery; you can see its brass vats behind the buffet.

The establishments, which apart from drinks offer a reasonable food menu, include *Piwnica pod Złotą Pipą (ul Floriańska 30)*; *Piwnica pod Ogródkiem (ul Jagiellońska 6)*; *Piec Art (ul Szewska 12)*; and *Klub Starego Teatru Osorya (ul Jagiellońska 5)*. All four are in cellars and all are amazing, particularly the Osorya.

If you are tired of medieval cellars and need some breath of the future, try the spanking new, cool double-level *In Vitro (ul Sienna 3)* with its silver-and-white glass décor, and acid jazz at times.

Should you need a good watering hole in Kazimierz (Map 5), try *Singer Club (ul Estery 20)*; *Ptaszyl (ul Szeroka 10)*; *Pub Fanaberia (ul Meiselsa 11)*; and *Łaźnia (ul Paulińska 28)*.

Back in the Old Town, *Hotel Elektor* boasts exquisite medieval cellars, which house a classy wine bar. Its selection of French and Rhine wines is among the best in town. There's also an upmarket Vinoteka in *Hotel Pod Różą*.

DISCOS

Popular haunts include *Equinox (☎ 421 17 71, ul Sławkowska 13/15)*; *Kredens (Rynek Główny 12)*; *Klub pod Papugami (☎ 422 08 06, ul Szpitalna 1)*; and *Music Bar 9 (ul Szewska 9)*.

Also popular are *Rock Club Yellow Submarine (ul Grodzka 50)*; *Rock & Roll Club (ul Grodzka 50)*; and *Klub Pasja (☎ 423 04 83, ul Szewska 5)*.

Most discos operate nightly, usually except Mondays. Most student clubs run discos on Friday and Saturday nights. *Klub Rotunda (☎ 633 35 38, ul Oleandry 1)*; and *Klub pod Przewiązką (☎ 637 45 02, ul Bydgoska 19B) are worth a try*.

GAY & LESBIAN VENUES

The best known gay and lesbian places include *Klub Hades (ul Starowiślna 60)* which holds Friday and Saturday discos from about 8 pm till late, frequented mostly by gays but also some lesbians; and the gay bar *Hali Gali (ul Karmelicka 10)* which is open nightly except Monday.

JAZZ & BLUES

The main jazz outlets include *Jazz Club u Muniaka (☎ 422 84 48, ul Floriańska 3)* and *Harris Piano Jazz Bar (☎ 421 57 41, Rynek Główny 28)*. Live jazz is usually played from Thursday to Saturday. Other places to check include *Rotunda Orlik Club (☎ 634 34 12, ul Oleandry 1)* on Tuesday; *Jazz Club Kornet (Al Krasińskiego 19)* on Wednesday; and *Chimera II (ul Gołębia 2)*.

Live blues can be found at *Klub u Luisa (Rynek Główny 13)* and *Klinika 35 (ul Św Tomasza 35)*.

FOLK & ETHNIC MUSIC

Polish folk music is still well cultivated in the countryside, particularly at the foothills of the Tatras, but not commonly heard in the cities. In Kraków, you'll mostly hear it in the street, performed by amateur ensembles decked out in folk costumes. In the tourist summer season, there's often a band playing at the entrance to Wawel, and there may be another at the main square.

Of other musical varieties, *klezmer* (traditional Jewish) music has become a very popular genre over recent years, with more than half a dozen local groups appearing on the scene. The best known of these is the *Kroke* trio, which began in 1992 and came to the fore when Spielberg filmed his *Schindler's List*, but these days the group is mostly on international tours, turning up at Kraków only occasionally. Other klezmer groups regularly play in the cafés on ul Szeroka in Kazimierz – check *Ariel*, *Alef*, *Austeria* and *Arka Noego* (Noah's Ark). Concerts normally start around 8 pm and there's a US$5 entry fee.

Other ethnic rhythms, such as Russian, Ukrainian, Gypsy, Irish and Georgian, are presented irregularly, both in the street and in some pubs and cafés, including the *Chimera II*.

CLASSICAL MUSIC

The *Filharmonia Krakowska (☎ 422 94 77, ul Zwierzyniecka 1)* is home to one of the best orchestras in the country. Concerts are held on Friday and Saturday and irregularly on other days, and tickets can be bought from the ticket office, open weekdays from 2 to 7 pm and Saturday one hour before the concerts.

CABARETS

Piwnica pod Baranami is a legendary cabaret operating uninterruptedly since 1956 and acclaimed as the best in the country. It continues despite the death (in 1997) of its long-time inspirer and animator, Piotr Skrzynecki. You may not grasp the finer points of the political satire, but the music, settings, movement and general atmosphere cut across linguistic boundaries. The group usually performs on Saturday nights in their cellar *Piwnica pod Baranami (Rynek Główny 27)*.

Tickets can be bought in WOK (☎ 421 25 00) at Rynek Główny 25 (Monday to Friday from noon to 5 pm), but they are hard to come by, so book as soon as they go on sale.

Other renowned local cabarets include *Loch Camelot* which performs in *Café Camelot (ul Św Tomasza 17)*; and *Jama Michalika* in the café *Jama Michalika (ul Floriańska 45)*.

CINEMA

Kraków has 18 movie houses, half of them in the centre. The cinemas that may have some art movies in their program include *Kino Mikro (ul Lea 5)*; *Kino Paradox (Krowoderska 8)*; and the *cinema club (ul Oleandry 1)* in the Rotunda Student Club.

THEATRE, OPERA & BALLET

Established in 1955, the avant-garde *Cricot 2* is Kraków's best known theatre outside the national borders, but it was dissolved after its creator and director, Tadeusz Kantor, died in 1990.

An advertisement for a theatre play.
Teatr Stary is known for its great performances.

Theatre buffs may be interested in visiting the *Cricoteka (☎ 422 83 32, ul Kanonicza 5)*, the centre which documents his works (see the Things to See & Do chapter).

In the mainstream, the *Teatr Stary* (Old Theatre) is the best known city theatre and has attracted the cream of the city's actors. It has a *main stage (☎ 422 40 40, ul Jagiellońska 1)* and two *small stages (☎ 421 19 98, ul Starowiślna 21* and *☎ 421 59 76, ul Sławkowska 14)*.

The *Słowacki Theatre (Teatr im Słowackiego; ☎ 422 45 75, Plac Św Ducha 1)* focuses on the Polish classics and on large-scale productions. This large and opulent building, a historical monument in itself, was totally renovated in 1991 and its interior is spectacular (see the Things to See & Do chapter). Opera and ballet performances are also staged here, as there's no proper opera house in Kraków.

The *Teatr STU (☎ 422 27 44, Al Krasińskiego 16)* started in the 1970s as an

Food is fresh and cheap at the daily markets, north and south of the Old Town.

Be sure to try *obwarzanki*. They're a local speciality sold from street carts and kiosks.

Rynek Główny has a huge population of pigeons but they aren't available for pigeon pie!

Kraków has had worldwide recognition for its experimental theatre. Its International Festival of Street Theatre takes over the Rynek Główny for several days in July.

'angry', politically involved, avant-garde student theatre and was immediately successful. Today it no longer deserves any of those adjectives, but nonetheless it's a solid professional troupe.

There are a dozen or so other theatres in the city, some of which may have interesting shows. Tickets can be bought directly from the theatres.

SPECTATOR SPORTS

Soccer is Poland's most popular spectator sport. The country had quite a strong national team in the 1970s, but its fortunes have since risen and fallen. Yet, the matches of the national league invariably fill up the stadiums. Kraków's main facility is the Wisła stadium in the Wisła sports complex and Kraków's Wisła team led the national league in 1999.

Soccer apart, there doesn't seem to be any particular sport that sends the nation crazy. Cycling is reasonably popular in some circles, as is basketball. Poland has had some international successes in athletics, and was once strong in boxing, wrestling and fencing. Kayaking and rowing are other sports in which Poles have gained occasional high scores in international competitions.

Interestingly, some of the hugely popular sports in some western countries, including cricket, baseball, rugby, football and golf, are almost unknown in Poland.

Shopping

CRAFTS

Poland offers quite a choice of handicrafts, made by local artisans and mostly sold through the chain of Cepelia shops, which exist in all large cities. The most common Polish crafts include papercuts, woodcarving, tapestries, embroidery, paintings on glass, pottery, and hand-painted wooden boxes and chests.

There are several Cepelia shops scattered around Kraków's central area, but the best place to go to is the Cloth Hall in the middle of the main square, where several dozen stands sell all imaginable Polish crafts.

AMBER

If there's a typical Polish precious stone it's probably amber, with the distinction that amber is not a precious stone at all. It's actually a fossilised tree resin of vegetable origin, which appears in a striking variety of colours from ivory and pale yellow to reddish and brownish tints. Amber is commonly used in silver jewellery, and sold through the Cepelia chain, jewellery shops and commercial art galleries. In Kraków, possibly the best place to start your shopping is, again, the Cloth Hall where some of the stalls sell amber jewellery, which may be good value.

CONTEMPORARY ART

Polish contemporary painting, original prints and sculpture are renowned internationally, as are Polish posters. They are presented and sold by private commercial art galleries. The galleries in Kraków, along with those in Warsaw, have the biggest and the most representative choice, and are therefore good places to get an insight into what's currently happening in Polish art and, if you wish, to buy some. There are several dozen commercial art galleries in Kraków including some considered to be among the best in Poland.

Among the most reputable art galleries specialising in paintings are the Starmach

KRZYSZTOF DYDYŃSKI

A craft shop in Cloth Hall with products by local artisans on display.

Gallery at ul Węgierska 5; Stawski Gallery at ul Miodowa 15; Rostworowski Gallery at ul Św Jana 20; Artemis at ul Starowiślna 21; and Marian Gołogórski Gallery at ul Grodzka 29. Labirynt has two places – ul Floriańska 36 and ul Józefa 15; and ZPAP Sukiennice is in the Cloth Hall.

The Andrzej Fejkiel Gallery, ul Grodzka 25, has the widest selection of prints in town, while the best choice of sculpture is offered by the Galeria Rzeźby ZAR, ul Bracka 15.

For a bit of fun, visit the Andrzej Mleczko Gallery at ul Św Jana 14, which displays and sells comic drawings by one of the most popular Polish satirical cartoonists.

Without doubt, the best choice of posters is at the Galeria Plakatu (Poster Gallery) at ul Stolarska 8/10. Here you will find works by Poland's most prominent poster makers. It's worth going to have a look even if you don't plan to purchase a poster.

ANTIQUES

The main seller of old art and antiques is a state-owned chain of shops called Desa. Some of these shops also have work by contemporary artists. Large Desa shops usually have an amazing variety of old jewellery, watches, furniture and whatever else you could imagine. Remember that it's officially forbidden to export any item manufactured before 9 May 1945, works of art and books included, unless you get a special permit. In Kraków, it can be obtained from the Wydział Ochrony Zabytków (Department of Monuments' Protection; ☎ 422 83 00), at Plac Wszystkich Świętych 3.

Kraków has several Desa antique shops that are good though not cheap. There are Desa shops at ul Grodzka 8, ul Mikołajska 10, ul Stolarska 17 and ul Floriańska 13, amongst others. The Desa shop in the backyard of ul Floriańska 13 has the best collection of Orthodox Church icons, some of which are easily museum pieces. The Antykwariat at ul Sławkowska 10 (corner of ul Św Tomasza) has a variety of old books, prints, maps, drawings and etchings.

BOOKS & MAPS

Poland publishes quite an assortment of well-edited and lavishly illustrated coffee-table books about the country, many also available in English and German. Several bookshops on Kraków's main square have a good choice of these books, including some alluring photographic accounts of Kraków (English versions available).

For English-language books, check the Księgarnia Columbus (☎ 421 62 71), ul Starowiślna 38; Księgarnia Językowa Szawal (☎ 421 53 61), ul Długa 1; English Book Centre (☎ 422 62 00), Plac Matejki 5; and the Inter Book (☎ 632 10 08), ul Karmelicka 27. The Księgarnia Edukator (☎ 421 53 17) in the French Institute at ul Św Jana 15 has the best selection of books in French.

The Księgarnia Odeon (☎ 429 12 93), ul Sienna 2; Księgarnia Znak (☎ 422 45 48) at

Sławkowska 1; and Księgarnia Hetmańska (☎ 430 24 53), Rynek Główny 17, have modest selections of books in English and a few in French.

For foreign-language newspapers and magazines, the best central place to check is the EMPiK, Rynek Główny 25.

The widest choice of publications related to Jewish issues is to be found at the Jarden Jewish Bookshop (Map 5; ☎ 421 71 66) at ul Szeroka 2 in Kazimierz.

Some of the best selection of regional and city maps is in Sklep Podróżnika at ul Jagiellońska 6 (☎ 429 14 85) and ul Szujskiego 2 (☎ 421 89 22); the latter is the cheapest place in Kraków which sells Lonely Planet guidebooks.

MUSIC

Polish music (pop, folk, jazz, classical and contemporary) is now commonly produced on CD and is easy to buy. Polish CDs cost about $10 to $15; imported CDs are $15 to $20. Cassettes are much cheaper than CDs, but avoid buying them from street stalls as these are of dubious quality.

For CDs with Polish music, check the Księgarnia Muzyczna Kurant at Rynek Główny 36; Music Corner at Rynek Główny 13; and the Salon Muzyczny Musica Antiqua at ul Senacka 6.

Jazz Compact at Rynek Główny 28 has the best selection of jazz to be found anywhere in Poland, including a representative offering of Polish jazz.

PHOTOGRAPHY & FILM

Some of the better stores selling cameras, photo equipment and accessories include the Big Fox at its three locations: ul Grodzka 51 (☎ 421 11 61); ul Karmelicka 28 (☎ 633 73 15); and ul Zwierzyniecka 31 (☎ 421 23 80).

Also try the Westfoto (☎ 423 22 82), ul Sławkowska 13/15 (enter from ul Św Marka). Sklep Foto, ul Wiślna 10, has a large if haphazard variety of mostly second-hand cameras and accessories including some amazing antique cameras.

A good and convenient place to buy Kodak film is EMPiK Kodak Express

SHOPPING

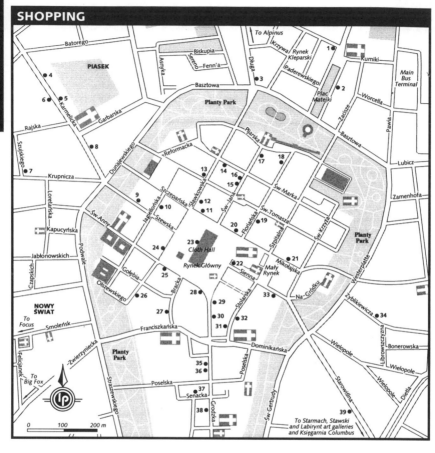

(☎ 422 85 06), Rynek Główny 46, which offers a reasonable choice and is fairly cheap. For Fuji film (including Velvia and Provia), check the Foto Studio (☎ 421 70 00), Plac Matejki 9; the Foto Expert (☎ 422 21 25), ul Karmelicka 13; as well as Focus (☎ 422 40 53), ul Smoleńsk 22 all of which stock films and keep them in the fridge.

CAMPING & OUTDOOR

If you happen to need a backpack, sleeping bag, trekking boots, a waterproof jacket or just a gas cartridge for your camping stove, probably the best place to check first is the

Sklep Górski Wierchy (☎ 429 67 05), ul Szewska 23, which is well stocked, very central and among the cheapest. Another good place to try is the Sklep Podróżnika (☎ 421 89 22), ul Szujskiego 2, which is also reasonably priced.

Other central places to consider include the Centrum Sportu Maks (☎ 421 71 01), ul Zyblikiewicza 2; and the Alpinus at its three locations: ul Sienna 15 (☎ 422 42 49), ul Karmelicka 33 (☎ 632 22 40) and ul Długa 50 (☎ 423 32 26).

The large shopping centres such as Géant, ul Bora Komorowskiego 37; and

CONTEMPORARY ART
- 15 Andrzej Mleczko Gallery
- 16 Rostworowski Gallery
- 18 Labirynt
- 23 ZPAP Sukiennice
- 27 Galeria Rzeźby ZAR
- 32 Galeria Plakatu (Poster Gallery)
- 35 Jan Fejkiel Gallery
- 36 Marian Gołogórski Gallery
- 39 Artemis

ANTIQUES
- 13 Antykwariat
- 19 Desa
- 21 Desa
- 30 Desa
- 31 Desa

BOOKS & MAPS
- 2 English Book Centre
- 3 Księgarnia Językowa Szawal
- 5 Inter Book
- 7 Sklep Podróżnika
- 10 Sklep Podróżnika
- 12 Księgarnia Znak
- 17 Księgarnia Edukator
- 22 Księgarnia Odeon
- 25 EMPiK
- 28 Księgarnia Hetmańska

MUSIC
- 11 Księgarnia Muzyczna Kurant
- 24 Jazz Compact
- 29 Music Corner

- 37 Salon Muzyczny Musica Antiqua

PHOTOGRAPHY & FILM
- 1 Foto Studio
- 6 Big Fox
- 8 Foto Expert
- 14 Westfoto
- 20 EMPiK Kodak Express
- 26 Sklep Foto
- 38 Big Fox

CAMPING & OUTDOOR
- 4 Alpinus
- 9 Sklep Górski Wierchy
- 33 Alpinus
- 34 Centrum Sportu Maks

Zakopianka, ul Zakopiańska 62, feature shops with sports, travel and camping gear.

MARKETS

A charming flea market is organised at Rynek Główny in summer, normally once a month over the weekend – check for dates after you arrive. It features a diverse collection of antiques and bric-a-brac.

Every Sunday a huge bazaar springs up in Kazimierz, at Plac Nowy and the surrounding streets. It's actually a gigantic garage sale, which gathers together hundreds of city dwellers to sell off their old stuff, mostly used clothing, from plastic sheets. Come in the morning as by midday it is already vanishing and by 2 pm all but rubbish is gone.

The daily market at Rynek Kleparski, just north of the Old Town, trades in food and is possibly the best central place for fresh fruits and vegetables. There is also a similar food market farther north, at Nowy Kleparz.

Excursions

Kraków is a convenient jumping-off point for various one-day trips to nearby places of interest, of which the Auschwitz death camp in Oświęcim is the most popular. Then you can get away from it all on the glorious walking trails in Ojców National Park. Many visitors take a few days to visit Zakopane and the Tatra Mountains, and some also go rafting in Dunajec Gorge. Finally, Częstochowa, the spiritual centre of Poland, draws in crowds of people, pilgrims and casual visitors alike, thanks to the miraculous Black Madonna.

All prices are given in US$.

OŚWIĘCIM
☎ 033

Oświęcim is a normal medium-sized industrial town about 60km west of Kraków. The Polish name may be unfamiliar to outsiders but the German one – Auschwitz – is not; the largest Nazi concentration camp was built here. This was the scene of the largest experiment in genocide in the history of humankind and the world's largest cemetery. It is possibly the most moving sight in Poland.

The Auschwitz camp was established in April 1940 in the prewar Polish army barracks on the outskirts of Oświęcim. It was originally destined to hold Polish political prisoners but it eventually became a gigantic centre for the extermination of European Jews. For this purpose, the much larger Birkenau (Brzezinka) camp, also referred to as Auschwitz II, was built in 1941-42, 2km west of Auschwitz, followed by another one in Monowitz (Monowice), several kilometres to the west of the town. About 40 smaller camps, branches of Auschwitz, were subsequently established all over the region. This death factory eliminated some 1.5 to two million people of 27 nationalities, about 85% to 90% of whom were Jews. The name Auschwitz is commonly used for the whole Auschwitz-Birkenau complex, both of which are open to the public.

Auschwitz

Auschwitz was only partially destroyed by the fleeing Nazis, and many of the original buildings stand to this day as a bleak document of the camp's history. A dozen of the 30 surviving prison blocks today house the museum; some blocks stage general exhibitions, while others are dedicated to victims from particular countries which lost citizens at Auschwitz.

During the communist era, the museum was conceived as an anti-fascist exhibition and the fact that most of the victims were Jewish was played down. Prominence was given to the 75,000 Polish Catholics killed here, at the expense of the Jewish dead. This approach has changed: block No 27, dedicated to the 'suffering and struggle of the Jews', now presents Auschwitz more correctly, as the place of martyrdom of the European Jewry.

From the visitors' centre in the entrance building, you enter the barbed-wire encampment through the gate with the cynical inscription 'Arbeit Macht Frei' (Work

KATE NOLAN

The grim entrance to Auschwitz is a precursor to the horror behind the gates.

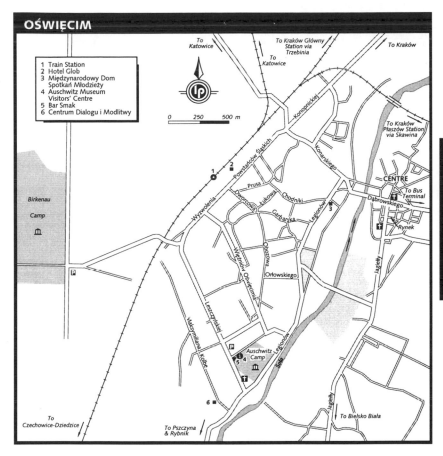

Makes Free), then visit exhibitions in the prison blocks and finally see the gas chamber and crematorium. You don't need much imagination to take in what happened here.

A 15 minute documentary about the liberation of the camp by Soviet troops on 27 January 1945 is screened in the cinema in the visitors' centre every half-hour, and a few times a day it is shown with a foreign-language soundtrack (English, French, German, Italian or Russian). Before you set off for the camp check with the information desk at the visitors' centre to find out what time your language version will be screened

– although the film's message is clear in any language.

The museum opens daily at 8 am and closes at 7 pm in June, July and August; at 6 pm in May and September; at 5 pm in March and November; at 4 pm in April and October; and at 3 pm in December, January and February. Admission is free; there's a $0.50 fee to enter the cinema. Photos, film and video are permitted free of charge throughout the camp. Anyone under 13 is advised by the museum management not to visit the camp, but the final decision is left to the accompanying adults. There's a cheap self-service Bar Smak by the entrance, facing the car park. There's also a *kantor*, a left-luggage room and several bookshops stocked with publications about the place.

Get a copy of a small brochure (available in a number of languages, including Polish, English, French and German) which is quite enough to get you around the grounds. Tours in English and German are organised daily at 11.30 am ($4 per person). Otherwise you can hire a foreign-language guide for your party at the information desk; $40 for Auschwitz-Birkenau (three hours).

From 15 April to late October, there is a special bus from Auschwitz to Birkenau ($0.40). It departs hourly from 10.30 am to 4.30 pm from outside the entrance to the visitors' centre, opposite Bar Smak. Alternatively, you can walk (2km) or take a taxi.

Birkenau

It was actually at Birkenau, not Auschwitz, that the extermination of large numbers of Jews took place. Vast (175 hectares), purpose-built and 'efficient', the camp had over 300 prison barracks and four huge gas chambers complete with crematoria. Each gas chamber accommodated 2000 people and there were electric lifts to raise the bodies to the ovens. The camp could hold 200,000 inmates at a time.

Though much was destroyed by the retreating Nazis, the size of the place, fenced off with long lines of barbed wire and watchtowers stretching almost as far as the eye can see, will give you some idea of the scale of the crime. Don't miss going to the top of the entrance gate for the view. Some of the surviving barracks are open to visitors. At the back of the complex is the monument to the dead, flanked on each side by the sinister remains of gas chambers.

In some ways, Birkenau is an even more shocking sight than Auschwitz. It can be visited in the same opening hours as Auschwitz and entry is free. Make sure to leave enough time (at least an hour) to walk around the camp – it is really vast.

There are no buses from Birkenau to the train station (2km); walk or go by taxi. Alternatively, take the same special bus back to Auschwitz (departing on the hour from 11 am to 5 pm) and change there for one of the frequent city buses to the station or take the direct PKS bus to Kraków.

Places to Stay & Eat

For most visitors, Auschwitz-Birkenau camp is a day trip, in most cases from Kraków, and *Bar Smak*, mentioned above, is all you need to keep you going. However, if you want to linger longer, Oświęcim has a choice of places to stay and eat.

The Catholic Church-built *Centrum Dialogu i Modlitwy* (☎ 43 10 00, ul Św Maksymiliana Kolbe 1), 700m south-west of the Auschwitz camp, provides comfortable and quiet accommodation in rooms of two, three, four, five, six and 10 beds (most with private bath) and a restaurant. Bed and breakfast costs $20 ($15 for students). You can also camp here ($6 per person).

Another good place is *Międzynarodowy Dom Spotkań Młodzieży* (*International Meeting House for the Youth;* ☎ 43 21 07, ul Legionów 11), 1km east of the train station. Built in 1986 by the Germans, the place essentially provides lodging for groups coming for longer stays, but anyone can be accommodated if there are vacancies. Singles/doubles/quads with bath cost $18/25/34; students pay $12/20/27, respectively. Inexpensive meals are served in the dining room on the premises. Camping is also possible here.

Hotel Glob (☎ 43 06 32, ul Powstańców Śląskich 16), outside the train station, has decent (if noisy) singles/doubles with bath for $25/36 and its own restaurant.

Getting There & Away

For most tourists, the jumping-off point for Oświęcim is Kraków, from where many tours to the camp are organised. There are a few early morning trains from Kraków Główny station via Trzebinia (65km) but then nothing till around 3 pm. More trains depart from Kraków Płaszów station via Skawina (also 65km), though they are not very regular either. Check the schedule the day before to plan properly. Frequent urban buses (Nos 24 to 29) run from Oświęcim train station to Auschwitz camp (1.7km), but none to Birkenau camp (2km).

Buses are more convenient as they run more regularly and will deliver you directly to the Auschwitz museum. There are about 10 PKS buses per day from Kraków to Oświęcim (64km); they pass by Oświęcim train station and Auschwitz museum before reaching the terminal on the far eastern outskirts of the town. Don't miss the stop, otherwise you'll have to backtrack 4km to the museum by the local bus, No 2 or 3, which is infrequent.

To get back to Kraków, take the PKS bus from the stop near the museum or, if there's none due soon, go by local bus to the train station and check that schedule in case a train is passing through first. Better still, take note of the schedules upon arrival in town and plan your visit accordingly.

OJCÓW NATIONAL PARK
☎ 012

At only 21 sq km, the Ojców National Park (Ojcowski Park Narodowy), about 20km north-west of Kraków, is Poland's second smallest, yet it's picturesque and varied. Encompassing some of the most beautiful parts of the Kraków-Częstochowa Upland, it is a showcase of the region: in its small area you'll find two castles, a number of caves, impressive rock formations and a wide variety of plant life. Most of the park is beech, fir, oak and hornbeam forest which is particularly photogenic in autumn.

Orientation

Most tourist attractions are along the road that runs through the park beside the Prądnik River, with Ojców and Pieskowa Skała, about 7km apart, being the main points of interest. Though buses run between these two localities, it is much better to walk the whole stretch, enjoying the sights and scenery.

Give yourself a full day in the park – it's a captivating place. Buy the *Ojcowski Park Narodowy* map (scale 1:22,500) in Kraków before setting off. The map includes all the marked trails and shows rocks, caves, gorges and the like.

Things to See

Ojców is the only village in the park. Its predominantly wooden houses are scattered across a slope above the river. The hill at the northern end of the village is crowned with the ruins of **Ojców Castle**, with its original 14th century entrance gate and an octagonal tower.

One of the two long buildings just south of the castle houses the **Natural History Museum** (Muzeum Przyrodnicze), focusing on the geology, archaeology, flora and fauna of the park, while a wooden house a few paces farther south is the **Regional Museum** (Muzeum Regionalne), which features the history and ethnography of the place.

The trail marked in black which heads southward from Ojców Castle will lead you in half an hour to the **Łokietek Cave** (Jaskinia Łokietka). About 250m long, the cave consists of one small and two large chambers, but there are no stalactites or stalagmites. The cave is artificially lit and can be visited from May to October between 9 am and 4 pm (longer in summer); guided tours take about half an hour.

Possibly more interesting and larger is the **Wierzchowska Górna Cave**, in the village of Wierzchowie outside the park boundaries, 5km south-west of Ojców; the yellow trail will take you there. It's the longest cave so far discovered in the whole region – 1km long – and about 370m of its length can be visited. It's open to the general public at similar times to the Łokietek Cave. The 50-minute tours begin on the hour. The temperature inside is 7.5°C year-round.

Two other caves are also open to the public: the **Dark Cave** (Jaskinia Ciemna), close to Ojców and easily reached by the green trail, and the **Bat Cave** (Jaskinia Nietoperzowa), farther away and accessible by the blue trail.

About 200m north of Ojców Castle is the **Chapel upon the Water** (Kaplica na Wodzie), positioned above the river bed where it was rebuilt from the former public baths. The chapel is open only for religious services on Sunday morning.

In the hamlet of Grodzisko about 2km to the north the road divides. You should take the left-hand fork skirting the river and look for the red trail that branches off the road to the right and heads uphill. It will take you to the small baroque **Church of the Blessed Salomea**, erected in the 17th century on the site of the former Convent of Poor Clares. The stone wall encircling the church is adorned with statues representing Salomea and her family. Behind the church is an unusual carved stone elephant (1686) supporting an obelisk on its back.

Follow the red trail, which will bring you back down to the road. Walk along it for several more kilometres to an 18m-tall limestone pillar known as **Hercules' Club** (Maczuga Herkulesa). A short distance beyond it is the **Pieskowa Skała Castle**. The castle was erected in the 14th century but the mighty fortress you see is the result of extensive rebuilding in the 16th century. It's the best preserved castle in the upland and the only one with more than bare walls. It houses a museum.

You first enter a large outer courtyard which is accessible free of charge daily from 8 am to 8 pm. From here you get to the arcaded inner courtyard and the museum (open from 10 am to 3 pm, except Monday). On display is European art from the Middle Ages to the mid-19th century, including furniture, tapestries, sculpture, painting and ceramics.

There's a restaurant-café in the outer courtyard of the castle, a good place to finish your sightseeing with a beer, coffee or something more substantial – the trout is recommended. In summer they open the terrace on the roof, providing a good view over the castle and the surrounding forest.

Places to Stay & Eat

Local people in Ojców rent out rooms in their homes but it can be hard to get one on summer weekends. The rooms can be arranged through the Ojcowianin travel agency (☎ 389 20 89) in the building of the regional museum. In the same building, the PTTK office (☎ 389 20 36) also handles private rooms.

Dom Wycieczkowy Zosia (☎ 389 20 08) in Złota Góra, 1km west of Ojców Castle,

is open in summer. Some 500m farther up the road is *Camping Złota Góra* (which has tents with beds) and *Zajazd* restaurant, both open from May to September. There are also a couple of restaurants in Ojców.

With your own transport, you can stay at either *Zajazd Krystyna (☎ 419 30 02)* in Bębło or *Zajazd Orle Gniazdo (☎ 419 10 37)* in Biały Kościół. Both these motels are located on the Kraków-Olkusz road, 2km south-west of the park, and both have restaurants.

Getting There & Away

There are about eight buses daily from Kraków to Ojców (22km), some of which continue up to Pieskowa Skała. Fewer buses run at weekends.

From Pieskowa Skała, you can take a bus back to Kraków (29km), or continue to Olkusz (16km) and from there farther north to Częstochowa. The bus stop is at the foot of the castle; check the schedule before visiting the castle to help you to plan your trip.

ZAKOPANE & THE TATRAS
☎ 018

The Tatras, 100km south of Kraków, are the highest range of the Carpathian Mountains and the only alpine type, with towering peaks and steep rocky sides dropping hundreds of metres to glacial lakes. There are no glaciers in the Tatras, but patches of snow remain all year. Winters are long, summers short and the weather erratic.

The whole range, roughly 60km long and 15km wide, stretches across the Polish-Slovakian border. A quarter of it is now Polish territory and was declared the Tatra National Park, which encompasses about 212 sq km. The park boasts more than a score of peaks that exceed 2000m, the highest of which is Mt Rysy (2499m).

Set at the northern foot of the Tatras, Zakopane (population 30,000) is the most famous mountain resort in Poland and the winter sports capital. The town attracts a couple of million tourists a year, with peaks in summer and winter. Though Zakopane is essentially a base for either skiing or hiking in the Tatras, the town itself is enjoyable

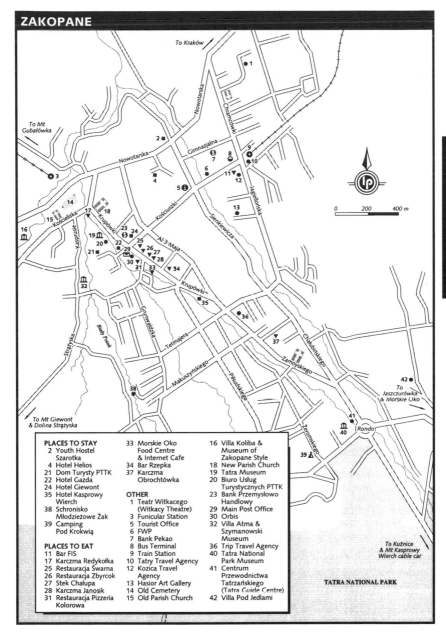

ZAKOPANE

EXCURSIONS

0   200   400 m

To Kraków
To Mt Gubałówka
To Mt Giewont & Dolina Strążyska
To Kuźnice & Mt Kasprowy Wierch cable car
To Jaszczurówka & Mörskie Uko

TATRA NATIONAL PARK

PLACES TO STAY
2 Youth Hostel Szarotka
4 Hotel Helios
21 Dom Turysty PTTK
22 Hotel Gazda
24 Hotel Giewont
35 Hotel Kasprowy Wierch
38 Schronisko Młodzieżowe Żak
39 Camping Pod Krokwią

PLACES TO EAT
11 Bar FIS
17 Karczma Redykołka
25 Restauracja Świarna
26 Restauracja Zbyrcok
27 Stek Chałupa
28 Karczma Janosik
31 Restauracja Pizzeria Kolorowa

33 Morskie Oko Food Centre & Internet Cafe
34 Bar Rzepka
37 Karczma Obrochtówka

OTHER
1 Teatr Witkacego (Witkacy Theatre)
3 Funicular Station
5 Tourist Office
6 FWP
7 Bank Pekao
8 Bus Terminal
9 Train Station
10 Tatry Travel Agency
12 Kozica Travel Agency
13 Hasior Art Gallery
14 Old Cemetery
15 Old Parish Church

16 Villa Koliba & Museum of Zakopane Style
18 New Parish Church
19 Tatra Museum
20 Biuro Usług Turystycznych PTTK
23 Bank Przemysłowo Handlowy
29 Main Post Office
30 Orbis
32 Villa Atma & Szymanowski Museum
36 Trip Travel Agency
40 Tatra National Park Museum
41 Centrum Przewodnictwa Tatrzańskiego (Tatra Guide Centre)
42 Villa Pod Jedlami

enough to hang around in for a while, and it has lots of tourist facilities.

Since the late 19th century, Zakopane has become popular with artists, many of whom came to settle and work here. The best known of these are the composer Karol Szymanowski and the writer and painter Witkacy. Witkacy's father, Stanisław Witkiewicz (1851-1915), was inspired by the traditional local architecture and created the so-called Zakopane style; some of the buildings he designed stand to this day.

Orientation

Zakopane, nestling below Mt Giewont at an altitude of 800m to 1000m, will be your base. The bus and train stations are adjacent in the north-east part of town. It's a 10 minute walk down ul Kościuszki to the town's heart, the pedestrian mall of Krupówki, lined with restaurants, cafés, boutiques and souvenir shops. It's always jammed with tourists parading around.

The funicular to Mt Gubałówka is just off the northern end of Krupówki. The cable car to Mt Kasprowy Wierch is at Kuźnice, 3km to the south.

Information

Tourist Office The helpful Centrum Informacji Turystycznej (☎ 201 22 11), ul Kościuszki 17, is open daily from 7 am to 9 pm.

Money Bank Pekao at ul Gimnazjalna 1 behind the bus terminal changes most major brands of travellers cheques and pays złoty advances on Visa and MasterCard. Bank Przemysłowo Handlowy at ul Krupówki 19 opposite Hotel Gazda changes cheques and accepts Visa card. As for cash, kantors dot ul Krupówki every 50m or so, and there are also a few ATMs.

If you are heading for Slovakia, buy some Slovak crowns in Zakopane.

Travel Agencies Centrum Przewodnictwa Tatrzańskiego (Tatra Guide Centre; ☎ 206 37 99) at ul Chałubińskiego 44 and the Biuro Usług Turystycznych PTTK (☎ 201 58 48) at ul Krupówki 12 can arrange mountain guides speaking English and Ger-

man, but advance notice is necessary. The cost depends on the difficulty of the hike or climb: from about $40 to $100 a day per group.

Orbis (☎ 201 50 51), ul Krupówki 22, sells domestic and international train tickets, arranges accommodation in private houses and selected holiday homes and organises tours. Teresa (☎ 201 43 01) at ul Kościuszki 7 specialises in international bus tickets.

Other useful travel agencies include the Trip (☎ 201 59 47) at ul Zamoyskiego 1 (international bus tickets, tours); the Tatry (☎ 201 43 43) at ul Chramcówki 35 just off the train station (private rooms, tours); the Giewont (☎ 206 35 66) at ul Kościuszki 4 (private rooms, tours); the Fregata (☎ 201 33 07) at ul Krupówki 81b (international tickets); and the Kozica (☎ 201 32 77) at ul Jagiellońska 1 right behind the Bar FIS (private rooms, tickets).

Many of these and other agencies will have tours to the Dunajec Gorge ($15 to $18 per person) and other popular regional tourist destinations.

Bookshop The best choice of maps and guidebooks on the Tatras and other mountain regions is to be found in Księgarnia Górska, the bookshop on the 1st floor of Dom Turysty PTTK.

Cybercafés Internet Café is on the 1st floor of the Morskie Oko gastronomic complex at ul Krupówki 30.

Things to See

The **Tatra Museum** (closed Monday), ul Krupówki 10, has several sections including history, ethnography, geology and flora and fauna and is thus a good introduction to the region.

On nearby ul Kościeliska is a charming **old parish church** (1847). Just behind it is the **old cemetery** with a number of amazing wooden tombs. Continue west along ul Kościeliska to the **Villa Koliba**, the first design (1892) of Witkiewicz in the Zakopane style. It now accommodates the **Museum of Zakopane Style** (closed Monday and Tuesday). Half a kilometre south-east, on ul

Kasprusie, is the **Villa Atma**, once the home of Szymanowski, today a museum (closed Monday) dedicated to the composer. Piano recitals are held here in summer.

The striking assemblages of Polish avant-garde artist Władysław Hasior can be seen at the **Hasior Art Gallery** (closed Monday and Tuesday), ul Jagiellońska 7, near the train station. A 20 minute walk south of here, next to the roundabout called Rondo, is the **Tatra National Park Museum** (closed Sunday) with an exhibition on the natural history of the park.

A short walk east up the hill will lead you to the **Villa Pod Jedlami**, another splendid house in the Zakopane style (the interior cannot be visited). Perhaps Witkiewicz's greatest achievement is the **Jaszczurówka Chapel**, about 1.5km farther east on the road to Morskie Oko.

Funicular to Mt Gubałówka

Mt Gubałówka (1120m) offers an excellent view over the Tatras and is a favourite destination for those tourists who don't feel like exercising their legs too much. The funicular, built in 1938, provides comfortable access to the top. It covers the 1388m-long route in less than five minutes, climbing 300m at the same time ($2.50 return trip).

Cable Car to Mt Kasprowy Wierch

Since it opened in 1935, almost every Polish tourist has made the cable car trip from Kuźnice to the summit of Mt Kasprowy Wierch (1985m) where you can stand with one foot in Poland and the other foot in Slovakia. The route is 4290m long with an intermediate station midway at Mt Myślenickie Turnie (1352m). The one-way journey takes 20 minutes, and you climb 936m in that time.

There's a great view from the top, clouds permitting, and also a restaurant. Many people return to Zakopane on foot down the Gąsienicowa Valley, and the most intrepid walk the ridges all the way across to Lake Morskie Oko via Pięć Stawów, a strenuous hike taking a full day in good weather.

The cable car normally operates from about mid-December to mid-May and from early June to late October (take these dates as a rough guide only). In midsummer it runs from 7.30 am to 8 pm; in winter from 7.30 am to 4 pm.

The one-way/return ticket costs $5/7. If you buy a return, your trip back is automatically reserved two hours after departure time. Tickets can be bought at the Kuźnice cableway station (for the same day only). You can also buy them in advance from Orbis and some other travel agencies, but normally only if you purchase some of their services. At peak tourist times (both summer and winter), tickets run out fast and there are usually long lines in Kuźnice; get there early. PKS buses go to Kuźnice frequently from the bus terminal, and there are also private minibuses that park in front of the Bar FIS.

Hiking in the Tatras

If you plan on hiking in the Tatras, get a copy of the *Tatrzański Park Narodowy* map, which shows all the walking trails in the area. In July and August, the Tatras can be overrun by tourists. Late spring and early autumn seem to be the best times to visit. Theoretically at least, you can expect better weather in autumn (September to October) when the rainfall is lower than in spring.

Like all alpine mountains, the Tatras can be dangerous, particularly during the snowy period, which is roughly November to May. Use common sense and go easy. Remember that the weather can be tricky, with snow or rain, thunderstorms, fog, strong wind etc occurring frequently and unpredictably. Bring good footwear, warm clothing and rain gear.

There are several picturesque small valleys south of Zakopane, the **Dolina Strążyska** being arguably the nicest. You can return the same way or transfer by the black trail to either of the neighbouring valleys. You can also go from the Strążyska by the red trail up to **Mt Giewont** (1909m, 3½ hours from Zakopane), and then walk down on the blue trail to Kuźnice in two hours.

EXCURSIONS

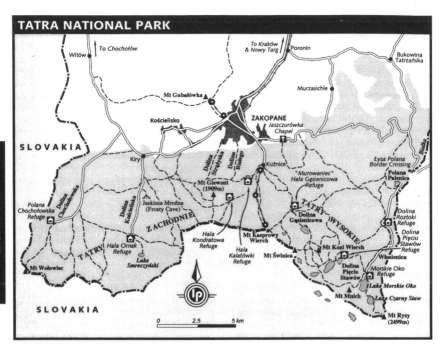

TATRA NATIONAL PARK

There are two long and beautiful forested valleys, the **Dolina Chochołowska** and the **Dolina Kościeliska**, in the western part of the park, known as Tatry Zachodnie (West Tatras). Each valley has a mountain refuge if you want to eat or stay for the night. Visit the **Jaskinia Mroźna** (Frosty Cave). Both valleys are serviced by PKS buses and private minibuses from Zakopane.

The Tatry Wysokie (High Tatras) to the east offer quite different scenery: a land of bare granite peaks with glacial lakes at their feet. One way to get there is to take the cable car to **Mt Kasprowy Wierch** and head eastward along the red trail to Mt Świnica (2301m), and on to the Zawrat pass (2½ hours from Mt Kasprowy). From Zawrat you can descend either north to the Dolina Gąsienicowa along the blue trail and back to Zakopane, or south (also by the blue trail) to the wonderful **Dolina Pięciu Stawów** (Five Lakes' Valley) where you'll find a mountain refuge (1¼ hours from

Zawrat). The blue trail heading west from the refuge will bring you to the emerald-green **Lake Morskie Oko** (Eye of the Sea), acclaimed as among the loveliest in the Tatras (1½ hours from the refuge).

A far easier way of getting to Morskie Oko is by road from Zakopane, and this is one of the most popular tourist trips in the Tatras. Hence, the lake is swamped with visitors in peak season, particularly July and August. PKS buses and private minibuses depart from Zakopane for the lake regularly and go as far as the car park at the Polana Palenica ($1.25, 30 minutes). From there a road continues uphill to the lake (9km), but no cars, bikes or buses are allowed farther up. You can walk the distance in two hours (it isn't steep), or you can take a horse-drawn carriage that brings you to Włosienica, 2km from the lake.

Horse-drawn carriages leave when they collect 15 people. The trip takes about 1¼ hours uphill and costs $7; to come down takes 45 minutes and costs $5. In summer, carriages go up until about 4 or 5 pm and return up to around 8 pm. In winter, transport is by horse-drawn four-seater sledges, which are more expensive than carriages.

The Morskie Oko mountain refuge at the lakeside serves hearty *bigos* (sauerkraut with meat) and drinks. A stone path circling the lake provides a lovely stroll (40 minutes). You can climb to the upper lake, Czarny Staw, in another 20 minutes or so. The trail continues steeply up to the top of **Mt Rysy** (2499m). In late summer, when the snow has finally gone, you can climb it in about four hours from the refuge.

Special Events

The International Festival of Mountain Folklore in late August is Zakopane's leading cultural event. In July, a series of concerts presenting music by Karol Szymanowski is held in the Villa Atma.

Places to Stay – Zakopane

Zakopane has heaps of places to stay and, except for occasional peaks, finding a bed is no problem. Even if hotels and hostels are full, there will still be some private rooms around. Incidentally, private rooms provide some of the cheapest and best accommodation in town.

As with all seasonal resorts, accommodation prices in Zakopane fluctuate (sometimes considerably) between the high and the off seasons, peaking in February, July, August and late December/early January. The prices in the text are for the high season.

Camping The all-year *Camping Pod Krokwią* (☎ 201 22 56, ul Żeromskiego) has large heated bungalows, each containing several double and triple rooms. They cost $10 per person in July and August (less in other months), but they are often full in that period. To get to the camping ground from the bus and train stations, you can take any bus to Kuźnice or Jaszczurówka and get off at Rondo.

Zakopane has several more camping grounds, including the all-year *Camping*

Harenda (☎ 206 84 06) on the Kraków road; the summer *Camping za Strugiem* (☎ 201 45 66, ul Za Strugiem 39)*; the *Camping u Daniela* (☎ 206 12 96) in Oberconiówka; and the *Auto Camping Comfort* (☎ 201 49 42, ul Kaszelewskiego 7) on the Kościeliska road.

Youth Hostels Zakopane has the year-round *Youth Hostel Szarotka* (☎ 206 62 03, ul Nowotarska 45)*, a 10 minute walk from the centre and the same distance from the stations. With some 250 beds (mostly in eight to 12-bed dorms), this is one of the largest hostels in the country, but it can still get packed, far exceeding its capacity in the high season. The hostel is frequently used by school groups.

The all-year *Schronisko Młodzieżowe Żak* (☎ 201 57 06, ul Marusarzówny 15) is in a quiet, verdant south-western suburb of the town. Run by Almatur, it's not a regular PTSM youth hostel, but it works on similar principles and costs the same. It has seven small dorms ($5 a bed) and two doubles ($6 a bed); bed sheets are $1.50 extra. The place is well run and friendly, and is little known, so it may be easier to find a bed here than in the Szarotka.

Other Hostels The very central 460 bed *Dom Turysty PTTK* (☎ 206 32 07, ☎ 206 32 81, ul Zaruskiego 5) has heaps of rooms of different sizes, mostly dormitories. Doubles/triples with bath cost $32/40, rooms with shower only go for $26/36, and those without bath can be got for $24/30. You can stay in a dorm with four/eight/28 beds for $8/6/5 per head. Like the Szarotka, the place can often be swamped with excited crowds of pre-teens. There's an 11 pm curfew.

Private Rooms The business of private rooms for hire is flourishing. It is run by most travel agencies, including the tourist office, Orbis, PTTK, Tatry and Kozica (see the Information section earlier). In the peak season, they probably won't want to fix up accommodation for a period shorter than three nights, but in the off season, this shouldn't apply. Expect a bed in a double room to cost $6 to $10 in the peak season. Check the location before deciding.

In season, there are usually quite a few locals hanging around the bus and train stations, who approach arriving passengers to offer them rooms in their homes. The prices given up-front may sometimes be absurdly inflated (particularly for foreigners), but they can be swiftly negotiated down to the normal level. As a rule, you shouldn't pay more than when renting a room through an agency. Again, check the location before setting out.

Many locals don't bother to hunt for arriving tourists; they simply put boards reading *pokoje*, *noclegi* or *zimmer frei* outside their homes. You'll find many such signs throughout the town. You'll also see a number of places called 'pensjonat' (pension), which may offer better facilities, but are usually more expensive and may insist on selling a bed-and-board package.

Holiday Homes There are plenty of holiday homes in Zakopane. These days, most of them are open to the general public, renting rooms either directly or through travel agencies. The major agent is FWP (☎ 201 27 63) which has its office in the DW Podhale at ul Kościuszki 19. It's open weekdays from 8 am to 5 pm (also on Saturday in season).

The office rents rooms in 11 FWP holiday homes scattered around the town. Rooms range from doubles to quads; some have private bath, while others don't. You can take just a room or room with board (three meals). As a rough guide, in July and August a bed in rooms without/with bath will cost $12/20; in the off season it will be $8/12. Add $10 for full board. One-night stays are OK.

Hotels Given the abundance of private rooms and holiday homes, plus other cheap options, few travellers bother to look at the hotels, which are perhaps more comfortable and offer more facilities, but are more expensive. There are a number of them including four central establishments: the *Hotel Gazda* (☎ 201 50 11, ul Zaruskiego 2); the Orbis-run *Hotel Giewont* (☎ 201 20 11, ul Kościuszki 1); *Hotel Kasprowy Wierch*

(☎ 201 27 38, ul Krupówki 50B); and the *Hotel Helios* (☎ 201 38 08, ul Słoneczna 2A). Any of these will cost around $40/60 for a single/double ($30/50 off season).

Places to Stay – Tatra National Park

Mountain Refuges Camping is not allowed in the park but there are eight PTTK mountain refuges, which provide simple accommodation ($5 to $8 per person in a dorm or $20 to $30 per double room). Most refuges are pretty small and fill up fast. In both midsummer and midwinter they are invariably packed far beyond capacity. No one is ever turned away, though you may have to crash on the bare floor. Don't arrive too late and bring along your own bed mat and sleeping bag. All refuges serve simple hot meals, but their kitchens and dining rooms close early, in some places at 7 pm.

The refuges are open year-round but some may be temporarily closed for repairs, usually in November. Before you set off, check the current situation at the PTTK office in Zakopane, which runs the refuges.

The easiest refuge to get to from Zakopane is the large and decent *Hala Kalatówki Refuge* (84 beds), a 30 minute walk from the Kuźnice cable-car station. Half an hour beyond Kalatówki on the trail to Giewont is the *Hala Kondratowa Refuge* (20 beds). For location and atmosphere it's great, but note the small size.

Hikers wishing to traverse the park might begin at the *Dolina Roztoki Refuge* (96 beds), accessible via the Morskie Oko bus. An early start from Zakopane, however, would allow you to visit Morskie Oko in the morning and stay at the *Morskie Oko Refuge*, or continue through to the *Dolina Pięciu Stawów Refuge* (70 beds). This is the highest (1700m) and the most scenically located refuge in the Polish Tatras. A leisurely day's walk north-west of Pięć Stawów is the *Murowaniec Hala Gąsienicowa Refuge* (100 beds), from which you can return to Zakopane. The Pięć Stawów and Hala Gąsienicowa are the most crowded refuges.

Don't try to take off in these old tubs at the Polish Aviation Museum. Nowa Huta is in the distance.

Fabulous Witkacy Theatre in Zakopane, named after the creator of Poland's Theatre of the Absurd.

People pay their respects with flowers and candles on All Saints Day at the Military Cemetery.

'Relax. You don't have to row back up the Dunajec Gorge. The rafts come apart to be trucked back.

Lake Morskie Oko in the Tatra Mountains.

Villa Koliba, a first design in the Zakopane style.

In the western part of the park are the **Hala Ornak Refuge** (75 beds) and **Polana Chochołowska Refuge** (161 beds), connected by trail.

Places to Eat

The central mall, ul Krupówki, boasts heaps of eateries, everything from hamburger stands to well appointed establishments. The proliferation of small fast-food outlets is astonishing, and there are also plenty of informal places in private homes in the back streets, displaying boards saying 'obiady domowe' (home-cooked lunches).

Among the cheapest places are the basic **Bar Mleczny** *(ul Krupówki 1)*; the **Bar Rzepka** *(ul Krupówki 43)*; the **Bistro Grota** *(ul Kościuszki 5)*; and the **Bufet** *(ul Kościuszki 13)* in the building of the Urząd Miasta (local government headquarters).

Slightly more expensive is the **Restauracja Świarna** *(ul Kościuszki 4)*. If you have arrived hungry by bus or train, the large drab **Bar FIS** can prove an emergency option for you.

The folksy **Stek Chałupa** *(ul Krupówki 33)* has popular Polish dishes at low prices. **Restauracja Pizzeria Kolorowa** has been totally revamped and is now a pleasant place to eat, and not only for pizza. **Morskie Oko**, a few steps up the mall, is a large food centre, with a vast restaurant in the basement.

There's a fair choice of reasonable restaurants serving typical Polish regional food, most of which are decorated accordingly and even the waiters are decked out in regional costumes.

Going from north to south, you have **Karczma Redykołka** *(ul Krupówki 2)*; **Restauracja Zbyrcok** *(ul Krupówki 29)*; **Karczma Janosik** *(ul Krupówki 35)*; and, probably the best of its kind, **Karczma Obrochtówka** *(ul Kraszewskiego 10A)*.

Don't miss trying the smoked sheep's-milk cheese sold at street stands all along ul Krupówki.

Entertainment

The **Teatr Witkacego** *(Witkacy Theatre; ul Chramcówki 15)* is one of the best theatres in Poland.

Getting There & Away

Most regional routes are covered by bus; the train is useful only for long-distance travel – to Warsaw for example.

Train There are several trains to Kraków (147km) but buses are faster and run more frequently. One train daily (in season two) runs to Warsaw (444km). Tickets are available from the station or from Orbis at ul Krupówki 22.

Bus The PKS fast buses run to Kraków (104km) every hour; the trip costs $3.50 and takes 2½ hours. There are also nine buses a day to Kraków operated by a private company (departing from ul Kościuszki 19). They are cheaper ($3) and a bit faster. Tickets are available from the office next to Kozica travel agency. PKS has introduced a useful direct bus to Kąty (for the Dunajec raft trip).

In the region around Zakopane, bus transport is relatively frequent. PKS buses can take you to the foot of the Kościeliska and Chochołowska valleys as well as to Polana Palenica near Lake Morskie Oko. There are also private minibuses leaving from in front of Bar FIS, which ply the most popular tourist routes.

There are a couple of buses per week to Budapest ($16; nine hours) and a daily morning bus to Poprad in Slovakia ($3), where you can catch the express train to Prague, departing around 11 am and arriving about 6.30 pm. You can also take any of the Polana Palenica PKS buses or private minibuses; get off at Łysa Polana (22km), cross the border on foot and continue by bus (regular transport) to Tatranská Lomnica (30km). Southbound this route is easy but northbound you could find the Polana Palenica bus to Zakopane crowded with day-trippers from Morskie Oko (and the taxi drivers want 20 times the bus fare).

DUNAJEC GORGE

Every year tens of thousands of people go rafting on the Dunajec River, along a stretch where the river cuts through the Pieniny Mountains just before turning north to flow towards the Vistula. The river runs along the Polish-Slovakian border here, winding through a spectacular deep gorge with high cliffs on both sides. The mix of deciduous trees and conifers makes lovely patterns of colour. This is not a white-water experience; the rapids are gentle and you won't get wet.

The trip begins in Kąty, and after a 15km journey you disembark in the spa town of Szczawnica. The 2½ hour raft trips operate from May to October with rafts leaving as soon as 10 people sign up ($8 per person). Each 10 seat raft consists of five wooden coffin-like sections lashed together, guided by two boatmen dressed in embroidered folk costumes. In Szczawnica, the sections are taken apart, loaded onto a truck and carried back to Kąty.

Dunajec raft trips are also offered from Ćervenÿ Kláštor in Slovakia, but the Slovakian trips are shorter and not as easily arranged.

Getting There & Away

The Dunajec Gorge is an easy day trip from Zakopane. Take the direct PKS bus from Zakopane to Kąty ($1.75). Alternatively, go to Nowy Targ (frequent service; 24km; 30 minutes; $1), then take one of the six daily Sromowce Niżne buses from Nowy Targ to Kąty (31km; one hour; $1). The landing at Kąty is fairly obvious with a large parking lot and a pavilion housing the ticket office and a snack bar.

At Szczawnica, where the trip ends, you can take the direct PKS bus back to Zakopane, or catch one of the 25 daily buses to Nowy Targ (38km; $1) and change there for a bus to Zakopane.

If you go to Nowy Targ, it is worth your while to stop midway at the village of Dębno Podhalańskie, to visit one of Poland's best timber Gothic churches.

There are five fast buses from Szczawnica direct to Kraków (118km), and a regular bus service to Nowy Sącz (48km).

There are plenty of tours organised from Zakopane; they include the raft trip and visits to the church in Dębno Podhalańskie and the ruined castle in Czorsztyn. They cost $16, which is a fair deal.

CZĘSTOCHOWA
☏ 034

Częstochowa, north-west of Kraków, is the spiritual heart of Poland and the country's national shrine. It owes its fame to the miraculous icon of the Black Madonna, kept in Jasna Góra (Bright Mountain) Monastery, which has been visited by pilgrims from all corners of the country and beyond for centuries. Today, Częstochowa attracts some of the largest pilgrimages in the world.

The monastery was founded in 1382 by the Paulites of Hungary, and the Black Madonna was brought soon after. The holy icon was damaged in 1430 by the Hussites, who slashed the face of the Madonna and broke the wooden panel. The picture was restored and repainted, but the scars on the face of the Virgin Mary were left as a reminder of the sacrilege.

Early in the 17th century the monastery was fortified, and it became one of the few places in the country which withstood the Swedish sieges of the 1650s, the miracle naturally being attributed to the Black Madonna and this contributing to still larger floods of pilgrims. In 1717 the Black Madonna was crowned the Queen of Poland.

After WWII, in an attempt to overshadow its religious status, the communists built Częstochowa into a major industrial centre. Today it's a city of 260,000 people which has a large steelworks and a number of other factories complete with a forest of smoky chimneys. Amid them, however, the tower of the Paulite monastery still proudly overlooks the city, showing pilgrims the way to the end of their journey.

Orientation

The main thoroughfare in the city centre is Al Najświętszej Marii Panny (or Al NMP), a wide, tree-lined avenue with Jasna Góra Monastery and the Black Madonna at its western end and St Sigismund's Church at the eastern end. Both the train and bus stations are south of the eastern part of Al NMP. It's about a 20 minute walk from either station to the monastery.

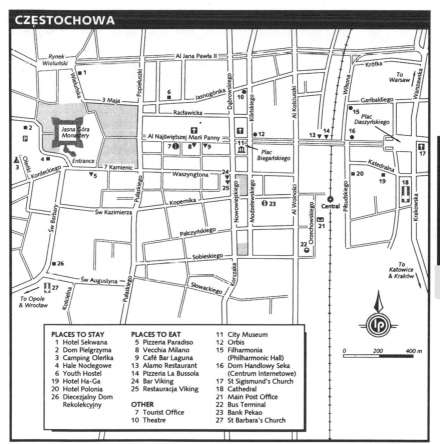

CZĘSTOCHOWA

PLACES TO STAY	PLACES TO EAT	11 City Museum
1 Hotel Sekwana	5 Pizzeria Paradiso	12 Orbis
2 Dom Pielgrzyma	8 Vecchia Milano	15 Filharmonia
3 Camping Oleńka	9 Café Bar Laguna	(Philharmonic Hall)
4 Hale Noclegowe	13 Alamo Restaurant	16 Dom Handlowy Seka
6 Youth Hostel	14 Pizzeria La Bussola	(Centrum Internetowe)
19 Hotel Ha-Ga	24 Bar Viking	17 St Sigismund's Church
20 Hotel Polonia	25 Restauracja Viking	18 Cathedral
26 Diecezjalny Dom		21 Main Post Office
Rekolekcyjny	OTHER	22 Bus Terminal
	7 Tourist Office	23 Bank Pekao
	10 Theatre	27 St Barbara's Church

Information

Tourist Office The Centrum Informacji Turystycznej (☎ 324 13 60, ☎/fax 324 34 12), Al NMP 65, is open each weekday from 9 am to 6 pm, Saturday from 10 am to 6 pm and Sunday (between 15 April and 15 October) from 10 am to 6 pm. The office is well stocked with maps from all over the country.

Money You'll find kantors and ATMs on Al NMP. Bank Pekao at ul Kopernika 19 changes travellers cheques and gives cash advances on Visa and MasterCard.

Cybercafés The Centrum Internetowe (☎ 366 48 13) is situated on the top floor of the Dom Handlowy Seka at Al NMP 12D. It is open daily till 10 pm.

Things to See

A vibrant symbol of Catholicism in a secular sea, **Jasna Góra Monastery** retains the appearance of a fortress. Inside the compound are a number of buildings including a church, a chapel and the monastery. The large baroque church you enter first is beautifully decorated, but the image of the Black Madonna is on the high altar of the adjacent chapel. Upstairs in the monastery is the Knights' Hall (Sala Rycerska) where you can examine a copy of the icon up close.

There are also three museums to visit within the defensive walls (all open daily): the Arsenal with a variety of old weapons; the 600th Anniversary Museum (Muzeum Sześćsetlecia) containing Lech Wałęsa's 1983 Nobel Peace Prize; and the Treasury (Skarbiec) featuring votive offerings presented by the faithful. You can also climb the monastery tower (the tallest church tower in Poland at 106m), open daily from April to November.

On weekends and holidays there are long lines to enter all three museums, and the crowds in the chapel may be so thick you're almost unable to enter, much less get near the icon.

The **City Museum** (closed Monday) in the old town hall (1828) on Plac Biegańskiego has an ethnographic collection and modern Polish painting, plus some temporary exhibitions.

Special Events

The major Marian feasts at Jasna Góra are 3 May, 16 July, 15 August, 26 August, 8 September, 12 September and 8 December, and on these days the monastery is packed with pilgrims. Particularly celebrated is the Assumption (15 August) when pilgrims come on foot to Częstochowa from all over Poland. Up to half a million of the faithful can flock to Jasna Góra for this feast.

Places to Stay

The all-year **Camping Oleńka** (☎ 324 74 95, ul Oleńki 10/30) near the monastery is good and has chalets. Rooms are $5/10 a single/double without bath, $23/30/37 for three/four/five people with bath, or you can pitch your tent for $3 per person. There's an inexpensive snack bar on the grounds.

The **youth hostel** (☎ 324 31 21, ul Jasnogórska 84/90) is also close to the monastery, but it's open only in July and August and has modest facilities.

Some of the cheapest accommodation available is provided by the Church-run **Hale Noclegowe** (☎ 365 66 88 ext 224, ul

TAMSIN WILSON

The miraculous Black Madonna, held at the Jasna Góra Monastery.

Klasztorna 1), just next to the monastery. You pay $3.50 per person for a four to nine-bed dorm with shared facilities and cold water only, and must be inside before the 10 pm curfew.

The Church's better lodging facility is **Dom Pielgrzyma** (Pilgrim's Home; ☎ 324 70 11), right behind the monastery. This large hostel has singles/doubles/triples with bath for $15/18/25, or you can pay $5 for a bed in a quad without bath. The door closes at 10 pm. There's a cafeteria on the premises. The **Diecezjalny Dom Rekolekcyjny** (☎ 324 11 77, ul Św Barbary 43), a 10 minute walk south of the monastery, offers similar conditions and also has a curfew.

The best place to stay in the monastery area is the small **Hotel Sekwana** (☎ 324 89 54, ul Wieluńska 24), which costs $40/60 a single/double with bath.

There are a few hotels close to the train station, including the *Hotel Ha-Ga* (☎ *324 61 73, ul Katedralna 9)*. It has singles/doubles/triples/quads with shared facilities for $13/15/18/20 and rooms with bath attached for $18/22/25/28. The best around here is *Hotel Polonia (also called Centralny*; ☎ *324 23 88, ul Piłsudskiego 9)*, opposite the station. It has been renovated and now costs $33/40/50/60 with bath and breakfast.

Places to Eat
In the monastery area, apart from the above-mentioned cafeteria of the *Dom Pielgrzyma* and the *Bar Oleńka* at the camping ground, there's a line of fast-food outlets on ul 7 Kamienic, including the pleasant *Pizzeria Paradiso*.

There are also quite a number of inexpensive eateries along Al NMP, including the *Café Bar Laguna (Al NMP 57)*; *Alamo Restaurant (Al NMP 16)*; and the *Pizzeria La Bussola* next door. Some of the best ice cream and cappuccinos in town can be found at the *Vecchia Milano (Al NMP 59)*.

The upmarket *Restauracja Viking (ul Nowowiejskiego 10)* is one of the best places to eat in the centre. It also runs the inexpensive *Bar Viking* just round the corner, which is good and has a few tables on the terrace.

The *Hotel Sekwana* has a pleasant and reasonably priced French restaurant – good value.

Getting There & Away
The new, purpose-built train station on ul Piłsudskiego handles half a dozen fast trains to Warsaw (235km) and about the same number of fast trains to Kraków (132km). Trains run every hour or so to Katowice (86km) from where there are connections to Kraków and Wrocław.

The bus terminal is close to the central train station. Buses departing from here include three daily to Kraków (114km), three to Wrocław (176km) and there is one bus to Zakopane (222km).

EXCURSIONS

Language

Polish is a western variety of the Slavonic languages (found in central and eastern Europe), such as Croatian, Czech, Russian, Serbian, Slovak and Slovene. It is the official national language of Poland and is spoken by over 99% of the population.

In medieval Poland, Latin was the lingua franca and the official language of Church and State. The Latin alphabet was adopted for written Polish but in order to represent the complex sounds of the language a number of diacritical marks had to be added. The visual appearance of Polish is pretty fearsome for people outside the Slavic circle, and it's no doubt a difficult language to master. It has a complicated grammar, with word endings changing depending on case, number and gender, and the rules abound with exceptions.

The Polish Alphabet

Polish letters with diacritical marks are treated as separate letters, and the order of the Polish alphabet is as follows:

a ą b c ć d e ę f g h i j k l ł m n ń o ó p (q) r s ś t u (v) w (x) y z ź ż

The letters **q**, **v** and **x** appear only in words of foreign origin.

Pronunciation

Written Polish is phonetically consistent, which means that the pronunciation of letters or clusters of letters doesn't vary from word to word. The stress almost always goes on the second-last syllable.

Vowels

Polish vowels are pure, consisting of one sound only, and are of roughly even length. Their approximate pronunciation is as follows:

a	as the 'u' in 'cut'
e	as in 'ten'
i	similar to the 'ee' in 'feet' but shorter
o	as in 'not'
u	as in 'put'
y	similar to the 'i' in 'bit'

There are three vowels which are common only to Polish:

ą	a highly nasalised vowel; a cross between the 'awn' in 'lawn' and the 'ong' in 'long'
ę	also highly nasalised; like the 'eng' in 'engage' (where the 'ng' is one sound, not 'n' followed by 'g'); pronounced as **e** when word-final
ó	the same as Polish **u**

Consonants

Most Polish consonants are pronounced as in English. However, there are some very fine distinctions between certain consonants in Polish which English speakers may find difficult to produce. The following guide gives approximations only of the correct pronunciation – your best bet is to listen to and learn from native speakers:

c	as the 'ts' in 'its'
ch	similar to 'ch' in Scottish *loch*
cz	as the 'ch' in 'church'
ć	similar to **c** but pronounced with the tongue a little further back on the roof of the mouth; pronounced as 'tsi' before vowels
dz	as the 'ds' in 'adds up'
dź	similar to **dz** but pronounced with the tongue a little further back on the roof of the mouth; pronounced as 'dzi' before vowels
dż	as the 'j' in 'jam'
g	as in 'get'
h	the same as **ch**
j	as the 'y' in 'yet'
ł	as the 'w' in 'wine'
ń	as the 'ni' in 'onion'; written as 'ni' before vowels

r	always trilled
rz	as the 's' in 'pleasure'
s	as in 'set'
sz	as the 'sh' in 'show'
ś	similar to s but not as strident; written as 'si' before vowels
w	as the 'v' in 'van'
ź	similar to z but not as strident; written as 'zi' before vowels
ż	the same as rz
szcz	the most awful-looking cluster – it's pronounced as the 'shch' in 'fresh cheese'

The following consonants are unvoiced when they are word-final: **b** is pronounced as **p**, **d** as **t**, **g** as **k**, **w** as **f**, **z** as **s** and **rz** as **sz**.

Finally, here's the favourite Polish tongue-twister for you to test your pronunciation skills on: *Chrząszcz brzmi w trzcinie* (The cockchafer buzzes in the weeds).

Greetings & Civilities

Good morning.	*Dzień dobry.*
Good evening.	*Dobry wieczór.*
Hello.	*Cześć.* (informal)
Goodbye.	*Do widzenia.*
Good night.	*Dobranoc.*
Yes.	*Tak.*
No.	*Nie.*
Please.	*Proszę.*
Thank you (very much).	*Dziękuję (bardzo).*
You're welcome.	*Proszę.*
How are you?	*Jak się Pan/ Pani miewa?* (m/f)
Very well, thank you.	*Dziękuję, bardzo dobrze.*
May I?	*Czy mogę?*
Excuse me/ I'm sorry.	*Przepraszam.*
OK.	*Dobrze.*

Basics

I	*ja*
you	*ty*
he/she	*on/ona*
we	*my*
you	*wy*
they	*oni/one*

What?	*Co?*
Where?	*Gdzie?*
When?	*Kiedy?*
Who?	*Kto?*
Why?	*Dlaczego?*
How?	*Jak?*
and	*i*
Mrs/Madam	*Pani*
Mister/Sir	*Pan*

Language Difficulties

Do you speak English?	*Czy Pan/Pani mówi po angielsku?* (m/f)
Does anyone here speak English?	*Czy ktoś tu mówi po angielsku?*
I don't speak Polish.	*Nie mówię po polsku.*
I understand.	*Rozumiem.*
I don't understand.	*Nie rozumiem.*
Please speak more slowly.	*Proszę mówić wolniej.*
Could you repeat that please?	*Proszę to powtórzyć.*
What does it mean?	*Co to znaczy?*
Please write that down.	*Proszę to napisać.*
How do you pronounce it?	*Jak się to wymawia?*

Getting Around

What time does the ... leave/ arrive?	*O której godzinie przychodzi/ odchodzi ...?*
plane	*samolot*
boat	*statek*
bus	*autobus*
train	*pociąg*
tram	*tramwaj*

Where is (the) ...?	*Gdzie jest ...?*
airport	*lotnisko*
train station	*stacja kolejowa*
bus station	*dworzec autobusowy*
bus stop	*przystanek autobusowy*
petrol station	*stacja benzynowa*

Two tickets to ... please.	*Poproszę dwa bilety do ...*

ticket	*bilet*
ticket office	*kasa biletowa*
timetable	*rozkład jazdy*
1st/2nd class	*pierwsza/druga klasa*
next	*następny*
first	*pierwszy*
last	*ostatni*
arrival	*przyjazd*
departure	*odjazd*
left-luggage room	*przechowalnia bagażu*
taxi	*taksówka*

How can I get to ...?	*Jak się dostać do ...?*
How far is it?	*Jak to daleko stąd?*
Please show me on the map.	*Proszę pokazać mi to na mapie.*
Turn left.	*Proszę skręcić w lewo.*
Turn right.	*Proszę skręcić w prawo.*
Go straight ahead.	*Proszę iść prosto.*

Where can I hire a ...?	*Gdzie mogę wypożyczyć ...?*
car	*samochód*
motorbike	*motocykl*
bicycle	*rower*

Out & About

town, city	*miasto*
village	*wieś*
road	*szosa, droga*
street	*ulica*
city centre	*centrum*
bridge	*most*
castle	*zamek*
cathedral	*katedra*
church	*kościół*
embassy	*ambasada*
monastery	*klasztor*
monument	*pomnik*
museum	*muzeum*
old town	*stare miasto*
old town square	*rynek*
open-air museum	*skansen*
palace	*pałac*
police station	*posterunek policji*
public toilet	*toaleta publiczna*
square	*plac*

Signs

WEJŚCIE	ENTRANCE
WYJŚCIE	EXIT
INFORMACJA	INFORMATION
OTWARTE	OPEN
ZAMKNIĘTE	CLOSED
WZBRONIONY	PROHIBITED
POSTERUNEK POLICJI	POLICE STATION
TOALETY	TOILETS
PANOWIE	MEN
PANIE	WOMEN

synagogue	*synagoga*
town hall	*ratusz*
university	*uniwersytet*
beach	*plaża*
cave	*jaskinia*
coast	*wybrzeże*
forest	*las/puszcza*
island	*wyspa*
lake	*jezioro*
mountain	*góra*
river	*rzeka*
valley	*dolina*
waterfall	*wodospad*

Accommodation

Do you have any rooms available?	*Czy są wolne pokoje?*
May I see the room?	*Czy mogę zobaczyć pokój?*
How much is it?	*Ile kosztuje?*
Does it include breakfast?	*Czy śniadanie jest wliczone?*

hotel	*hotel*
youth hostel	*schronisko młodzieżowe*
room	*pokój*
dormitory	*sala zbiorowa*
bathroom	*łazienka*
bed	*łóżko*
key	*klucz*
sheets	*pościel*
shower	*prysznic/natrysk*
toilet	*toaleta*

clean/dirty	*czysty/brudny*
good/poor, bad	*dobry/niedobry*
noisy/quiet	*głośny/cichy*
hot/cold	*gorący/zimny*

Post & Communications

post office	*poczta*
postcard	*pocztówka*
letter	*list*
parcel	*paczka*
stamp	*znaczek*
air mail	*poczta lotnicza*
registered letter	*list polecony*
letter box	*skrzynka pocztowa*
international call	*rozmowa międzynarodowa*
long distance call	*rozmowa międzymiastowa*
public telephone	*automat telefoniczny*
telephone card	*karta telefoniczna*
token	*żeton*

Money

bank	*bank*
money	*pieniądze*
cash	*gotówka*
travellers cheque	*czek podróżny*
commission	*prowizja*
credit card	*karta kredytowa*
ATM	*bankomat*

Shopping

Do you have ...?	*Czy są ...?*
How much is it?	*Ile to kosztuje?*
I (don't) like it.	*(Nie) podoba mi się.*
shop	*sklep*
shopping centre	*centrum handlowe*
market	*targ/bazar*
pharmacy	*apteka*
price	*cena*
cheap/expensive	*tani/drogi*
big/small	*duży/mały*
many/much	*dużo*
a few	*kilka*
a little	*trochę*
enough	*wystarczy*
more/less	*więcej/mniej*

Food

I'm a vegetarian.	*Jestem jaroszem.*
the bill	*rachunek*
cup	*filiżanka*
dish	*danie*
fork	*widelec*
glass	*szklanka*
knife	*nóż*
menu	*jadłospis*
plate	*talerz*
spoon	*łyżka*
teaspoon	*łyżeczka*
bread	*chleb*
butter	*masło*
egg	*jajko*
fish	*ryba*
fruit	*owoce*
ham	*szynka*
meat	*mięso*
milk	*mleko*
pepper	*pieprz*
potatoes	*ziemniaki*
rice	*ryż*
salad	*sałatka, surówka*
salt	*sól*
sandwich	*kanapka*
sausage	*kiełbasa*
sugar	*cukier*
vegetables	*warzywa, jarzyny*
water	*woda*

Time & Date

What is the time?	*Która godzina?*
time	*czas*
minute	*minuta*
hour	*godzina*
day	*dzień*
week	*tydzień*
month	*miesiąc*
year	*rok*
now	*teraz*
today	*dzisiaj, dziś*
tonight	*dziś wieczorem*
tomorrow	*jutro*
yesterday	*wczoraj*
this week	*w tym tygodniu*
next week	*w przyszłym tygodniu*
last week	*w zeszłym tygodniu*
morning	*rano*
afternoon	*popołudnie*

Emergencies

Please call a doctor/the police.
Proszę wezwać lekarza/policję.
Where is the nearest hospital?
Gdzie jest najbliższy szpital?
Could you help me please?
Proszę mi pomóc.
I don't feel well.
Źle się czuję.
I have a fever.
Mam gorączkę.
Could I use the telephone?
Czy mogę skorzystać z telefonu?
I want to contact my embassy.
Chcę się skontaktować z moją ambasadą.
Please leave me alone!
Proszę mnie zostawić!

accident	*wypadek*
ambulance	*karetka pogotowia*
dentist	*dentysta*
doctor	*lekarz*
hospital	*szpital*
medicine	*lek/lekarstwo*
police	*policja*

evening	*wieczór*
night	*noc*
midday	*południe*
midnight	*północ*
sunrise	*wschód*
sunset	*zachód*

Monday	*poniedziałek*
Tuesday	*wtorek*
Wednesday	*środa*
Thursday	*czwartek*
Friday	*piątek*
Saturday	*sobota*
Sunday	*niedziela*

January	*styczeń*
February	*luty*
March	*marzec*
April	*kwiecień*
May	*maj*
June	*czerwiec*
July	*lipiec*
August	*sierpień*
September	*wrzesień*
October	*październik*
November	*listopad*
December	*grudzień*

summer	*lato*
autumn	*jesień*
winter	*zima*
spring	*wiosna*

Numbers

¼	*jedna czwarta*
½	*jedna druga*
0	*zero*
1	*jeden*
2	*dwa*
3	*trzy*
4	*cztery*
5	*pięć*
6	*sześć*
7	*siedem*
8	*osiem*
9	*dziewięć*
10	*dziesięć*
11	*jedenaście*
12	*dwanaście*
13	*trzynaście*
14	*czternaście*
15	*piętnaście*
16	*szesnaście*
17	*siedemnaście*
18	*osiemnaście*
19	*dziewiętnaście*
20	*dwadzieścia*
21	*dwadzieścia jeden*
22	*dwadzieścia dwa*
30	*trzydzieści*
100	*sto*
1000	*tysiąc*
100,000	*sto tysięcy*

one million	*milion*

1st	*pierwszy*
2nd	*drugi*
3rd	*trzeci*
percent	*procent*
once	*raz*
twice	*dwa razy*
three times	*trzy razy*
often/seldom	*często/rzadko*

Glossary

For further Polish terms, see the Language and the Places to Eat chapters.

Aleja or **Aleje** – avenue, main city street; abbreviated to Al in addresses and on maps
Almatur – the nationwide Student Travel & Tourist Bureau

bankomat – ATM
bar mleczny – milk bar; a self-service basic soup kitchen with mostly vegetarian dishes
barszcz – beetroot soup; one of Poland's national dishes
basen – swimming pool
bigos – sauerkraut and meat; another national dish
bilet – ticket
biuro turystyczne – travel agency
biuro zakwaterowania – office that arranges private accommodation

Cepelia – a network of shops with artefacts by local artisans
cerkiew – (plural *cerkwie*), an Orthodox or Uniate church
cocktail bar – type of café that serves cakes, pastries, milk shakes, ice creams and other sweeties
cukiernia – cake shop

Desa – state-owned chain of old art and antique traders
dla niepalących – for nonsmokers
dom kultury – cultural centre
dom wczasowy or **dom wypoczynkowy** – holiday home
dom wycieczkowy – term applied to PTTK-run hostels
domek campingowy – cabin, bungalow, chalet

grosz – unit of Polish currency, abbreviated to gr; see also *złoty*

jadłodajnia – small budget eatery serving hearty home-cooked meals
jadłospis – menu

kantor – private currency-exchange office
kasa – ticket office
kawiarnia – café
kierunek zwiedzania – direction of sightseeing (a common board in museums)
kino – cinema
kiosk Ruch – newsagency
kolegiata – collegiate church
kort (tenisowy) – (tennis) court
kościół – church
księgarnia – bookshop
kwatery agroturystyczne – agrotourist accommodation; increasingly numerous and popular
kwatery prywatne – rooms in private houses rented out to tourists

Lajkonik – Kraków's legendary figure looking like a Tatar khan on a horse
LOT – Polish Airlines

miejscówka – reserved seat ticket
miód pitny – mead; a traditional Polish beverage made by fermenting malt in honeyed water

na zdrowie! – 'to the health'; what Poles say before drinking; cheers!

odjazdy – departures (on transport schedules)
ogródek – 'small garden'; open-air section of a café, bar and restaurant
Orbis – the largest travel company in Poland
otwarte – open

pensjonat – pension or private guesthouse, usually small
peron – railway platform
piekarnia – bakery
pierogi – dumplings made from noodle dough, stuffed and boiled
piwnica – cellar, often a brick vault dating from medieval times; there are plenty of these in Kraków
PKP (Polskie Koleje Państwowe) – Polish State Railways

PKS (Państwowa Komunikacja Samochodowa) – the state bus company
poczta – post office
Polonia – general term applied to the Polish community living outside Poland
powiat – sub-province; an administrative division
pralnia – dry cleaner, laundry
prowizja – the commission on bank transactions
przechowalnia bagażu – left-luggage room
przewodnik – guide (a person) or guidebook
przychodnia – outpatient clinic
przyjazdy – arrivals (on transport schedules)
PTSM – Polish Youth Hostel Association
PTTK – Polish Tourists Association
PZM or **PZMot** (Polski Związek Motorowy) – Polish Motoring Association

rachunek – bill or check
rozkład jazdy – transport timetable
Rynek – Old Town Square

schronisko górskie – mountain refuge, usually run by PTTK
schronisko młodzieżowe – youth hostel
Sejm – lower house of parliament
skansen – open-air museum of traditional architecture
sklep – shop
smacznego – said before eating; *bon appetit*

specjalność zakładu – on a menu, speciality of the house
stadnina koni – horse stable
stanica wodna – waterside hostel, usually with boats, kayaks and related facilities
stołówka – canteen; restaurant or cafeteria of a hostel etc
szlachta – gentry or feudal nobility in 17th to 18th century Poland
szopka – Nativity scene, usually in a church-like form made of cardboard, tinfoil etc

Święty/a – Saint; abbreviated to Św (St)
Święty Mikołaj – Santa Claus

ulgowy (bilet) – discounted (ticket)
ulica – street; abbreviated to ul in addresses (and placed before the proper name); usually omitted on maps

wódka – vodka; the No 1 Polish brew
województwo – province; an administrative division (there are 16 in Poland), further divided into *powiat*

zakaz palenia – no smoking
zakaz wstępu – no entry
zamknięte – closed
zdrój – spa
złoty – unit of Polish currency; abbreviated to zł; divided into 100 *grosz*
zniżka studencka – student discount

żeton – token used in public telephones
żubr – the European bison

Lonely Planet Journeys

Journeys is a unique collection of travel writing – published by the company that understands travel better than anyone else. It is a series for anyone who has ever experienced – or dreamed of – the magical moment when they encountered a strange culture or saw a place for the first time. They are tales to read while you're planning a trip, while you're on the road or while you're in an armchair in front of a fire.

These outstanding titles explore our planet through the eyes of a diverse group of international writers. JOURNEYS books catch the spirit of a place, illuminate a culture, recount a crazy adventure or introduce a fascinating way of life. They always entertain, and always enrich the experience of travel.

MALI BLUES
Traveling to an African Beat
Lieve Joris (translated by Sam Garrett)

Drought, rebel uprisings, ethnic conflict: these are the predominant images of West Africa. But as Lieve Joris travels in Senegal, Mauritania and Mali, she meets survivors, fascinating individuals charting new ways of living between tradition and modernity. With her remarkable gift for drawing out people's stories, Joris brilliantly captures the rhythms of a world that refuses to give in.

THE GATES OF DAMASCUS
Lieve Joris (translated by Sam Garrett)

This best-selling book is a beautifully drawn portrait of day-to-day life in modern Syria. Through her intimate contact with local people, Lieve Joris draws us into the fascinating world that lies behind the gates of Damascus. Hala's husband is a political prisoner, jailed for his opposition to the Assad regime; through the author's friendship with Hala we see how Syrian politics impacts on the lives of ordinary people.

THE OLIVE GROVE
Travels in Greece
Katherine Kizilos

Katherine Kizilos travels to fabled islands, troubled border zones and her family's village deep in the mountains. She vividly evokes breathtaking landscapes, generous people and passionate politics, capturing the complexities of a country she loves.

'**beautifully captures the real tensions of Greece**' – *Sunday Times*

KINGDOM OF THE FILM STARS
Journey into Jordan
Annie Caulfield

Kingdom of the Film Stars is a travel book and a love story. With honesty and humour, Annie Caulfield writes of travelling in Jordan and falling in love with a Bedouin with film-star looks.

She offers fascinating insights into the country – from the tent life of traditional women to the hustle of downtown Amman – and unpicks tight-woven western myths about the Arab world.

LONELY PLANET

Phrasebooks

L onely Planet phrasebooks are packed with essential words and phrases to help travellers communicate with the locals. With colour tabs for quick reference, an extensive vocabulary and use of script, these handy pocket-sized language guides cover day-to-day travel situations.

- handy pocket-sized books
- easy to understand Pronunciation chapter
- clear & comprehensive Grammar chapter
- romanisation alongside script to allow ease of pronunciation
- script throughout so users can point to phrases for every situation
- full of cultural information and tips for the traveller

'... vital for a real DIY spirit and attitude in language learning'
— *Backpacker*

'the phrasebooks have good cultural backgrounders and offer solid advice for challenging situations in remote locations'
— *San Francisco Examiner*

Arabic (Egyptian) ● Arabic (Moroccan) ● Australian *(Australian English, Aboriginal and Torres Strait languages)* ● Baltic States *(Estonian, Latvian, Lithuanian)* ● Bengali ● Brazilian ● British ● Burmese ● Cantonese ● Central Asia (Uyghur, Uzbek, Kyrghiz, Kazak, Pashto, Tadjik ● Central Europe *(Czech, French, German, Hungarian, Italian, Slovak)* ● Eastern Europe *(Bulgarian, Czech, Hungarian, Polish, Romanian, Slovak)* ● Ethiopian (Amharic) ● Fijian ● French ● German ● Greek ● Hebrew ● Hill Tribes ● Hindi & Urdu ● Indonesian ● Italian ● Japanese ● Korean ● Lao ● Latin American Spanish ● Malay ● Mandarin ● Mediterranean Europe *(Albanian, Croatian, Greek, Italian, Macedonian, Maltese, Serbian, Slovene)* ● Mongolian ● Nepali ● Pidgin ● Pilipino (Tagalog) ● Quechua ● Russian ● Scandinavian Europe *(Danish, Finnish, Icelandic, Norwegian, Swedish)* ● South-East Asia *(Burmese, Indonesian, Khmer, Lao, Malay, Tagalog Pilipino, Thai, Vietnamese)* ● South Pacific Languages ● Spanish (Castilian) *(also includes Catalan, Galician and Basque)* ● Sri Lanka ● Swahili ● Thai ● Tibetan ● Turkish ● Ukrainian ● USA *(US English, Vernacular, Native American languages, Hawaiian)* ● Vietnamese ● Western Europe *(Basque, Catalan, Dutch, French, German, Greek, Irish, Italian, Portuguese, Scottish Gaelic, Spanish (Castilian), Welsh)*

LONELY PLANET

Lonely Planet Travel Atlases

L onely Planet has long been famous for the number and quality of its guidebook maps. Now we've gone one step further and produced a handy companion series: Lonely Planet travel atlases – maps of a country produced in book form.

Unlike other maps, which look good but lead travellers astray, our travel atlases have been researched on the road by Lonely Planet's experienced team of writers. All details are carefully checked to ensure the atlas corresponds with the equivalent Lonely Planet guidebook.

- full-colour throughout
- maps researched and checked by Lonely Planet authors
- place names correspond with Lonely Planet guidebooks
- no confusing spelling differences
- legend and travelling information in English, French, German, Japanese and Spanish
- size: 230 x 160 mm

Available now: Chile & Easter Island ● Egypt ● India & Bangladesh ● Israel & the Palestinian Territories ● Jordan, Syria & Lebanon ● Kenya ● Laos ● Portugal ● South Africa, Lesotho & Swaziland ● Thailand ● Turkey ● Vietnam ● Zimbabwe, Botswana & Namibia

Lonely Planet TV Series & Videos

L onely Planet travel guides have been brought to life on television screens around the world. Like our guides, the programs are based on the joy of independent travel and look honestly at some of the most exciting, picturesque and frustrating places in the world. Each show is presented by one of three travellers from Australia, England or the USA and combines an innovative mixture of video, Super-8 film, atmospheric soundscapes and original music.

Videos of each episode – containing additional footage not shown on television – are available from good book and video shops, but the availability of individual videos varies with regional screening schedules.

Video destinations include: Alaska ● American Rockies ● Argentina ● Australia – The South-East ● Baja California & the Copper Canyon ● Brazil ● Central Asia ● Chile & Easter Island ● Corsica, Sicily & Sardinia – The Mediterranean Islands ● East Africa (Tanzania & Zanzibar) ● Cuba ● Ecuador & the Galapagos Islands ● Ethiopia ● Greenland & Iceland ● Hungary & Romania ● Indonesia ● Israel & the Sinai Desert ● Jamaica ● Japan ● La Ruta Maya ● London ● The Middle East (Syria, Jordan & Lebanon ● Morocco ● New York City ● Northern Spain ● North India ● Outback Australia ● Pacific Islands (Fiji, Solomon Islands & Vanuatu) ● Pakistan ● Peru ● The Philippines ● South Africa & Lesotho ● South India ● South West China ● South West USA ● Trekking in Uganda & Congo ● Turkey ● Vietnam ● West Africa ● Zimbabwe, Botswana & Namibia

The Lonely Planet TV series is produced by: Pilot Productions
The Old Studio
18 Middle Row
London W10 5AT, UK

Lonely Planet Online

Whether you've just begun planning your next trip, or you're chasing down specific info on currency regulations or visa requirements, check out Lonely Planet Online for up-to-the-minute travel information.

As well as miniguides to more than 250 destinations, you'll find maps, photos, travel news, health and visa updates, travel advisories and discussion of the ecological and political issues you need to be aware of as you travel. You'll also find timely upgrades to popular guidebooks that you can print out and stick in the back of your book.

There's an online travellers' forum (The Thorn Tree) where you can share your experience of life on the road, meet travel companions and ask other travellers for their recommendations and advice.

There's also a complete and up-to-date list of all Lonely Planet travel products including travel guides, diving and snorkeling guides, phrasebooks, atlases, travel literature and videos, and a simple online ordering facility if you can't find the book you want elsewhere.

Lonely Planet Diving & Snorkeling Guides

Beautifully illustrated with full-colour photos throughout, Lonely Planet's Pisces books explore the world's best diving and snorkeling areas and prepare divers for what to expect when they get there, both topside and underwater.

Dive sites are described in detail with specifics on depths, visibility, level of difficulty, special conditions, underwater photography tips and common and unusual marine life present. You'll also find practical logistical information and coverage on topside activities and attractions, sections on diving health and safety, plus listings for diving services, live-aboards, dive resorts and tourist offices.

Guides by Region

onely Planet is known worldwide for publishing practical, reliable and no-nonsense travel information in our guides and on our Web site. The Lonely Planet list covers just about every accessible part of the world. Currently there are thirteen series: travel guides, shoestring guides, walking guides, city guides, phrasebooks, audio packs, city maps, travel atlases, diving & snorkeling guides, restaurant guides, first-time travel guides, healthy travel and travel literature.

AFRICA Africa on a shoestring ● Africa – the South ● Arabic (Egyptian) phrasebook ● Arabic (Moroccan) phrasebook ● Cairo ● Cape Town ● Cape Town city map● Central Africa ● East Africa ● Egypt ● Egypt travel atlas ● Ethiopian (Amharic) phrasebook ● The Gambia & Senegal ● Healthy Travel Africa ● Kenya ● Kenya travel atlas ● Malawi, Mozambique & Zambia ● Morocco ● North Africa ● South Africa, Lesotho & Swaziland ● South Africa, Lesotho & Swaziland travel atlas ● Swahili phrasebook ● Tanzania, Zanzibar & Pemba ● Trekking in East Africa ● Tunisia ● West Africa ● Zimbabwe, Botswana & Namibia ● Zimbabwe, Botswana & Namibia travel atlas
Travel Literature: The Rainbird: A Central African Journey ● Songs to an African Sunset: A Zimbabwean Story ● Mali Blues: Traveling to an African Beat

AUSTRALIA & THE PACIFIC Auckland ● Australia ● Australian phrasebook ● Bushwalking in Australia ● Bushwalking in Papua New Guinea ● Fiji ● Fijian phrasebook ● Islands of Australia's Great Barrier Reef ● Melbourne ● Melbourne city map ● Micronesia ● New Caledonia ● New South Wales & the ACT ● New Zealand ● Northern Territory ● Outback Australia ● Out To Eat – Melbourne ● Papua New Guinea ● Pidgin phrasebook ● Queensland ● Rarotonga & the Cook Islands ● Samoa ● Solomon Islands ● South Australia ● South Pacific Languages phrasebook ● Sydney ● Sydney city map ● Tahiti & French Polynesia ● Tasmania ● Tonga ● Tramping in New Zealand ● Vanuatu ● Victoria ● Western Australia
Travel Literature: Islands in the Clouds ● Kiwi Tracks: A New Zealand Journey ● Sean & David's Long Drive

CENTRAL AMERICA & THE CARIBBEAN Bahamas, Turks & Caicos ● Bermuda ● Central America on a shoestring ● Costa Rica ● Cuba ● Dominican Republic & Haiti ● Eastern Caribbean ● Guatemala, Belize & Yucatán: La Ruta Maya ● Jamaica ● Mexico ● Mexico City ● Panama ● Puerto Rico
Travel Literature: Green Dreams: Travels in Central America

EUROPE Amsterdam ● Amsterdam city map ● Andalucía ● Austria ● Baltic States phrasebook ● Barcelona ● Berlin ● Berlin city map ● Britain ● British phrasebook ● Brussels, Bruges & Antwerp ● Budapest city map ● Canary Islands ● Central Europe ● Central Europe phrasebook ● Corsica ● Croatia ● Czech & Slovak Republics ● Denmark ● Dublin ● Eastern Europe ● Eastern Europe phrasebook ● Edinburgh ● Estonia, Latvia & Lithuania ● Europe on a shoestring ● Finland ● France ● French phrasebook ● Germany ● German phrasebook ● Greece ● Greek phrasebook ● Hungary ● Iceland, Greenland & the Faroe Islands ● Ireland ● Italian phrasebook ● Italy ● Lisbon ● London ● London city map ● Mediterranean Europe ● Mediterranean Europe phrasebook ● Norway ● Paris ● Paris city map ● Poland ● Portugal ● Portugal travel atlas ● Prague ● Prague city map ● Provence & the Côte d'Azur ● Romania & Moldova ● Rome ● Russia, Ukraine & Belarus ● Russian phrasebook ● Scandinavian & Baltic Europe ● Scandinavian Europe phrasebook ● Scotland ● Slovenia ● Spain ● Spanish phrasebook ● St Petersburg ● Switzerland ● Trekking in Spain ● Ukrainian phrasebook ● Vienna ● Walking in Britain ● Walking in Ireland ● Walking in Italy ● Walking in Spain ● Walking in Switzerland ● Western Europe ● Western Europe phrasebook
Travel Literature: The Olive Grove: Travels in Greece

INDIAN SUBCONTINENT Bangladesh ● Bengali phrasebook ● Bhutan ● Delhi ● Goa ● Hindi & Urdu phrasebook ● India ● India & Bangladesh travel atlas ● Indian Himalaya ● Karakoram Highway ● Kerala ● Mumbai (Bombay) ● Nepal ● Nepali phrasebook ● Pakistan ● Rajasthan ● Read This First: Asia & India ● South India ● Sri Lanka ● Sri Lanka phrasebook ● Trekking in the Indian Himalaya ● Trekking in the Karakoram & Hindukush ● Trekking in the Nepal Himalaya
Travel Literature: In Rajasthan ● Shopping for Buddhas

LONELY PLANET

Mail Order

Lonely Planet products are distributed worldwide. They are also available by mail order from Lonely Planet, so if you have difficulty finding a title please write to us. North and South American residents should write to 150 Linden St, Oakland, CA 94607, USA; European and African residents should write to 10a Spring Place, London NW5 3BH, UK; and residents of other countries to PO Box 617, Hawthorn, Victoria 3122, Australia.

ISLANDS OF THE INDIAN OCEAN Madagascar & Comoros ● Maldives ● Mauritius, Réunion & Seychelles

MIDDLE EAST & CENTRAL ASIA Arab Gulf States ● Central Asia ● Central Asia phrasebook ● Hebrew phrasebook ● Iran ● Israel & the Palestinian Territories ● Israel & the Palestinian Territories travel atlas ● Istanbul ● Istanbul to Cairo ● Jerusalem ● Jordan & Syria ● Jordan, Syria & Lebanon travel atlas ● Lebanon ● Middle East on a shoestring ● Syria ● Turkey ● Turkey travel atlas ● Turkish phrasebook ● Yemen
Travel Literature: The Gates of Damascus ● Kingdom of the Film Stars: Journey into Jordan

NORTH AMERICA Alaska ● Backpacking in Alaska ● Baja California ● California & Nevada ● Canada ● Chicago ● Chicago city map ● Deep South ● Florida ● Hawaii ● Honolulu ● Las Vegas ● Los Angeles ● Miami ● New England ● New Orleans ● New York City ● New York city map ● New York, New Jersey & Pennsylvania ● Pacific Northwest USA ● Puerto Rico ● Rocky Mountain ● San Francisco ● San Francisco city map ● Seattle ● Southwest USA ● Texas ● USA ● USA phrasebook ● Vancouver ● Washington, DC & the Capital Region ● Washington DC city map
Travel Literature: Drive Thru America

NORTH-EAST ASIA Beijing ● Cantonese phrasebook ● China ● Hong Kong ● Hong Kong city map ● Hong Kong, Macau & Guangzhou ● Japan ● Japanese phrasebook ● Japanese audio pack ● Korea ● Korean phrasebook ● Kyoto ● Mandarin phrasebook ● Mongolia ● Mongolian phrasebook ● North-East Asia on a shoestring ● Seoul ● South-West China ● Taiwan ● Tibet ● Tibetan phrasebook ● Tokyo
Travel Literature: Lost Japan

SOUTH AMERICA Argentina, Uruguay & Paraguay ● Bolivia ● Brazil ● Brazilian phrasebook ● Buenos Aires ● Chile & Easter Island ● Chile & Easter Island travel atlas ● Colombia ● Ecuador & the Galapagos Islands ● Latin American Spanish phrasebook ● Peru ● Quechua phrasebook ● Rio de Janeiro ● Rio de Janeiro city map ● South America on a shoestring ● Trekking in the Patagonian Andes ● Venezuela
Travel Literature: Full Circle: A South American Journey

SOUTH-EAST ASIA Bali & Lombok ● Bangkok ● Bangkok city map ● Burmese phrasebook ● Cambodia ● Hanoi ● Healthy Travel Asia & India ● Hill Tribes phrasebook ● Ho Chi Minh City ● Indonesia ● Indonesia's Eastern Islands ● Indonesian phrasebook ● Indonesian audio pack ● Jakarta ● Java ● Laos ● Lao phrasebook ● Laos travel atlas ● Malay phrasebook ● Malaysia, Singapore & Brunei ● Myanmar (Burma) ● Philippines ● Pilipino (Tagalog) phrasebook ● Singapore ● South-East Asia on a shoestring ● South-East Asia phrasebook ● Thailand ● Thailand's Islands & Beaches ● Thailand travel atlas ● Thai phrasebook ● Thai audio pack ● Vietnam ● Vietnamese phrasebook ● Vietnam travel atlas

ALSO AVAILABLE: Antarctica ● The Arctic ● Brief Encounters: Stories of Love, Sex & Travel ● Chasing Rickshaws ● Lonely Planet Unpacked ● Not the Only Planet: Travel Stories from Science Fiction ● Sacred India ● Travel with Children ● Traveller's Tales

FREE Lonely Planet Newsletters

W e love hearing from you and think you'd like to hear from us.

Planet Talk

Our FREE quarterly printed newsletter is full of tips from travellers and anecdotes from Lonely Planet guidebook authors. Every issue is packed with up-to-date travel news and advice, and includes:

- a postcard from Lonely Planet co-founder Tony Wheeler
- a swag of mail from travellers
- a look at life on the road through the eyes of a Lonely Planet author
- topical health advice
- prizes for the best travel yarn
- news about forthcoming Lonely Planet events
- a complete list of Lonely Planet books and other titles

To join our mailing list, residents of the UK, Europe and Africa can email us at go@lonelyplanet.co.uk; residents of North and South America can email us at info@lonelyplanet.com; the rest of the world can email us at talk2us@lonelyplanet.com.au, or contact any Lonely Planet office.

Comet

O ur FREE monthly email newsletter brings you all the latest travel news, features, interviews, competitions, destination ideas, travellers' tips & tales, Q&As, raging debates and related links. Find out what's new on the Lonely Planet Web site and which books are about to hit the shelves.

Subscribe from your desktop: www.lonelyplanet.com/comet

Index

Text

A

accommodation 111-17
  budget 111-14
  mid-range 114-15
  top-end 115-17
activities 108-9
air travel 56-60
  airport, see Balice airport
  departure tax 56
  glossary 58-9
alcoholic drinks 120-1
amber 130
antiques 131
Archaeological Museum 80
Archdiocesan Museum 82
architecture 23-4
art 130-1
arts, the 19-28
Auschwitz 134-6
  museum 134-6

B

Balice airport 31, 56, 65
ballet 128-9
Barbican 76
battle of Grunwald 12
Benedictine Abbey 103
Bernardine church 89
bicycle 63, 67
Birkenau 136
Black Madonna 146-9
boat 67
Boleslaus the Brave 11
Błonia 98
Bonifrater church 92
books 42-3, 131
Botanical Garden, Wesoła 102
Boznańska, Olga 20
Bukowski, Jan 102
Bunker of Art 78
bus travel 61-2
business hours 50-1

C

cabaret 128
cafés 125

Camaldolese monks 103
camping 111-12
  camping goods 132
Capucine church 97
car travel 62-3, 66
  parking 66
  private vehicles 63
  rental 66
  road rules 62
Carmelite church 97
Catherine the Great 99
Centrum Informacji Turysty-
  cznej, see tourist offices
chambers of commerce 55
Chapel of Our Lady of the
  Rosary 80
Chapel upon the Water 137
children 47-9
Chopin, Frédéric 19, 51
Chromy, Bronisław 26, 89, 107
Church of Our Lady of Często-
  chowa 107
Church of Our Lady Queen of
  Poland 107
Church of SS Peter & Paul 24,
  80-1
Church of the Blessed Salomea
  138
Church of the Holy Cross 24
Church of the Nuns of the
  Visitation 100
Church of the Reformed
  Franciscans 76-7
cinema 27-8, 128
Cistercian Abbey 106
climate 17
Cloth Hall 70-1
Collegium Luridicum & Zoolog-
  ical Museum 81
Collegium Maius 24, 78
Collegium Novum 79
Conrad, Joseph 22
Copernicus, Nicolaus 12, 20
Corpus Christi church 91
crafts 130
Cricot 2 27, 128
Cricoteka 80, 128
cultural centres 49
Cultural Information Centre 126
customs 35
Czartoryski Museum 76

Czorsztyn 146
Częstochowa 146-9, **147**
  getting there 149
  information 147
  Jasna Góra Monastery 147
  places to stay 148-9
  special events 148
Czyżyny 102

D

da Vinci, Leonardo 77
dangers & annoyances 49-50
  reporting theft 50
Dębno Podhalańskie 146
death camps 15, 48
  Auschwitz 15, 134-6
  Płaszów 15
  Birkenau 136
departure tax 56
disabled travellers 47
discos 127
discounts
  hostel card 33
  student card 33
documents 32-3
  photocopies 33
Dolina Chochołowska 142
Dolina Kościeliska 142
Dolina Pięciu Stawów 142
Dolina Strążyska 141
Dominican Church 79-80
drinks 120-1
driving licence 33
Długosz, Jan 20
Dunajec Gorge 145

E

ecology 17
economy 18
electricity 45
email & Internet access 41-2
embassies & consulates 34
environment 15, 17-18
  aluminium works 17
  Ministry of Environmental
    Protection 17
  steelworks 15-17, 18, 106
  Vistula 17
Ethnographic Museum 54

Bold indicates maps.

Ethnographic Museum, Kazimierz 92

F
festivals 51-3
Filharmonia Krakowska 128
fitness centres 109
Florian Gate 75-6
food 118-25
    budget eateries 121-3
    cuisine 118
    eating habits 118
    meat dishes 123
    mid-range eateries 123-4
    top end eateries 124-5
    vegetarian dishes 124
Franciscan Church 79

G
Gallery of 19th Century Polish
    Painting 70-1
gay travellers 47
    venues 127
geography 17
Geological Museum 80
ghettos 15, 94
Górecki, Henryk 19
government & politics 18
Grodzisko 138
Grunwald Monument 98

H
Hasior, Władysław 141
health 33, 46-7
    health card 33
    insurance 46
    medical services 46-7
    vaccinations 33
hejnał 74
Hermitage of the Camaldolese
    Monks 103
hiking 141-3
Historical Museum, Kraków 72
history 10-16
    communist rule 15-16
    decline 12-13
    Kraków's origins 10-11
    medieval times 11-12
    postcommunist 16-19
    the golden age 12
    the partitians 13
    WWI 13-14
    WWII 14-15
hitching 63-4
horse riding 109

hostels 112-13
House of the Medical
    Association 102
House under the Globe 100
House under the Singing Frog
    97

I
insurance 33, 46
International Cultural Centre 47
Internet resources 41-2
Isaac's Synagogue 92

J
jadłodajnias 121
Jagiellonian University 11, 48
Jasna Góra Monastery 146-9
Jesuit Church 102
Jewish Cemetery, New 93
Jewish-Polish history 91
    museum 92

K
Kąty 146
Kalwaria Zebrzydowska 51
Kantor, Tadeusz 20, 25, 27, 51,
    80
Kazimierz 89-93
    Christian Quarter 90-2
    Jewish Quarter 92-3
    Jewish-Polish history 91
Kazimierz Wielki III, King 11, 91
Kieślowski, Krzysztof 19, 28
Kievan Rus 11
Kleparz 98-100
Kościuszko, Tadeusz 13, 20,
    96, 99
    Kościuszko's mound 98
Komeda, Krzysztof 19
Krakus' Mound 96
Kuźnice 140, 141

L
Lajkonik 52, 53
Lake Morskie Oko 142-3
language 30, 151-5
    language courses 109-10
Las Wolski 103-7
laundry 45
left luggage 45
legal matters 50
Lem, Stanisław 20
Lenin, Vladimir 14
lesbian travellers 47
literature 22-3

Loreto House 97
Lutosławski, Witold 19

M
magazines 43
Main Market Square, see
    Rynek Główny
Malczewski, Jacek 20, 90
maps 31, 131
markets 133
Matejko, Jan 20, 25, 70, 97
    Matejko House 74
medical services 46-7
Mehoffer, Józef 20, 26, 81, 97
    Mehoffer House 97
Michałowski, Piotr 25
Mickiewicz, Adam 20, 22, 71-2
    monument 71-2
Military Cemetery 101
Miłosz, Czesław 20, 22-3
miraculous icons
    Black Madonna 146
    Jesus of Nazareth statue 92
    Our Lady of the Sand
        painting 97
    painting of the Virgin 80
    St Stanislaus' pond 90
    wooden statue of Christ 106
Missionaries' church 89
Młoda Polska, see Young
    Poland movement
money 35-8
    cash 35
    costs 37
    exchange rates 35
    taxes 38
    tipping 37
    travellers cheques 36
Moniuszko, Stanisław 19
motorcycle travel, see car
    travel
Mrożek, Sławomir 20, 22
Mt Giewont 140, 141
Mt Gubałówka 140, 141
Mt Kasprowy Wierch 140, 141
Mt Rysy 138, 143
Museum of History and Culture of Kraków Jewry 92
Museum of Kraków's Theatre
    74
Museum of National Remembrance 93
Museum of Pharmacy 74
music 19, 127-8, 131
    classical 128
    folk & ethnic 127-8
    jazz & blues 127

N

National Museum, Kraków 70
  Main Building 97
Nativity scenes 54, 92
Natural History Museum 89
newspapers 43
Nowa Huta 15-16, 24, 104 7
  cultural centre 107
  steelworks 15-17, 18, 106
Nowodworski Collegium 79
Nowosielski, Jerzy 20, 25, 81
Nowy Targ 146

O

Oświęcim 134-7, **135**
  getting there 136-7
  places to stay 136
obwarzanki 122
Ojców caves 10, 137
Ojców National Park 137-8
  castles 137-8
  museums 137
  places to stay 138
Łokietek Cave 137
Old Synagogue 92
Old Theatre, see Teatr Stary
Old Town 69-82
opera 128-9
organised tours 64, 67-8

P

painting & sculpture 24-7
Palace of Art 78
Passion play 51
passport 32, 50
  emergency passports 50
Płaszów 95
Pauline Church 90
Penderecki, Krzysztof 20
photography 44, 131-2
  film & equipment 44
Piarist church 76
Pieskowa Skała Castle 138
Piłsudski, Józef 13-14, 21, 96, 105
Piłsudski's Mound 104
Planty, the 69
Podgórze 93-6
Podkowiński, Władysław 70, 71
Polański, Roman 19, 21, 28
Pope John Paul II 16, 96
Poper's Synagogue 93

population & people 18
post & communications 38-41
posters 27, 130-1
Pravda 14
Preisner, Zbigniew 19, 21
private rooms 113-14
public holidays 51
public transport 65
pubs & bars 126-7

R

Rabbi Moses 93
radio 43-4
Rakowicki cemetery 100
religion 29-30
Remuh cemetery 93
Remuh Synagogue 93
Resurrectionist Seminary 96
rhinoceros 90
roads 62-3
rock climbing 109
Royal Republic, the 12-13
Rynek Główny 31, 69-74
Rząsa, Antoni 107

S

salt mine 107
  Chapel of the Blessed Kinga 107
  lakes 107
  museum 108
Schindler's Factory 94-5
Schindler's List 28, 91
  tour 68
senior travellers 47
shopping 130-3, **132**
Sigismund chapel 25
Sigismund Tower 84
Skrzynecki, Piotr 21, 128
soccer 129
society & conduct 28-9
Solidarity (Solidarność) 16
Słowacki Theatre 26, 128
Słowacki, Juliusz 21, 22
Spielberg, Steven 94
sports 129
St Adalbert's church 71
St Andrew's church 23, 81
St Anne's church 24, 78
St Barbara's church 73
St Bartholomew's church 107
St Benedict's church 95
St Catherine's church 24, 90
St Florian 101
St Florian's church 100
St Giles' church 82

St Hyacinthus' chapel 80
St Mark's church 76
St Mary's church 24, 72-4, **73**
St Nicholas' church 101
St Stanislaus, bishop 90
St Vladimir's Foundation 81
Stare Miasto, see Old Town
steelworks, see Nowa Huta
Stoss, Veit 15, 21, 24, 89
Stradom 89-92
swimming 108-9
Szczawnica 146
Szołajski House 77
szopki 53, 54
Szymanowski, Karol 19, 21, 90 140, 143
  Villa Atma 141
Szymborska, Wisława 21, 23

T

Talowski, Teodor 97
Tatra Mountains 31, 138-45
Tatra National Park 138-45, **142**
  places to stay 144-5
  museum 140-1
taxis 66-7
Teatr Stary 27, 77, 128
Teatr STU 129
telephone 40-1
  eKno 41
  fax 41
television 43-4
Tempel Reformed Synagogue 93
tennis 109
theatre 128-9
tickets & passes 65
  Ruch kiosks 65
  ticket inspectors 65
time 44-5
tourist offices 31-2
  KART 31
Town Hall Tower 71
train travel 60-1
Tyniec 102-3

U

universities 48
Urbaniak, Michał 19

V

vegetarian cuisine 124
video 44
visas 32-3
Vistula (Wisła) 17

Bold indicates maps.

W

Wajda, Andrzej 21, 27, 28
walking 137
Wanda's Mound 96
Wałęsa, Lech 16
water 18, 46
  Oligocene water 18
Wawel 23-5, 82-9
  chakra 86
  dragon's den 89
  guide services 82
Wawel Castle 85-9
  history 87
  Royal Chambers 87
Wawel Cathedral 82-5, **85**
  coronations 83
weights & measures 45

Wesoła 101-2
Wieliczka 107-8
  museum 108
  salt mine 107
Wieniawski, Henryk 19
Wierzchowska Górna Cave 137
Witkacy Theatre 27, 145
Witkiewicz, Stanisław
  (Witkacy) 22
Witkiewicz, Stanisław 140
  Villa Koliba 141
Wojtyła, Karol 21
women travellers 47
work 54-5
Wyspiański Museum 80
Wyspiański, Stanisław 21, 22,
  26, 51, 81, 90, 97, 116

Y

Young Poland movement 13,
  20-1, 25-6, 80, 100

Z

Zakopane 138-45, **139**
  getting there 145
  information 140
  places to eat 145
  places to stay 143-4
  special events 143
  things to see 140-1
Zoological Garden 104
Zucher's Synagogue 94
Zwierzyniec 98
  churches 98
  Kościuszko's Mound 98

Boxed Text

Bagels 122
Centre of Japanese Art &
  Technology 'Manggha' 49
Chopin Open 51
Emergency 50
Hejnał 74
High Altar of St Mary's Church
  73
Highlights 69
How Much is a Double Room
  with Bath? 114
How Much Will It Cost Me? 38
International Cultural Centre
  47
Wawel Chakra 86
Jagiellonian University –
  Poland's Alma Mater 48
Jewish Ghetto 94
Kazimierz's Chequered Jewish-
  Polish History 91
Kraków in Figures 18
Kraków vs Warsaw 29
Kraków's Mounds 96
Kraków's National Museum 70

Kraków's Szopki – The Art of
  Nativity Scenes 54
Kraków's Who's Who 20-1
Lajkonik – Kraków's Legendary
  Figure 53
Lenin in Kraków 14
Leonardo da Vinci's *Enigmatic
  Lady with Ermine* 77
Marshal Józef Piłsudski –
  Father of the Second Re-
  public 105
Meats, Meats & More Meats
  123
Nowa Huta – A Communist
  Fantasy 106
One Ticket Please ... 60
Płaszów Concentration Camp
  95
Poland's Phone Area Codes 40
Poster Art 27
So You Wanna be a Camal-
  dolese Monk ... 103
Some Tips About Changing
  Cash 36

Some Tips About Restaurant
  Menus 119
St Florian – the Patron Saint of
  Firefighters 101
St Stanislaus – the Patron Saint
  of Poland 84
Tadeusz Kościuszko – Polish-
  American Hero of Indepen-
  dence 99
The Painting that Scandalised
  the Public 71
Two Towers of St Mary's
  Church 72
Vegetarians, Don't Worry 124
Wawel Coronations 83
Wawel Dragon 88
Welcome to the Polish Pub 126
Wisława Szymborska – 1996
  Nobel Prizewinner 23
Woolly Rhinoceros 90
Wyspiański's Stained-Glass
  Windows 81
Young Poland 26
Your Ticket, Please ... 65

Wawel, symbol of Poland's national identity, is approached by a lane at the top of ul Kanonicza.

Church & Convent of the Premonstratensian Nuns, Zwierzyniec, are reflected in the Vistula waters.

Excursion boats leave from the wharf where the banks of the Vistula run up to Wawel.

KRZYSZTOF DYDYŃSKI

KRZYSZTOF DYDYŃSKI

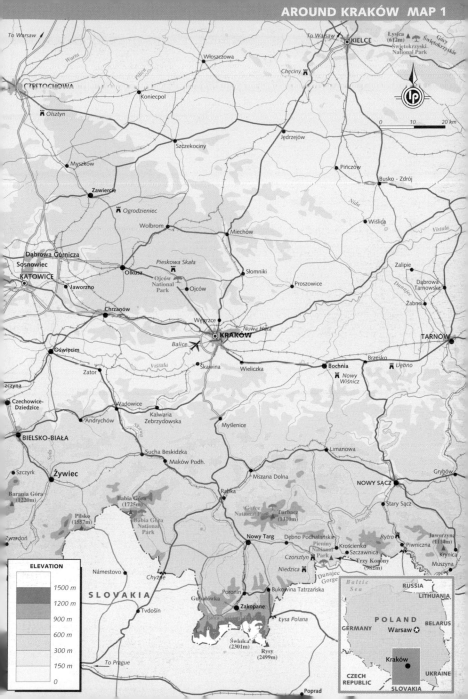

AROUND KRAKÓW MAP 1

MAP 2 GREATER KRAKÓW

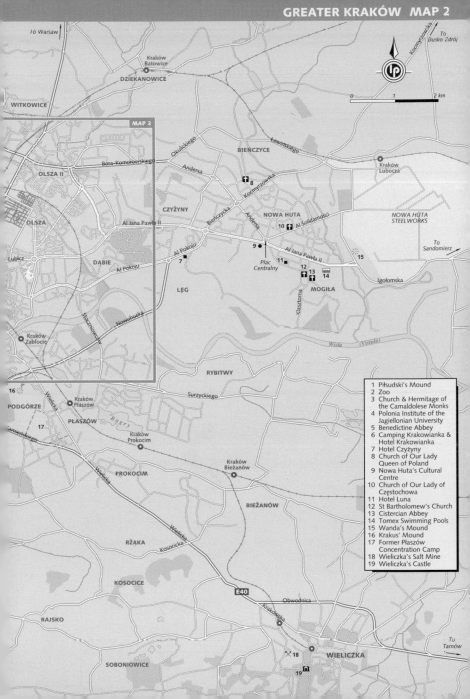

GREATER KRAKÓW MAP 2

1 Piłsudski's Mound
2 Zoo
3 Church & Hermitage of the Camaldolese Monks
4 Polonia Institute of the Jagiellonian University
5 Benedictine Abbey
6 Camping Krakowianka & Hotel Krakowianka
7 Hotel Czyżyny
8 Church of Our Lady Queen of Poland
9 Nowa Huta's Cultural Centre
10 Church of Our Lady of Częstochowa
11 Hotel Luna
12 St Bartholomew's Church
13 Cistercian Abbey
14 Tomex Swimming Pools
15 Wanda's Mound
16 Krakus' Mound
17 Former Płaszów Concentration Camp
18 Wieliczka's Salt Mine
19 Wieliczka's Castle

MAP 3 INNER KRAKÓW

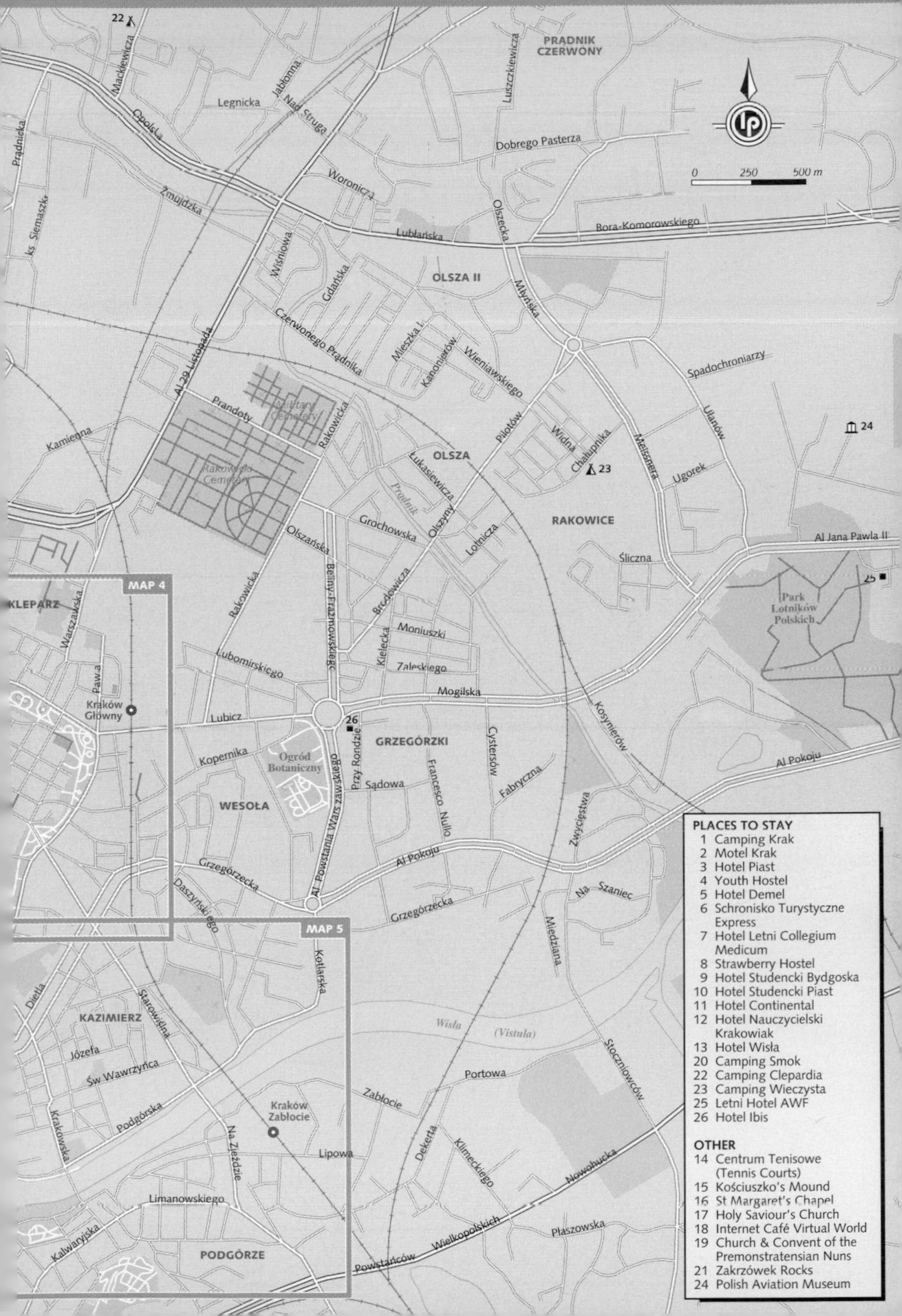
PRĄDNIK CZERWONY
OLSZA II
OLSZA
RAKOWICE
GRZEGÓRZKI
WESOŁA
KLEPARZ
KAZIMIERZ
PODGÓRZE
MAP 4
MAP 5
0 250 500 m
Mackiewicza
Legnicka
Jabłonna
Nad Strugą
Opolska
Prądnicka
Żmujdzka
ks. Siemaszki
Woronicza
Dobrego Pasterza
Łuszczkiewicza
Olszecka
Bora-Komorowskiego
Lublańska
Wiśniowa
Gdańska
Czerwonego Prądnika
Al 29 Listopada
Mieszka I
Kanonierów
Wieniawskiego
Młyńska
Spadochroniarzy
Ułanów
Meissnera
Prandoty
Military Cemetery
Rakowicka
Rakowicki Cemetery
Kamienna
Łukasiewicza
Pilotów
Widna
Chałupnika
Ugorek
Prądnik
Grochowska
Olszyny
Lotnicza
Olszańska
Beliny-Prażmowskiego
Bratysławska
Al Jana Pawła II
Śliczna
Park Lotników Polskich
Warszawska
Moniuszki
Kielecka
Zaleskiego
Lubomirskiego
Pawia
Kraków Główny
Mogilska
Lubicz
Kopernika
Ogród Botaniczny
Al Powstania Warszawskiego
Przy Rondzie
Sądowa
Francesco Nullo
Cystersów
Fabryczna
Kosynierów
Al Pokoju
Zwycięstwa
Grzegórzecka
Daszyńskiego
Na Szaniec
Miedziana
Kotlarska
Dietla
Starowiślna
Wisła (Vistula)
Józefa
Św Wawrzyńca
Stoczniowców
Portowa
Zabłocie
Kraków Zabłocie
Podgórska
Krakowska
Na Zjeździe
Lipowa
Dekerta
Klimeckiego
Nowohucka
Limanowskiego
Kalwaryjska
Powstańców Wielkopolskich
Płaszowska
22
23
24
25
26
PLACES TO STAY
1 Camping Krak
2 Motel Krak
3 Hotel Piast
4 Youth Hostel
5 Hotel Demel
6 Schronisko Turystyczne Express
7 Hotel Letni Collegium Medicum
8 Strawberry Hostel
9 Hotel Studencki Bydgoska
10 Hotel Studencki Piast
11 Hotel Continental
12 Hotel Nauczycielski Krakowiak
13 Hotel Wisła
20 Camping Smok
22 Camping Clepardia
23 Camping Wieczysta
25 Letni Hotel AWF
26 Hotel Ibis
OTHER
14 Centrum Tenisowe (Tennis Courts)
15 Kościuszko's Mound
16 St Margaret's Chapel
17 Holy Saviour's Church
18 Internet Café Virtual World
19 Church & Convent of the Premonstratensian Nuns
21 Zakrzówek Rocks
24 Polish Aviation Museum

MAP 4 OLD TOWN & AROUND

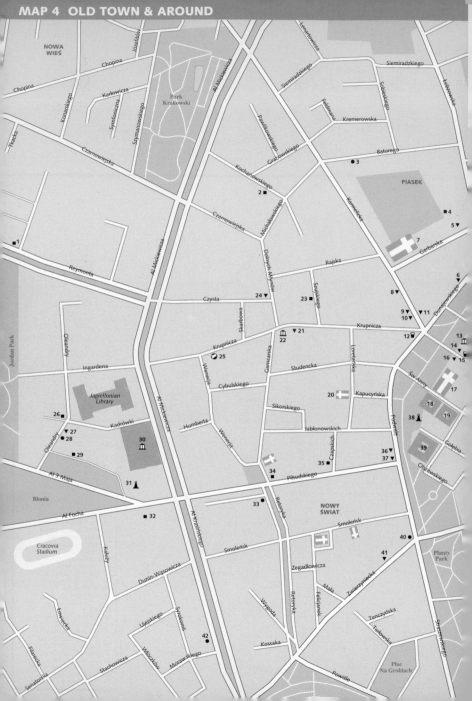

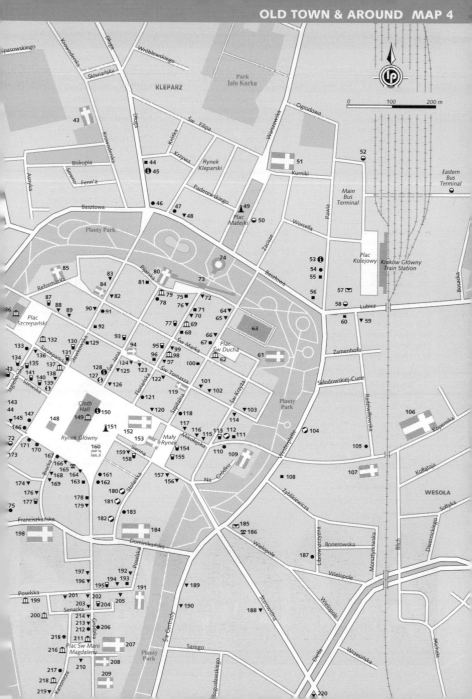

MAP 4 OLD TOWN & AROUND

PLACES TO STAY
1 Hotel Studencki Nawojka
2 Dom Wycieczkowy Chałupnik
4 Bursa im St Pigonia
23 Hotel Logos
26 Youth Hostel
29 Hotel Studencki Żaczek
32 Hotel Cracovia
34 Hotel Fortuna Bis
35 Hotel Fortuna
44 Pokoje Gościnne Jordan
55 Hotel Warszawski
56 Hotel Polonia
60 Hotel Europejski
67 Hotel Pollera
68 Hotel Pokoje Gościnne SARPu
71 Dom Gościnny UJ
75 Hotel Polski
81 Hotel Francuski
92 Grand Hotel
96 Hotel Pod Różą
100 Hotel Elektor
108 Dom Turysty PTTK
111 Hotel Wit Stwosz
129 Hotel Saski
163 Dom Polonii
178 Hotel Rezydent
193 Hotel Wawel-Tourist

PLACES TO EAT
5 Restauracyjka Pigoniówka
6 Bar Mleczny Warszawianka
8 Bar Rybny
9 Tribeca Coffe
10 King Pie
11 Ristorante Avanti
14 Naleśniqi
16 Kawiarnia u Zalipianek
21 Bar Wegetariański Vega
24 Bar Mleczny Górnik
27 Jadłodajnia Oleandry
36 Bar Bistro Różowy Słoń
37 Bar Mleczny Barcelona
41 Gospoda na Zwierzyńcu
48 Bar Dam
59 Restauracja Pod Wieżyczką
64 Jadłodajnia Sąsiedzi
65 Bar Bistro Różowy Słoń
66 Kawiarnia Buschmann
70 Jama Michalika
72 McDonald's
76 La Croissanterine Fleury Michon
82 Kuchnia Staropolska u Babci Maliny
83 Restauracja Cyrano de Bergerac
88 Jadłodajnia Jak u Mamy
89 Bar Azjatycki Asia
90 King Pie
97 Bar Mleczny Dworzanin
99 Bar Orientalny Lychee
101 Café Larousse
102 Jadłodajnia Bistro Stop
103 Kawiarnia Esplanada
114 El Paso Tex Mex Saloon
115 Jadłodajnia u Stasi & Pizzeria Cyklop
116 Jadłodajnia u Górala
117 Restauracja u Szkota
120 Naleśniqi
122 Sklep z Kawą Pożegnanie z Afryką
123 Café Camelot
124 Restauracja Cherubino
125 Grill Aladyn
126 Pizzeria Grace
136 Bistro Piccolo Chicken Grill
138 Restauracja Tetmajerowska
143 Jadłodajnia Kuchcik
144 Pizzeria Grace
145 Salad Bar & Restauracja Chimera
156 Pizzeria Grace
157 Jadłodajnia Anna Kwaśniewska
159 Bar Bistro Różowy Słoń
164 Ristorante da Pietro
166 Restauracja Wentzl
168 Gospoda CK Dezerter
169 Restauracja Guliwer
173 Surrestaurant Szuflada
174 Chimera II
176 Café Botanica
179 Akropolis Grill
188 Taco Mexicano
189 Kawiarnia Filmowa Graffiti
190 Bar Wegetariański Vega
192 Restauracja Korsykańska Paese
194 Taco Mexicano
196 Restauracja Pod Aniołami
197 Kawiarnia Wiśniowy Sad
201 Caffeteria Pod Błękitnym Kotem
202 Ristorante Caruso
203 Bar Mleczny Pod Temidą
205 Ristorante Corleone
210 Pizza Hut
213 Bar Grodzki
214 Marhaba Grill
219 Demmers Teehaus
220 Bar Mleczny Pod Filarkami

BARS & CLUBS
12 CK Browar
15 Klub Kulturalny
28 Rotunda Student Club
77 Piwnica Pod Złotą Pipą
87 @tmosfera
91 Equinox
93 Pub Pod Papugami
95 Pub Pod Jemiołą
113 Black Gallery
118 Klub Pod Papugami
121 Jazz Club u Muniaka
130 Free Pub

KRZYSZTOF DYDYŃSKI

Watching the activity in the square or just taking a break, under the arches of the Cloth Hall.

131 Pub u Kacpra
134 Klub Starego Teatru Osorya
135 Piwnica Pod Ogródkiem
140 Klub Pasja
141 Music Bar 9
142 Piec Art
147 Harris Piano Jazz Bar
154 Pub Uwaga
155 Nowy Kuzyn
158 In Vitro
161 Kredens
162 Klub u Louisa (Internet Café)
177 Piwnica Pod Kominkiem
195 Old Pub
204 Fischer Pub
206 Rock & Roll Club & Rock
    Club Yellow Submarine

CHURCHES

7 Carmelite Church
17 St Anne's Church
20 Capucine Church
43 Church of the Nuns of the
    Visitation
51 St Florian's Church
61 Church of the Holy Cross
80 Piarist Church
84 St Mark's Church
85 Church of the Reformed
    Franciscans
94 St John's Church
106 Jesuit Church
107 St Nicholas' Church
109 Church of Our Lady of the
    Snow
119 St Thomas' Church
152 St Mary's Church
153 St Barbara's Church
160 St Adalbert's Church
184 Dominican Church
191 St Joseph's Church
198 Franciscan Church
207 Church of SS Peter & Paul

208 St Andrew's Church
209 St Martin's Church

OTHER

3 Kompit (Internet Café)
13 Bunker of Art
18 Nowodworski Collegium
19 Collegium Maius
22 Mehoffer House
25 Austrian Consulate
30 National Museum's Main
    Building
31 Monument to Stanisław
    Wyspiański
33 House Under the Singing
    Frog
38 Monument to Nicolaus
    Copernicus
39 Collegium Novum
40 Filharmonia Krakowska
42 Teatr STU
45 Jordan Travel Agency, Tourist
    Office & Bike Rental
46 House Under the Globe
47 LOT Airlines Office & Avis Car
    Rental
49 Grunwald Monument
50 Bus No 100 to Kościuszko's
    Mound
52 Lux-Bus Minibus to Wieliczka
53 KART Tourist Office
54 Waweltur
57 Post Office
58 Bus No 152 to Airport
62 Museum of Kraków's Theatre
63 Słowacki Theatre
69 Matejko House
73 Florian Gate
74 Barbican
78 French Institute
79 Czartoryski Museum
86 Palace of Art
98 Museum of Pharmacy

104 Russian Consulate
105 House of the Medical
    Association
110 Łódź Internet Café
112 Hungarian Consulate
127 Orbis & American Express
128 Cultural Information Centre
132 Szołajski House
133 Teatr Stary (Old Theatre)
137 Historical Museum of Kraków
139 Bank Pekao
146 Piwnica Pod Baranami
148 Town Hall Tower
149 Gallery of 19th Century
    Polish Painting
150 Dexter Travel Agency &
    Tourist Office
151 Monument to Adam Mick-
    iewicz
165 Telekomunikacja Polska
167 Goethe Institute
170 EMPiK & International
    Cultural Centre
171 British Council
172 Minibuses to Nowa Huta
175 Archbishop Palace
180 German Consulate
181 US Consulate
182 French Consulate
183 Poster Gallery
185 Main Post Office
186 Main Telephone Centre
187 Kawiarnia Internetowa
    Magiel
199 Archaeological Museum
200 Geological Museum
211 Collegium Iuridicum &
    Zoological Museum
212 Italian Institute of Culture
215 Cricoteka
216 Wyspiański Museum
217 St Vladimir's Foundation
218 Archdiocesan Museum

Arts and crafts in the Cloth Hall. Upstairs is the Gallery of 19th Century Polish Painting.

KRZYSZTOF DYDYŃSKI

MAP 5 STRADOM, KAZIMIERZ & PODGÓRZE

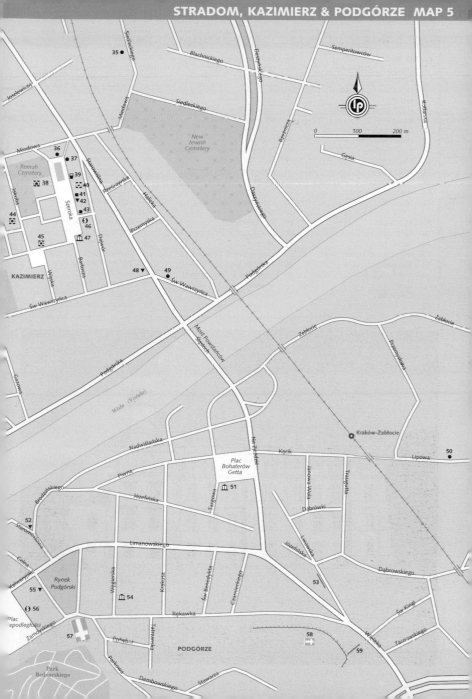

MAP 5 STRADOM, KAZIMIERZ & PODGÓRZE

PLACES TO STAY
1 Pensjonat i Restauracja Rycerska
3 Hotel Royal (two-star section)
5 Hotel Royal (three-star section)
12 Hotel Pensjonat Kazimierz
13 Hotel Franciszek
24 Hotel Regent
27 Mini Hotel
33 Hotel Forum
34 Hotel Korona
41 Hotel & Café Alef
43 Hotel Ester

PLACES TO EAT
8 Bar Hoang Hai
14 Bistro Pod 13-ką
15 Restauracja Chłopskie Jadło
19 Restauracja Ganges
28 Restauracjo Orientalna Thien Long
42 Café Ariel
48 Bar Mleczny Syrena

52 Restauracja A Dong
55 Jadłodajnia Amicus

OTHER
2 St Giles' Church
4 Natural History Museum
6 Missionaries' Church
7 Bernadine Church
9 InternetCity.com
10 Tempel Reformed Synagogue
11 Kupa Synagogue
16 Nadwiślan Tennis Courts
17 Centre of Japanese Art & Technology 'Manggha'
18 Excursion Boat Landing
20 Łaźnia
21 Pub Fanaberia
22 Jewish Cultural Centre
23 Singer Club
25 Corpus Christi Church
26 St Catherine's Church
29 Town Hall & Ethnographic Museum
30 Pauline Church (Skałka)
31 Ukrainian Consulate

32 Bonifrater Church
35 Olsza Tennis Courts
36 Jarden Jewish Bookshop & Arka Noego
37 Café Austeria
38 Remuh Synagogue
39 Ptaszyl
40 Poper's Synagogue
44 Isaac's Synagogue
45 High Synagogue
46 Bank Pekao
47 Old Synagogue & Museum of History and Culture of Kraków Jewry
49 Café Internet u Mozilli
50 Former Schindler's Factory
51 Museum of National Remembrance
53 Surviving Part of Ghetto Wall
54 Stelmach Gallery (Former Zucher's Synagogue)
56 Bank Pekao
57 St Joseph's Church
58 St Benedict's Church
59 Surviving Part of Ghetto Wall

KRZYSTOF DYDYŃSKI

The Town Hall in Kazimierz, built in the 14th century, today houses the Ethnographic Museum.

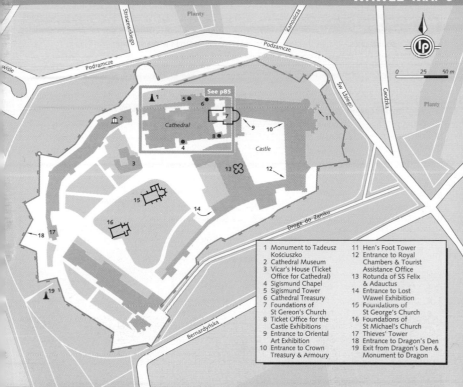

1 Monument to Tadeusz Kościuszko
2 Cathedral Museum
3 Vicar's House (Ticket Office for Cathedral)
4 Sigismund Chapel
5 Sigismund Tower
6 Cathedral Treasury
7 Foundations of St Gereon's Church
8 Ticket Office for the Castle Exhibitions
9 Entrance to Oriental Art Exhibition
10 Entrance to Crown Treasury & Armoury
11 Hen's Foot Tower
12 Entrance to Royal Chambers & Tourist Assistance Office
13 Rotunda of SS Felix & Adauctus
14 Entrance to Lost Wawel Exhibition
15 Foundations of St George's Church
16 Foundations of St Michael's Church
17 Thieves' Tower
18 Entrance to Dragon's Den
19 Exit from Dragon's Den & Monument to Dragon

Wawel Castle, political and cultural centre of Poland until the 17th century.

KRZYSZTOF DYDYŃSKI

MAP LEGEND

BOUNDARIES

............International
............State
............Disputed

HYDROGRAPHY

............Coastline
............River, Creek
............Lake
............Intermittent Lake
............Salt Lake
............Canal
............Rapids
............Spring
............Waterfalls

ROUTES & TRANSPORT

............Freeway
............Highway
............Major Road
............Minor Road
............Unsealed Road
............City Freeway
............City Highway
............City Road
............City Street, Lane

............Pedestrian Mall
............Tunnel
............Train Route & Station
............Metro & Station
............Tramway
............Cable Car or Chairlift
............Walking Track
............Walking Tour
............Ferry Route

AREA FEATURES

............Building
............Park, Gardens
............Cemetery

............Market
............Beach
............Urban Area

MAP SYMBOLS

○ **CAPITAL** ....National Capital
◉ **CAPITAL** ....State Capital
● **CITY** ....City
● **Town** ....Town
● **Village** ....Village
○ ....Point of Interest

■ ....Place to Stay
Δ ....Camping Ground
⌂ ....Caravan Park
⌂ ....Hut or Chalet

▼ ....Place to Eat
⬤ ....Pub or Bar

✈ ....Airport
............Ancient or City Wall
............Archaeological Site
............Bank
............Castle or Fort
............Church
............Cliff or Escarpment
............Embassy
............Hospital
............Lookout
............Mine
▲ ....Mountain or Hill
🏛 ....Museum
←............One Way Street

Ⓟ ....Parking
)(............Pass
★ ....Police Station
............Post Office
............Refuge
❖ ....Shopping Centre
............Stately Home
............Swimming Pool
............Synagogue
☎ ....Telephone
............Toilet
❶ ....Tourist Information
............Transport
............Zoo

Note: not all symbols displayed above appear in this book

LONELY PLANET OFFICES

Australia
PO Box 617, Hawthorn, Victoria 3122
☎ 03 9819 1877 fax 03 9819 6459
email: talk2us@lonelyplanet.com.au

USA
150 Linden St, Oakland, CA 94607
☎ 510 893 8555 TOLL FREE: 800 275 8555
fax 510 893 8572
email: info@lonelyplanet.com

UK
10a Spring Place, London NW5 3BH
☎ 020 7428 4800 fax 020 7428 4828
email: go@lonelyplanet.co.uk

France
1 rue du Dahomey, 75011 Paris
☎ 01 55 25 33 00 fax 01 55 25 33 01
email: bip@lonelyplanet.fr
www.lonelyplanet.fr

World Wide Web: www.lonelyplanet.com *or* AOL keyword: lp
Lonely Planet Images: lpi@lonelyplanet.com.au